Money Diaries

REFINERY29

Money Diaries

Everything You've Ever Wanted to Know About Your Finances . . . and Everyone Else's

Lindsey Stanberry

TOUCHSTONE

NEW YORK   LONDON   TORONTO   SYDNEY   NEW DELHI

Touchstone
An Imprint of Simon & Schuster, Inc.
1230 Avenue of the Americas
New York, NY 10020

This publication contains the opinions and ideas of its author. It is sold with the understanding that neither the author nor the publisher is engaged in rendering legal, tax, investment, insurance, financial, accounting, or other professional advice or services. If the reader requires such advice or services, a competent professional should be consulted. Relevant laws vary from state to state. The strategies outlined in this book may not be suitable for every individual, and are not guaranteed or warranted to produce any particular results.

No warranty is made with respect to the accuracy or completeness of the information contained herein, and both the author and the publisher specifically disclaim any responsibility for any liability, loss, or risk, personal or otherwise, which is incurred as a consequence, directly or indirectly, of the use and application of any of the contents of this book.

All names of diarists and other nonexpert contributors have been changed.

Some sections of this book were previously published on Refinery29.

First Touchstone trade paperback edition September 2018

TOUCHSTONE and colophon are registered trademarks of Simon & Schuster, Inc.

For information about special discounts for bulk purchases, please contact Simon & Schuster Special Sales at 1-866-506-1949 or business@simonandschuster.com.

The Simon & Schuster Speakers Bureau can bring authors to your live event. For more information or to book an event, contact the Simon & Schuster Speakers Bureau at 1-866-248-3049 or visit our website at www.simonspeakers.com.

Interior design by Ly Ngo
Illustrations by Abbie Winters

Manufactured in the United States of America

10 9 8 7 6 5 4 3 2 1

Library of Congress Cataloging-in-Publication Data

Names: Stanberry, Lindsey, author. | Refinery29 (Firm), issuing body.
Title: Refinery29 money diaries : everything you ever wanted to know about
    your finances . . . and everyone else's / by Lindsey Stanberry.
Other titles: Money diaries
Description: New York : Touchstone, [2018] |
Identifiers: LCCN 2018026872 (print) | LCCN 2018028738 (ebook) | ISBN
    9781501198007 (Ebook) | ISBN 9781501197994 (pbk.)
Subjects: LCSH: Finance, Personal.
Classification: LCC HG179 (ebook) | LCC HG179 .S55856 2018 (print) | DDC
    332.024—dc23
LC record available at https://lccn.loc.gov/2018026872

ISBN 978-1-5011-9799-4
ISBN 978-1-5011-9800-7 (ebook)

To the amazing women who share their stories and their diaries with Refinery29. Thank you for helping us start a revolution.

To Ken, who taught me the joy of saving money; and to Desmond, who has given me the best reason to spend it.

Contents

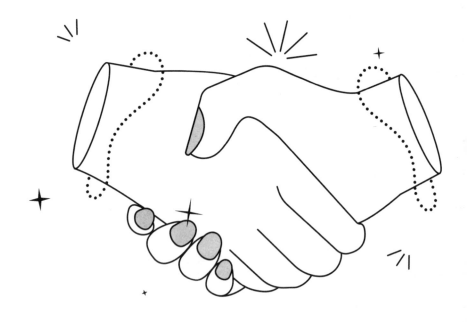

INTRODUCTION

If you had told seventeen-year-old Lindsey that one day I would write a book about personal finance, I would have laughed you out of the room. I could have told you a dozen reasons or more why I would never be qualified to give such advice: I'm terrible at calculus; the stock market is confusing; and I'm way too creative to care about such a boring topic. Yet here I am, twenty years later, completely fascinated by money; specifically, how women make, spend, invest, save, and generally feel about cold, hard cash. My teenage self had it all wrong: there's little to no connection between balancing your bank account and understanding calculus, and you can both be creative and care about making money. (I still think the stock market is complicated, but we'll get to that later.)

As the founding editor of Refinery29's Work & Money vertical, my days are spent dreaming about how we can finally put to rest the pervasive, frustrating, and BS myth that we women are incapable of managing our finances. Other stale stereotypes on my personal moratorium list? The idea that girls are bad at math. Or that millennials can't be trusted with credit. Or that it's not polite to talk about money or own our breadwinner status.

If I do my job well, you will close this book understanding the beauty of a fully funded emergency account, maxing your match, and investing in your long-term goals—and you'll have a hell of a good time doing it all. The truth is, we might not all get the six- or seven-figure happy ending of our dreams. But with a vision of what that could look like, some expert advice to help you find a clear path to get there, and a powerful community of young women living it right alongside of you, you will be a step ahead of most people.

Oftentimes, it's starting that's the hardest part, but I'm here by your side, and I'm not judging. I can't promise this book will make anyone rich, but it should make you *richer*. Let's begin!

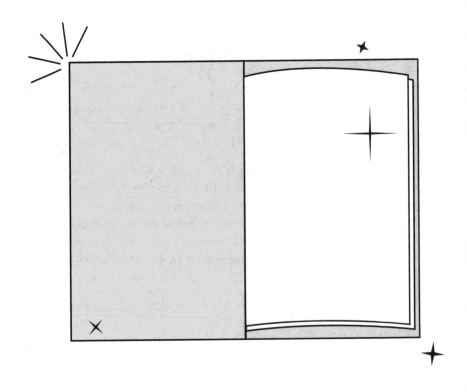

Over the next 300 pages, we're going to cover a lot of ground. I'm going to encourage you to have some tough conversations, to reevaluate how you spend your money, and ultimately, to take control of your finances. I'll also be sharing my own story alongside Money Diaries and interviews with millennial women about their feelings about this taboo topic.

But this isn't all going to be touchy-feely. I want you to actually use this book to help you save money. Sprinkled throughout, I've included thirty-two money challenges that will help you save $528 by the time you finish this book. Though you might want to tackle several of these challenges at once (open a high-yield savings account the same day you check your credit score, for example), I intend for you to save the recommended dollar amount one day at a time, making it an even more manageable process. In the end, you'll never have to save more than $32 in a day, but the total adds up quickly, and the momentum can be motivating.

I know that $528 is a lot of money, and it might not be a goal that everyone can achieve in a little more than a month. If you're living paycheck to paycheck, try saving the recommended dollar amount every other day, or even once a week.

Even if you don't hit that $528 goal, I hope you'll be inspired to think and talk about money, as these are the first steps to true financial empowerment.

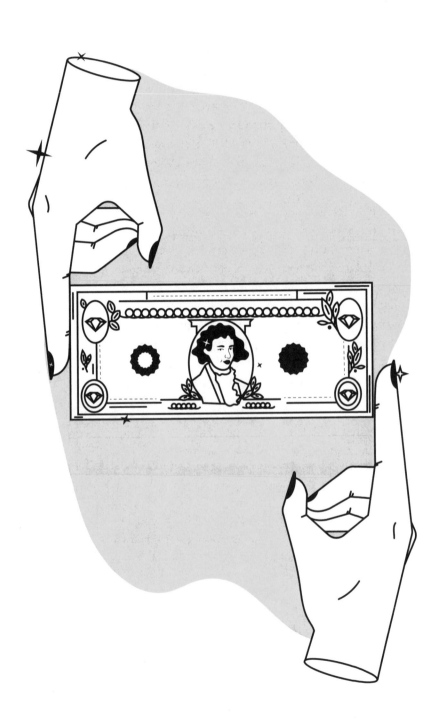

CHAPTER 1

Life & Money
(Or How to Afford Life)

I love to talk about money, but until we launched Money Diaries in January 2016, I didn't really know that other women felt the same way. The runaway success of the series—where millennial women share the intimate details of their financial lives—clearly struck a nerve.

It's probably not that surprising. After all, it's fun to read Money Diaries because you get a peek into someone else's world. We marvel at—and judge—the diarist as she navigates her week, spending too much on avocado toast or dutifully meal prepping on Sundays. We admire those who set aside more than 10 percent for retirement or are aggressively paying down student loans. We finally get an answer to the question that nags many of us: How do they afford their lives?

I imagine a lot of you opened this book for the diaries, but I hope you'll stay for the education and frank conversations about personal finance. Though most of us care a lot about our money, it's still a rather unpopular conversation topic—in a 2017 Refinery29 survey, we found that only 18 percent of millennial women talk about money with their friends at all.

Maybe that's because money is emotional. But just because it makes you squirm doesn't mean you can ignore it. And my hope is that by talking openly and honestly about it here, in the pages of this book, we'll begin to feel even more confident about how we spend and save.

In this chapter, we'll dive into the nitty-gritty (how often to check your bank balance) and even get a little philosophical (money mantra, anyone?). It's just the beginning. Throughout the book, you'll find the tools you need to get more comfortable with your finances so that you can afford the life you want.

A Week in Los Angeles, CA, on an **$86,000** Salary

OCCUPATION:
Senior copywriter
INDUSTRY: Advertising
AGE: 29
LOCATION: Los Angeles, CA
ANNUAL SALARY: $86,000 +
~$15,000 from my side hustle
**PAYCHECK AMOUNT
(TWICE A MONTH):** $2,250 +
$1,000 from my side jobs once a
month

**GENERAL FINANCIAL
INFORMATION:**
Checking Account Balance:
~$2,500
Savings Account Balance:
~$12,000 (I save $500–$1,000
each month. I'm working toward
having 6–12 months of salary in
savings in case something were
to happen and I lost my job. *Or
in case I want to buy a house
someday?* (Hahaha never going to
happen.) I am . . . nowhere close
to that.)

HOUSING:
Rent: $2,150 (I KNOW
OMG. But I live alone in a really
cute one-bedroom in a great part

of town, exactly one block from
my best friend, so I just deal with
it. My rent includes heat and hot
water.)
Electricity and Gas: $40
Internet and Cable: $120
Renter's Insurance: $0 (Yikes, I
know I really need to do this!!!)
Phone: $0 (Dad still pays, and
I think if I just never bring it up
maybe he will never ask me to
finally be a grown-up?)

TRANSPORTATION:
Car Payment: $0
(It's paid off!)
Car Insurance: $150
Parking: $22/year (The lot for my
building was full when I moved in,
so I negotiated down the cost of
my rent by $100/month. I park on
the street and pay $22 to the city
of West Hollywood for a residen-
tial parking permit.)

HEALTH & SELF-CARE:
Health Insurance: $35/
paycheck
Dental Insurance: $10/paycheck
Eye Insurance: $5/paycheck
FSA: $500/year

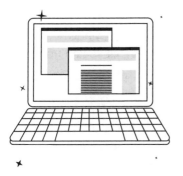

Hulu: $11.99 (No commercials because I'm bougie like that.)
Netflix: $10.99
Amazon Prime: $99/year

 DEBT:
Student Loan Debt
Total: $0 (My parents handled 90 percent of it, and I had loans for the other 10 percent, which were paid off within 4 years of graduating.)
Credit Card Debt Total: $0

ClassPass: $60 (5 classes/month. It's Southern California so I just try to hike a lot because it's free and I can do it all year round. Screw seasons!)
Tampons: $10 (I pay for a subscription for organic, all-cotton ones.)
Therapy: $2,560/year (I go twice a month at $200/session until I meet my $1,600 out-of-network deductible. Then it's partially covered by my insurance and I pay $60/session.)

 RETIREMENT:
401(k) Contribution: $250 paycheck (employer matches up to 6 percent)
401(k) Total: $16,000
IRA: $10,000 (I don't contribute now that I've got a 401(k).)

 **MISCELLANEOUS:**
Charitable Donations: $100 to Planned Parenthood, KPCC (local NPR station), and a couple other nonprofits that help women run for office. #girlpower

SUBSCRIPTIONS:
Spotify: $0 (I mooch.)

| DAY ONE |

6:35 a.m.—Alarm goes off, waking me out of a WEIRD dream where I was swimming through a water house with some coworkers. WTF is a water house? Anyway, I roll over and give my perfect, sweet, handsome boyfriend a big kiss as he compliments me on how cute I look while I sleep. KIDDING. I stretch out in my bed, single AF, and read the entire Internet before finally getting up.

8:15 a.m.—I'm at work earlier than almost anyone because I like the quiet, and it makes me feel superior to my coworkers. I eat an English muffin with goat cheese and tomatoes that I brought from home, plus a cutie, the fruit kind, not the human kind, and office coffee.

9:30 a.m.—It's a slow week at work. I look for Christmas presents for my dad to get my mom. Somehow this has become my job. I send him an email full of good options. He'll pick which ones he wants to buy, then I'll purchase and wrap them, and he'll pay me back. I realize this is unfair emotional labor that I am probably being tasked with because I am a woman, but at the same time—it's my dad. I owe him for basically everything in my life.

12 p.m.—Lunch! Salad from TJ's. I'm two days from starting my period so I'm extra hungry. I also eat some veggie chips and brownie brittle from the office snack stash.

2 p.m.—I recently ordered a really awesome print. One of my friends hung a print at her house using a bulldog clip, and it looked cute, so I buy a big rose gold one on Amazon to copy her. **$12.95**

3 p.m.—After writing a bunch of tweets for a client's content calendar, I eat a Honeycrisp apple with chia+flax peanut butter that I brought from home. I know sometimes people are like, "This fruit is so good, it tastes like candy!" And it's like, "No, ma'am, CANDY tastes like candy." But Honeycrisp apples are almost that good.

4 p.m.—I contribute $10 to a fund to help one of my coworkers change her flight home from a trip so she can make it to the office Christmas party. **$10**

6:45 p.m.—I booked a workout class through ClassPass at a ladies-only gym. Love it! BOY, BYE. I'm going to this gym forever.

7:45 p.m.—I go straight from class to my BFF's house for our weekly group dinner. We take turns providing the food. Tonight, one of my friends brought sandwiches from Mendocino Farms. Everyone has to deal with how sweaty/smelly I am while we chat and watch reality TV.

10:30 p.m.—Home and shower before heading to bed! I watch some *30 Rock* as I fall asleep.

DAILY TOTAL: $22.95

| DAY TWO |

6:30 a.m.—Yesterday, I decided to cancel both my 6 a.m. workout and my therapy appointment. My therapist is out of network and VERY expensive. I decide my mental health can survive a week without that big cost—especially since I keep buying Christmas presents. Anyway—it means I wake up at my normal time.

7:15 a.m.—It's a "chilly" 60 degrees and Santa Ana windy, which in SoCal equals fall. But by the time I drive over the hill into the Valley, I realize I'm driving into a literal chimney. The winds sparked huge

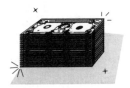

wildfires just north and the entire Valley is full of smoke. I hold my breath as I run into Peet's for a coffee and maple chicken sausage breakfast sando. **$7.15**

12 p.m.—Slow days mean I'm basically just watching the clock until it's a nonembarrassing time to eat lunch. I make it to 12 on the dot before eating my TJ's sando and carrots. I usually don't buy this much prepackaged stuff for lunch, but this week I was lazy.

2 p.m.—The smoke is making it too difficult to work/breathe/live right now, so everyone leaves the office to go work from home. Back in West Hollywood, the sky is relatively clear. I hope everyone in the path of the blaze is okay! I work the rest of the day from home—which means taking notes on two new episodes of shows I work on, while spying on some dogs outside.

4 p.m.—Oops, I bought some cool boots from Express on sale. **$45**

6:30 p.m.—I take a boxing class. It's free thanks to a friend who sent me a code! There are parts where we're supposed to unleash our rage on the heavy bag, but I'm not feeling super ragey.

8:30 p.m.—Shower and blow-dry my hair. I make whole wheat pasta with Brussels sprouts and garlic for dinner. I also do a couple hours of work for my side hustle—editing and writing. My mom keeps just offering up my services to her friends, willy-nilly. I help edit a brochure for a high school choir group for one of my mom's friends. YOU'RE WELCOME, KAREN. THAT USUALLY COSTS PEOPLE LIKE $50. Kidding. I'm happy to help.

10 p.m.—My dad finally picked the presents he wants for my mom. I buy them ($315) and he transfers me money to cover it—plus some extra money as a birthday present since my birthday is in two weeks! Woo!

DAILY TOTAL: $52.15

| **DAY THREE** |

8 a.m.—A new fire sparked overnight and it's nearer to the office. After some confusion about whether I need to go in, I call a Lyft to work. With all the madness, I almost forget it's our office Christmas party tonight, and I'll be getting ready at a coworker's house before heading straight there. I'm mad that it's on a Wednesday, but I guess I'll just have to deal with being hungover at work tomorrow.

We get $25 in travel money since the company doesn't want anyone driving drunk, but the rides from my office to the venue and then home will eat that up. I pay for this one myself. **$30**

8:30 a.m.—Breakfast! An English muffin and coffee from home.

12 p.m.—There are only, like, five people in the office due to the fires. The few of us who came in decide to go out to lunch. I get a salmon burger. **$21**

3 p.m.—Might as well get a manicure. **$20**

5 p.m.—Leave the office a tiny bit early to head to my coworker's house. We drink wine while we put on our fancy outfits and do our hair and makeup. We stop for wine and snacks, which I cover for the group. **$35**

7 p.m.—Lyft to the party (split with two coworkers and expensed). Our Lyft got a flat tire along the way, and we had to change cars! Nonstop thrills over here. The rest of the night is a blur. At some point, I do all of the following: eat 1,200 tater tots, wink awkwardly at a coworker, avoid talking to my boss, lose a raffle, and do a lot of whiskey shots. **$37** (expensed)

11:30 p.m.—We go from the party venue to another bar. I get myself and a coworker a vodka soda. This is a bad idea. **$17**

1 a.m.—I Lyft home (expensed) and drunkenly eat a microwaved frozen burrito in my bed. I am terrified for tomorrow. **$14** (expensed)

DAILY TOTAL: $123

DAY FOUR

6:30 a.m.—Ohhhhhh no.
6:45 a.m.—NOPE.
7:30 a.m.—Wow, this is really happening. A new day has come. I need to go to work.
9:30 a.m.—I crawl into work where my office is holding a "team breakfast," which they have never done before. I have a suspicion it is to lure hungover people into the office instead of sleeping all morning. I make it there for eggs and stuff. 75 percent of the office is wearing their sunglasses indoors. The struggle is real.
10:30 a.m.—Sit quietly at my desk and concentrate on not dying.
12 p.m.—Order a breakfast burrito with some coworkers. **$8**
3:30 p.m.—Take advantage of my boss's offsite meeting to sneak home to nap for the rest of the workday. It's the company's fault for doing this party on a weeknight!

7 p.m.—My dinner plans canceled, and I could not be happier. I eat leftover pasta with Brussels sprouts plus a LOT of M&Ms. Fun fact: they cure hangovers.
8 p.m.—After reading a ton of articles about the fires, I donate to a charity that's helping families who've been evacuated or lost their homes. **$50**

DAILY TOTAL: $58

DAY FIVE

8 a.m.—I pick up a quinoa, banana, pomegranate, almond, and honey bowl from a place by my work. Plus coffee. **$9**
12 p.m.—Eat the last Trader Joe's sandwich I had in my fridge, along with some carrots and another cutie.
2 p.m.—Walk to CVS for chapstick. **$2**
4 p.m.—Pay a $15 fee for late canceling a ClassPass class. I thought it might make me feel better to sweat out the rest of my hangover, but I'm starting to feel like I might be coming down with something. GREAT. **$15**
6 p.m.—Take some NyQuil and sleep forever.

DAILY TOTAL: $26

| DAY SIX |

8 a.m.—Well, my achey bones and fever make it clear: I have the flu. After freaking out that I have meningitis, I go to urgent care just in case and they send me home with a "you have the flu, please grow up." I pay the co-pay. **$50**

10 a.m.—I call to move my bikini wax to later in the week. The front-desk person takes pity on me and waives the cancellation fee. I love him.

11:30 a.m.—I DO make it out of the house for brunch for one of my best friends' birthday. Friends get mimosas and Bloody Marys, I get hot tea and try not to touch anyone. We all split the bill and cover our friend's meal. **$52**

7 p.m.—I slowly get dressed for a friend's Christmas party before realizing I'm a crazy person who is about to get a whole house full of people sick like some flu terrorist. I bow out last minute, change back into pajamas, and go to bed.

8 p.m.—I'm not one of those cool people who lose their appetite when they are sick. I order some yellow curry and pad Thai through Postmates and have a little before falling asleep. **$40**

DAILY TOTAL: $142

| DAY SEVEN |

9 a.m.—Wake up feeling slightly better and decide I am up for a walk since I haven't exercised since Tuesday. I am also craving a donut *and* a breakfast sandwich. I walk a mile to the fancy Pavilions super-market and make it happen. **$8**

11 a.m.—By the time I walk back home with my food, I am covered in sweat. Perhaps I was not as cured as I thought I was. I settle in to watch TV forever.

3 p.m.—I manage to do some work for my side hustle. Gotta get those hours in! I aim for 20 a month. Sometimes I get less, sometimes more. Depends on the clients, really.

5:30 p.m.—Time to do some work for my main job. It never ends! This Sunday was essentially a workday so I allow myself a half a glass of wine while I finish some things up as a reward.

10:30 p.m.—Time for bed. Take an aspirin and hope to feel better tomorrow. BYE!

DAILY TOTAL: $8

THE BREAKDOWN

TOTAL SPENT: $432.10

FOOD AND DRINK: $197.15

ENTERTAINMENT: $10

HOME AND HEALTH: $77.95

CLOTHES AND BEAUTY: $67

TRANSPORTATION: $30

OTHER: $50

THE FOLLOW-UP

You live alone. What made you decide to live without a roommate?
I had been living with roommates until I moved in with my boyfriend, and then we broke up really suddenly. At the time, all of my friends were living with their S.O.s or had pretty stable living situations. I just didn't want to do the whole Craigslist roommate thing. I needed some room to recover, and I didn't want to feel awkward in my own space. I also think it's a nice sign of adulthood.

What kind of reactions do you get when you tell people you live alone?
Among my friend group, I'm the only one who lives alone. I think they're all pretty shocked. I also make more money than most of my friends. I think half of my friends would love to; the other half think I'm crazy. They hear how much I spend on rent, and they think it's shocking.

Have there ever been moments where you thought maybe it wasn't financially worth it?
That's why I'm really focused on rainy-day savings. If I lost my job, I would definitely have to consider moving. But the way I look at it is,

hopefully, my salary only goes up from here. I hope to only make more money from here on.

Are there financial sacrifices you make in order to make living alone possible?
I definitely work a lot more at the side job. I never say no to work. I've been lucky because that's pretty stable, but it's a lot of evenings and weekends. Never ends.

Who do you talk to about money? Your parents? Friends?
I talk to my parents about some things. They are great resources and full of advice, but they have a way of making me feel like I'm spending too frivolously. My dad really wants me to buy property, but I don't feel like I'm in a place where I can afford it. They know how much I make and to them it sounds like a lot, but I don't think they fully grasp how expensive it is to live in LA. And while saving and getting onto the property ladder are goals of mine, I won't sacrifice having a fun/fulfilling life in the meantime—even if that means it takes longer to get where I want to be.

What surprised you most about doing a Money Diary?
I was honestly surprised by how quickly the small purchases add up. There were days where I thought I'd spent practically no money, only to realize that I'd spent $60 on random shit! Now I'm trying for more $0 spending days!

In order to get comfortable with your finances, we're going to start at the very beginning, getting a better sense of where we stand. Maybe you just got your first job and want to kick things off on a high note. Maybe you've got some debt, and you feel a wave of nausea every time you get a statement. Maybe you're pretty happy with your money management, but you want to start planning for even bigger goals. Whatever your status, coming clean about your financial picture is the first step to clarity and success.

So where to begin? Let's start with the numbers you need to know. And then we can dig a little deeper into what exactly they mean.

I'm still devoted to writing everything down with pen and paper, but an Excel spreadsheet or a Google doc works, too. You can also take notes here in the book—feel free to mark it up, carry it everywhere, share it with your accountant, your financial adviser, or your friends.

It might take an hour or so to collect all these numbers, especially if you have to set up online accounts or retrieve passwords. I made a note beside each account how often you should check in to see how you're doing. I like to look at my checking account balance every day, but that might make some people anxious. It's important to review your paycheck a few times a year, especially if you get a raise, increase your 401(k) contribution, or make other changes. The most important thing is to always have a sense of where you stand financially.

11
—

**CHECKING
ACCOUNT BALANCE
REGULARLY**

**401(K) BALANCE
FOUR TIMES A YEAR**

**CREDIT CARD DEBT
MONTHLY**

**SAVINGS ACCOUNT
BALANCE
REGULARLY**

**ADDITIONAL RETIREMENT
ACCOUNT BALANCES
FOUR TIMES A YEAR**

**PERSONAL LOAN DEBT
MONTHLY**

**STUDENT LOAN DEBT
YEARLY**

**CREDIT SCORE
FOUR TIMES A YEAR**

**ANNUAL SALARY
TWO TIMES A YEAR**

**INVESTMENT
ACCOUNT BALANCES
FOUR TIMES A YEAR
(IT'S OKAY IF YOU DON'T
HAVE ANYTHING TO WRITE
HERE—WE'LL WORK ON
THAT IN CHAPTER 9.)**

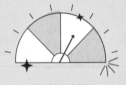

**REGULAR
ANNUAL EXPENSES
YEARLY
(IF YOU PAY A LUMP SUM
FOR INSURANCE [LIFE,
HOME, ETC.], PROPERTY
TAXES, ETC.)**

**REGULAR MONTHLY
EXPENSES
ONE TO FOUR TIMES A YEAR
(RENT/MORTGAGE,
UTILITIES, TRANSPORTATION
COSTS, SUBSCRIPTIONS,
GYM MEMBERSHIPS,
PRESCRIPTIONS, ETC.)**

Jane Doe
100 Main Street
New York City, NY 12345

Pay	Current	Hours
Regular Pay	600.00	40.00

Deductions	Current	YTD
Insurance	35.00	35.00

Taxes Withheld	Current	YTD
Federal Income Tax	69.82	69.82
Social Security	35.03	35.03
Medicare	8.19	8.19
Income Tax	28.25	28.25

Employer Taxes	Current	YTD
FSA	3.39	3.39
Social Security Employer	35.03	35.03
Medicare Employer	8.19	8.19
401K	30.00	30.00

Net Pay: $ 393.71

01 PAYCHECK DETAILS
TWO TIMES A YEAR
(OR ANYTIME YOUR
PAYCHECK CHANGES
UNEXPECTEDLY!)

02 INSURANCE DEDUCTIONS
(INCLUDING VISION, DENTAL, MEDICAL, LIFE, DISABILITY, ETC.)

03 NET PAY
(THIS IS THE AMOUNT DEPOSITED IN YOUR ACCOUNT.)

04 FSA DEDUCTIONS
(INCLUDING HSA, DEPENDENT CARE, TRANSIT, ETC.)

05 TAX DEDUCTIONS
(DEPENDING ON WHERE YOU LIVE, THIS MIGHT INCLUDE STATE AND CITY TAXES.)

06 401(K) DEDUCTIONS
(THIS DOESN'T INCLUDE YOUR EMPLOYER MATCH.)

Finished writing? There you go: your financial profile. How do you feel? Whenever I review this info, I usually feel a little mixed. I always see a few areas that could improve (I'm an oversaver who should definitely consider investing more), a few places where I worry I'm wasting money (hello, sad desk salad), and a few places where I'm totally killing it (shout-out to that fully funded emergency account). I expect that's pretty normal, as there's always *something* to work on.

But if this review makes you feel bad, let's remember that we're so much more than these numbers. I would never suggest that money shouldn't make you emotional—but let's not base our self-worth on dollars and cents. I know you're more interesting than that, and I am, too. You are not defined by the number in your checking account or your salary or your credit score.

It's really important to know this information. We can't become better at managing our money if we're not real about where we are in the first place.

THIS IS A GOOD TIME TO:

Write down all your account info and log-in details in one safe place. It's good to have in case there's ever an emergency and your family/next of kin/etc. needs to access it.

While you're at it, save $1
Total saved so far: $1

Find Your Money Mantra

TIME: *15–30 minutes (no need to rush this)*
TOOLS: *Pen and paper*

If you're rolling your eyes at "money mantra," give me a minute to explain. This isn't some New Age, spiritual bullshit. As Priya Malani, the founder of the millennial-minded Stash Wealth, first told me, it's a statement that helps you remember why having control of your finances is so important.

Hip-hop lyrics make perfect money mantras. Just take Missy Elliott's 1997 song "Hit 'Em wit da Hee," where she blows off some dude, reassuring him that "I got my own account and my bills in large amount." And that's something every woman should aspire to.

Five years ago, I took a $20,000 pay cut to work for a tiny startup so I could make a career change. Thankfully, my husband, Ken, and I had enough saved up that I could take that risk—and it turned out to be a life-changing decision. My money mantra is: *I always want to have enough in savings that I can take a risk.*

Managing your money can feel overwhelming at times, which is why it's so important to center yourself and remember the ultimate goal is planning for the future, not dwelling on the past.

Here are a few examples, but you should feel free to come up with your own.

- I am going to pay down my debt once and for all.
- I want to build an emergency fund, so I don't have to rely on my parents/partner/friends/credit card next time the shit hits the fan.

- I want to start saving so I can quit my job and travel the world/buy a house/insert your goal here.
- I want to be rich.

Write down your money mantra, and keep it handy—maybe on a Post-it note in your planner or taped to your bathroom mirror. Revise it from time to time as you accomplish goals or your wants and needs change.

While you're at it, save $2
Total saved so far: $3

Budgets are bullshit. And like diets—another thing your friends at Refinery29 do not believe in—budgets set us up to fail. There's nothing I hate more than when a financial planner starts comparing money management to getting a beach body. Yuck.

I'm not going to tell you not to buy a latte, but I will say that understanding how much money you earn and how much you spend every month is really important to achieving financial security. There are some guidelines you can follow that will help you make sure you're spending and saving in a way that works for you and isn't oppressive or overly prescriptive.

The 50/30/20 rule was first made popular by Elizabeth Warren (yes, the US senator and potential presidential candidate) and her daughter, Amelia Warren Tyagi, in their 2005 book *All Your Worth: The Ultimate Lifetime Money Plan*. I will spare you a "nevertheless, she persisted" joke here and just add that it's become a classic framework in personal finance over the past decade. Many of the financial advisers I tapped for the book reference the rule with their clients.

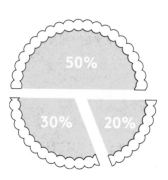

The rule breaks things down as follows:

- **50 percent** of your after-tax spending goes to **fixed expenses** such as your rent/mortgage, transportation (car expenses or public transit costs), insurance (including health, car, renter's or home, life, etc.), and food. If/when you have kids, you'd add mandatory child care (i.e., not the babysitter you hire for date night) to this bucket.

- **30 percent** of your after-tax spending goes to **flexible expenses** such as your gym membership, cable bill, clothing needs, travel, etc. This is the spending you do because you *can*, not because you have to. Credit card debt goes in this bucket

- **20 percent** of your after-tax spending goes to **future expenses** such as your emergency fund, retirement accounts, investment accounts, etc. Student loan debt goes in this bucket.

Want to figure out your own 50/30/20 plan? The math isn't that hard. You just need to pull the following numbers:

GROSS ANNUAL INCOME = _____ *(that's how much you bring home before taxes)*

APPROXIMATE TAX RATE PERCENTAGE = _____
(To find this number, just google "tax rate percentage"—there are a few websites that can help you calculate the number, as well as info on the IRS website.)

> **GROSS INCOME ×**
> **(1 – TAX RATE PERCENTAGE) =**
> **SPENDABLE YEARLY INCOME**

For example:

$$\$60,000 \times (1 - 0.25) = \$45,000$$

(Silly note here, but just a reminder that you should use a decimal for the percentage rate—so if you're in a 25 percent bracket, the decimal is 0.25. I promise this is about the hardest math you'll do in this book!)

SPENDABLE INCOME/12 = SPENDABLE MONTHLY INCOME

$45,000/12 = $3,750

(If you don't want to do this math, you can also just look at your paycheck, after taxes but before all your deductions.)

Once you've got that number, you can figure out your 50/30/20 plan.

SPENDABLE MONTHLY INCOME × 0.5 = BUDGET FOR FIXED EXPENSES

SPENDABLE MONTHLY INCOME × 0.3 = BUDGET FOR FLEXIBLE EXPENSES

SPENDABLE MONTHLY INCOME × 0.2 = BUDGET FOR FUTURE EXPENSES

So if you make $60,000 a year and pay an effective tax rate of 25 percent, you have $45,000 in spendable income a year. That breaks down to $3,750 per month after taxes:

- $1,875 should go to your fixed expenses, such as housing, transportation, groceries, insurance, etc.
- $1,125 should go to your flexible expenses, such as dining out, new shoes, or even a vacation.
- $750 should be split among your retirement accounts, savings, and paying down any student loan debt.

Manisha Thakor, the founder and CEO of MoneyZen, says that many of her clients panic when they see that 20 percent bucket because they aren't saving anywhere near that much. But it is a goal worth working toward.

If your fixed expenses exceed 50 percent (mine sure do!), you should only dip into your 30 percent flexible expenses to make up the difference. Priya has tweaked the 50/30/20 rule to an 80/20 rule. Since many of her clients were spending so much on fixed expenses, she encourages them to spend 80 percent of their income on their day-to-day expenses, from rent to lunch. The remaining 20 percent goes to future expenses (everything from retirement to long-term goals). If you've got debt, Priya tweaks the equation to 70/20/10: 70 percent for today, 20 percent to paying off debt, and 10 percent for the future.

Unfortunately, Priya and Manisha both found that people are more likely to compromise the amount they are saving than cut back on their wants. That's not really so surprising, right? It's easy to fall into bad habits—ordering lunch every day or giving in to an impulse buy. I'm also quick to justify certain expenses: I work hard, so I deserve that expensive gym membership even though I never go because I'm too busy working hard to actually use it.

These might seem like silly examples, but as I'll mention again and again throughout the book, the small expenses do add up (just as small savings can grow over time). Some of you might argue that there's just no way you could save another cent because of debt or the high cost of living or because you simply don't want to give up those little pleasures (or big indulgences) that make life better. But as a result your savings suffer, and in the long term, the future you suffers.

Manisha has an antidote to the overspending problem that she calls joy-based spending. It's a three-step process that takes a little time, but I promise, it's worth the effort.

Step 1: Take the highlighter test.

Track your spending for a period of time (do a Money Diary!)—Manisha recommends a month, but a weekend will work if that's all you can stomach.

When the time period is up, don't pull out a calculator—and definitely don't start stressing out about your spending—but get a highlighter. Go through the list and highlight any expenses that don't inspire you to do a happy dance.

Usually, the first things highlighted are bills, Manisha says. The answer there is the one we've all heard a thousand times (but don't always do), which is to call the provider and renegotiate your rate. If you're paying for Hulu *and* Netflix *and* Amazon Prime *and* HBOGO, do you still really need cable? Can you negotiate with the cable company for a more reasonable rate?

But going further down the list, Manisha's clients notice other expenditures that definitely don't make them feel sparkling. Like crazy-expensive drinks with a couple of women who actually make you feel like crap about yourself. Or that $2 mat fee you pay every time you go to yoga, even though you own a yoga mat you could take along. Those are the kinds of expenses you could cut and lose no joy.

We've all got these kinds of lifestyle-type expenses that we can ax, and it doesn't feel like deprivation. Just make sure to reallocate that money to your savings, not just spend it on something else. You can even do something as small as transferring $2 to savings every time you take your yoga mat to class.

Then there are the big expenses that are worth considering. Do you feel joy when you pay your rent or mortgage? If you do, it could be worth the cuts you have to make in the other areas of your life. If you don't, maybe it's time to move? Manisha sees people consistently buying houses that are too big for their needs, without really considering how much they can

comfortably afford. We'll tackle this a bit more in chapter 7, but for reference, you shouldn't be buying a home that is more than three to four times your yearly household income. If you live in a city, it might be closer to five to six times.

Curious about the car equivalent? Don't buy a vehicle that is more than one-third your annual income. So if you're making $60,000, you really shouldn't buy a car that costs more than $20,000. Manisha routinely meets people who are making $50,000 a year, driving a $35,000 car, and wondering why they can't make ends meet. "The reason is they're driving it," she tells me.

The highlighter test can be overwhelming. Even though you're supposed to be focused on the expenditures that bring you joy, you automatically spend a lot of time reviewing the waste. Don't forget to take a little time to appreciate the purchases you've made that bring you happiness. I get a lot of joy from the $37 I pay monthly for my *New York Times* subscription. Maybe the $4.50 you spent on a latte was worth it because you caught up with an old colleague who might have a new job opportunity for you. Or you feel pride every time you look at the $20 houseplant you haven't yet killed. The goal is to be mindful of your spending but not obsessive.

Step 2: Calculate your hourly wage.

Manisha first came across the idea for her clients to look at their spending through the lens of their hourly wage after she read about it in the classic personal finance book *Your Money or Your Life* by Joe Dominguez and Vicki Robin. The idea is that when we spend the money we earn, we are, karmically speaking, spending our life's energy. The process of paying attention to your money isn't about deprivation, it's about honoring all the time that was spent earning that money and making sure it's going toward the things in life that make you happy.

How do you calculate your hourly wage? Most full-time employees work around 2,000 hours a year. Divide your gross income by 2,000 to get your pretax hourly wage. If your pretax salary is $60,000, your pretax hourly wage is $30. So if you see a dress that costs $300, you can think to yourself: *I'd have to work more than ten hours to buy this dress. Do I really want it?*

There's no judgment on answering yes, but you have to decide. Odds are, there are plenty of impulse buys you might not throw into your cart *just because* they won't really feel like such a steal when looked at in this light. Take that cute West Elm throw pillow for $35. If you're making $45,000 a year, your hourly wage is $22.50, which means it will take more than an hour of work to pay for that pillow. Or think about a bigger expense, such as the ten-class ClassPass package at $135 a month. You'd have to work almost a full day to pay for those classes. If you're not consistently using all ten a month, maybe it's time to look into a different (less expensive) workout program.

Step 3: Quit comparing yourself to others.

The last step is a little more conceptual (and honestly a lot harder). Manisha points out that pop culture—especially movies and TV—presents lifestyles that are completely incompatible with the jobs the characters hold. It's unlikely Lena Dunham's character on *Girls* could afford the rent on her Brooklyn apartment. But we rarely think about all the other expenditures those fictional characters regularly make, from their designer clothing to immaculate blowouts to fancy vacations. Maybe we don't even realize that we're doing it, but it's easy to get caught up in thinking that we *should* be able to afford those lifestyles.

But not only is pop culture impacting the way we spend, so is social media. Nobody shares the bad stuff on Instagram—the dented car that required $1,000 in repairs or the sofa your new kitten destroyed. Instead, it seems as though it's all luxury travel and finely decorated homes—made worse by influencers who are paid for those lust-worthy posts. God help your 20 percent future expenses.

Manisha points out that we're trapped between the media we consume on a personal level and the media we consume more broadly on a societal level, with constant "perfect" images that aren't rooted in reality. Once you let go of the notion that pop culture is real life and that social media shows the whole picture, you can let go of some of the anxiety that you're not keeping up financially.

Look, it's not always going to be fun to stay within your 50/30/20 plan. Who doesn't want to indulge from time to time? But being more mindful—knowing your hourly wage, ignoring social media fallacies, and thinking before you swipe your credit card—can have a huge impact on your overall financial picture.

THIS IS A GOOD TIME TO:

Do an audit of your expenses to see how much you're really spending. Many financial advisers will suggest you review three months' worth of expenses because although certain items (rent, cable bill, etc.) are the same each month, other costs (clothing, food, electricity) will probably go up and down. Adding up your three-month total in each category and dividing by three helps you get a more realistic monthly average. This will take a while, so budget an hour or more.

While you're at it, save $3
Total saved so far: $6

"REAL WEALTH IS ABOUT BEING ABLE TO MAKE CHOICES"

How much money is enough to lead a happy life? A 2017 study from Purdue University found that $105,000 is the ideal individual income,[1] but I'd argue it's a highly personal question that a survey can't really determine. Ellen,* 31, brings in around $70,000 a year working long hours at three jobs—but she loves it. For her, a child of divorce, who faced severe income insecurity as a kid, working and saving provides a kind of financial safety net she's always craved. Refinery29's editor Jessica Chou interviewed Ellen about the bumpy path she followed to find this happiness.

How did your childhood impact how you view money today?

Growing up, I had a really wonderful life, but when I was about ten, my parents went through a nasty divorce. My father was very successful, but my mother suffered from mental health issues. Things weren't working out, and they split very suddenly. We went from upper middle class to sleeping in cars and crashing in people's basements.

I vowed that would never happen to me or my children. I grew up with the principles of being extremely frugal. You don't deserve anything you don't work for; if it's broken, you try to fix it before buying a new one. And if you're strong enough to work, you work as much as you can and save as much money as you can.

---

*All names of diarists and other nonexpert contributors have been changed.

When you were younger, did you make any money mistakes?

I went through a period of time where I was spending money I didn't have because I wanted to look like I had made it. I moved to Colorado for grad school, and there were a lot of kids who had a lot of money. I was going out and drinking top-shelf whiskey after class, buying four-dollar coffees every single day. When I first met my husband, he invited me to go skiing. I wanted to impress him so badly that I went out and got a credit card and bought ski gear. I didn't even shop around. I went in and I said, "I have a date with a man who invited me to go skiing. Dress me." It was awful.

What was the turning point?

My student loans. I was taking out an extra $5,000 to $8,000 a year and not working as much, because I thought, *Well, my friends aren't working. I'm a grad student, I don't have time to work.* Then I looked at the bill, and it was around $71,000 total for undergrad and grad school. I thought, *That's a down payment on a house. I can't do this. I can't keep adding to this debt.* It was a huge wake-up call.

How did your spending habits change?

I cut out the drinking, the partying, the spending. I didn't buy anything I didn't need.

Can you describe what real wealth means to you?

Real wealth is about being able to make choices. In my high school and college years, I always equated people who had money with these lavish lifestyles. I wanted to go out and have these fancy dinners and amazing vacations and wear all the nice clothes. But the richest people that I've met, they're wearing the same blue jeans for thirty years. They wake up before dawn and work until after dark, providing for their families. They don't live richly in the way I used to think rich meant, but they live with incredible happiness. There's always food in the fridge, and always compassion and generosity. They save so they can have the flexibility to live the life they want and not have to answer to anybody except their own family. That to me is what real wealth is.

How did you learn about personal finance?
Really, I learned from trial and error. I remember looking at my student loan debt and thinking, *Okay, I need to figure this out.* When I met my husband, he was already very adept at budgeting. He was also a big help when it came to paying off debt. A few years ago, I had a horrific mountain bike accident where I shattered my leg and almost lost it. It was going to be about $4,000 after my insurance kicked in, so I set up a plan to pay it off. I took out a 2 percent cash-back credit card, put all the medical debt on that, got the cash back, and paid it back before the interest rate kicked in. Little things like that are a huge help.

When was the first time you actually felt financially stable?
It sounds silly, but just a year ago, I went to go get a coffee, and one of my friends called me and said, "Hey, can you pick up a few more for the team?" I remember being able to do that and not even thinking twice about it. When I was a child, that would have been a big deal. I wouldn't have had the extra $10. That felt like making it. It's those little moments, and the nice thing about the little moments is you never feel like, *Oh, I've made it, I can just stop.* Your dreams and your goals change, but the way you get there never changes. You live frugally and save really hard.

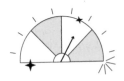

I'm willing to bet you know your SAT score but not your credit score. For a grown-up, there are few more important numbers to know. Your credit score determines whether you're eligible for everything from a credit card to a mortgage, and in some cases, employers even look at it when making hiring decisions. Over the past few years, it's become easier than ever to track your score—without damaging it.

According to Priya, knowing your score and how to improve it can save you tens, even hundreds, of thousands of dollars over your lifetime.

Your credit score is made up of several factors, she explains, but there are three main components to make up how your score is calculated:

Reliability: Do you pay on time?

Credit utilization rate (CUR): Are you maxing out how much credit is available to you? The general rule is to stay at or below 30 percent. So if you have a $10,000 credit limit, try not to charge more than $3,000 each month. If you do find yourself spending more (while staying within your 50/30/20 plan), call your credit card company and ask them to increase your spending limit.

Credit history: How long have you been managing credit? It's important to have a long credit history to prove your reliability over time.

Credit scores are like test scores, Priya says; the higher your score, the better you're doing. Every credit agency sets its own range and corresponding "creditworthiness" score, and lenders have their own standards they consult when determining how they manage risk. So although there is not one standardized credit score, the higher the better.

If you find yourself with a lower score than you expected (say you fall into the average or below average range), Priya suggests giving yourself a quick bump by increasing the frequency of paying down your debt. For instance, pay off your credit card balance every two weeks instead of once a month, and you should see your score increase pretty quickly.

THIS IS A GOOD TIME TO:

Check your credit score. It's easier than ever—more and more banks and financial institutions, including Capital One and Turbo, let you check it for free. They will also let you set up alerts so you can easily monitor if it goes up or down.

While you're at it, save $4
Total saved so far: $10

I didn't get my first credit card until I was out of college. I was afraid of the marketers who came to campus giving away free T-shirts and promises of easy money. I liked to shop, so it was inevitable that if I had a credit card, I'd run up thousands of dollars of debt, right? And my mom, my main source of financial advice, discouraged me. She didn't think I needed more than a debit card, and so for all of college, that's what I used.

But all that time, I wasn't building credit. So when I graduated, I didn't have any debt, but I did have a really hard time getting a credit card. I was rejected again and again, and I finally had to sign up for a card that required me to put down a cash deposit. In the years since, I've opened a few more cards. It turned out that even though I love to shop, I've never been tempted to use credit for something that I couldn't afford to pay off in full at the end of the month.

I've talked with quite a few women who aren't using credit cards at all. They use debit cards instead, for much the same reason that I did in college—because credit card debt seems terrifying. Research suggests my friends aren't alone: a 2016 Bankrate study found that just 33 percent of millennials have a credit card.[2]

The reality is, you do need a credit card in order to establish a good credit score, and it's better to start sooner than later, Priya says. If you want to get a credit card but have no credit history, here are three good options. Whatever route you take, make sure you're able to pay off the balance on time each month so you're not hit with high interest rates and late fees.

1. Get a secured card. This is what I did way back in the day when I was first trying to establish credit. With a secured card, you set aside a few hundred dollars into a savings account that becomes collateral for the credit card company. This amount dictates your credit limit, and if you don't make a payment, the credit card company can access those funds to cover your balance. It sounds like a debit card, but this little piece of plastic is actually helping you build credit.

2. Have a family member cosign. A lot of people ask an older sibling or parent to cosign on their first card, because it shows the credit card company that they have someone who has their back, financially. One thing to keep in mind when you have a family member cosign: it puts the cosigner's credit score on the line, so you'll want to be extra careful to pay the bills off in full and on time so you don't have a negative impact on their credit score.

3. Get a low-limit card. You might not be able to book a luxury vacation on one of these cards, but they will help you build credit. Usually, if you pay your balance consistently for six to eight months, the credit card company will automatically raise your line of credit (or you can call and ask for it to be raised).

THIS IS A GOOD TIME TO:

Pay with points! Maybe the best (and worst) thing about signing in to Amazon or Seamless these days is that you can easily pay for your purchase with credit card points. But getting cash back is another great reason to use your credit card instead of a debit card. When you pay with points, it almost feels as if you're getting something for free.

While you're at it, save $5
Total saved so far: $15

Take a Money Mental Health Day

TIME: *Anywhere from fifteen minutes to a full morning*
TOOLS: *Bills, account info, log-in details, etc.*

When I was talking with Shannon McLay, the founder of Financial Gym, about how her clients frequently rack up annoying bank fees, she mentioned that she encourages them to take a money mental health day every three to four months to keep their money management under control. I'd rather spend my precious time off doing something more fun than rolling over my 401(k), but maybe that explains why I struggle to get these little projects done. If you're responsible enough to tackle these problems as they come up, you don't need a money mental health day. If you're more like me and never, ever cross them off your daily to-do list, maybe it's time to dedicate some real time to getting it done.

On these money mental health days, make a list of all your outstanding financial issues and start working your way through it. Here are some places to start:

- Call your bank and ask it to refund any fees you are paying.*

---

*A note on bank fees, while we're (sort of) on the topic: you shouldn't be paying them, full stop. If your bank is charging you for your checking account and refuses to waive the fees, start shopping for a new bank. If you get hit with an unexpected fee, call customer service. The catch is, you actually have to ask, "Can you refund my fees?" Customer service reps can often help, but only if you say those magic words.

Also, be polite when you call. It can be hard (I get cranky when I make phone calls, too), but it's worth it.

- Call your insurance company (home or auto) and ask for a lower rate.
- Call your cell phone company and ask for a lower rate.
- Call your cable company and ask for a lower rate.
- Call your credit card company and ask for a lower interest rate if you're carrying a balance.
- If you have medical bills, call and ask to set up a payment plan.
- Cancel any subscriptions you aren't using.
- Check your credit score.
- Roll over any old 401(k) accounts.
- File any outstanding claims to your HSA or FSA accounts.

These tasks are superannoying, and it's easy to say "I'm too busy." But taking the time to make these calls can save you a lot. Plus, once you make your first call and save some cash, the success can be addictive!

While you're at it, save $6
Total saved so far: $21

Love & Money
(Or How Not to Fight About $$$)

Here's a financial truth about me: I make more money than my husband, Ken. A lot more. It happened rather suddenly, and sometimes it's a little weird. He's always been superfrugal (see his no-cab-taking, happy-hour-drinking, peanut-butter-every-day ways), and I've always gone along with it because we didn't make very much. But now that I make more, sometimes I want to spend money and not feel guilty. Even several years into our relationship the "mine, yours, ours" question still pops up from time to time.

There's also still a lot of societal pressure for men to be the primary breadwinners even though the number of households relying on two incomes has grown to 46 percent from 30 percent in 1970, according to a 2015 Pew Research Center study.[1] Though Ken's masculinity (and my femininity!) isn't threatened by our salary disparities, other women (and men) might not be comfortable in our situation. Gender politics play a big part in relationships, from that very first date and the question of who picks up the tab. Yet there's still a staggering number of people who don't even know their spouse's salary.[2]

In this chapter, we'll explore some of the challenges women face when it comes to love and money, from navigating the "Who pays the bill?" conundrum to deciding how to combine your income. Communication is key—and the first step is having open and honest conversations about the matter. Sounds a lot like any other consensual adult decision, doesn't it?

A Couple in Brooklyn with a $21,000 Difference in Salaries

PARTNER 1 (J)

OCCUPATION: Associate producer
INDUSTRY: Video production
AGE: 26
LOCATION: Brooklyn, NY
SALARY: $1,150 per week (roughly $59,000/year)
PAYCHECK AMOUNT (EVERY TWO WEEKS): $1,561

PARTNER 2 (B)

OCCUPATION: Accountant
INDUSTRY: Public accounting
AGE: 26
LOCATION: Brooklyn, NY
ANNUAL SALARY: $80,000
PAYCHECK (TWICE A MONTH): $2,043

J'S GENERAL FINANCIAL INFORMATION:

Checking Account Balance: $1,500
Savings Account Balance: ~$500

B'S GENERAL FINANCIAL INFORMATION:

Checking Account Balance: $2,000
Savings Account Balance: $25,000

SHARED HOUSING EXPENSES:

Rent: $2,250 (We split the rent on a one-bedroom apartment based on income. J pays $1,000 and B pays $1,250. Rent includes heat and hot water.)
Internet: $44 (split evenly)
Gas: $18 (split evenly)
Electricity: $40–$160 (split evenly)

SHARED SUBSCRIPTIONS:

Spotify: $11 (B pays)
Amazon Prime: $99/year (B pays)
Hulu: We sign up for free trials whenever there's a show we want to watch.

Netflix: We use our parents' accounts.
HBOGO: We use our parents' accounts.

J'S MONTHLY EXPENSES:

Transportation: $121 (for a 30-day unlimited-ride MetroCard)
Phone: $30 (I'm on my parents' plan, so I pay them.)
Health Insurance: $182
ClassPass: $90 (but frozen this month because I'm traveling)

J'S DEBT:
Student Loan Debt

Total: ~$6,000 (My parents paid for college but made me take out a (very) small loan each year so I would have some responsibility in my education.)
Student Loan Payment: $238
Credit Card Debt Total: ~$4,000
Credit Card Minimum Payment: $300

J'S RETIREMENT:
401(k) Total: $0

B'S MONTHLY EXPENSES:

Transportation: $121 (for a 30-day unlimited-ride MetroCard; deducted from paycheck, pretax)
Phone: $30
Health Insurance: $17/paycheck
Dental Insurance: $5/paycheck
Eye Insurance: $1/paycheck

B'S DEBT:
Student Loan Debt

Total: $0
Credit Card Debt Total: $0

B'S RETIREMENT:
401(k) Contribution: $61/paycheck (3 percent + company match)
401(k) Total: $4,250

| DAY ONE (J) |

7 a.m.—I'm working from home today, as I got back from a press trip to Europe late last night. Going to Europe for a long weekend is not a normal part of my life. There are a couple of perks that come with my job, and this was a BIG one.

8 a.m.—I decide to work from a local café. I must still be in Europe mode, because I feel entitled to a cappuccino and a scenic view while I work. There is an incident in Manhattan, and the trains are very delayed. I suggest my boyfriend, B., have breakfast with me since he can't get to work for a couple of hours anyway.

9 a.m.—We bring our laptops and order breakfast. B. decides to work from home, too. He lost his wallet last night, so I pay. Normally we split tabs like this, but occasionally one of us will pick up the whole thing. **$37**

2 p.m.—We take a break from work to go grocery shopping. I shop primarily at Trader Joe's because I love its products and prices. I'm the only one who

grocery shops, unless B. is picking up ingredients for dinner. I make my lunch every day, B. buys his at work; therefore, I usually pay for the groceries since I use the majority of them. Today, we get zucchini noodles for a baked shrimp scampi, smoothie ingredients, black bean burritos and guac, eggs, egg whites, cheese, pancake mix, and tomato soup. **$55.50**

3 p.m.—We grab half a sourdough loaf from the bakery. I pay. **$4.25**

6 p.m.—B. makes us grilled cheese and tomato soup. Normally, I meal prep for the week, but I'm too jet-lagged.

8 p.m.—We want to watch a Christmas movie and decide on *The Holiday*, which B. has never seen. Halfway through we decide we want hot chocolate. We have the instant mix, but I think it tastes better with a splash of milk. I convince B. to run downstairs for some. There's a credit card minimum, so we scrounge up some cash. I only have a dollar and three quarters, so we pull some more quarters from our laundry coin stash and hope it's enough. **$1.75 + $1.50 in laundry quarters**

DAILY TOTAL: $98.50

DAY ONE (B)

8 a.m.—Last night, I took a train to the Giants game in New Jersey and on the way to the game I dropped my wallet somewhere. I realized this seconds after I got off the train as the doors closed in my face. It was one of those moments where you're doing something that you've done a thousand times but one thing throws everything out of whack (in this case I was typing my credit card info into an app to pay for my train ticket). Luckily, my friends covered me for the day and I was able to get swiped into the subway on my way home. I lost my driver's license and credit cards, my work ID, a $100 gift card, $50 in cash, my MetroCard, and some other items of sentimental value. Luckily, I have my passport (which is expiring in a month) and $200 in cash. So this is going to be an old-fashioned week of purchasing whatever I need, in person, at a store. Fuck me.

9 a.m.—Although I am down in the dumps about my wallet, I go to a nice breakfast with my woman. She spots me! Thanks!

10 a.m.—Just kidding, forgot to cancel my credit card. Let me just buy a present for my nephew before I call to cancel. Kid's piano. **$27.99**

10:30 a.m.—Aaaand one more gift for the girlfriend. And now she'll know how much I'm spending on this gift. It was 50 percent off! Sweater and sexy underwear. **$58.95**

2 p.m.—Hit the grocery store for a few nights of cooking this week. I didn't pay, but my lovely girlfriend spent about $55. I carried the bags :)

DAILY TOTAL: $86.94

DAY TWO (J)

6 a.m.—I wake up, shower, and start working. I'm on set today and want to get some work done beforehand.

8 a.m.—B. wakes up and showers. I make scrambled eggs with mushrooms and Parmesan. I also toast the leftover sourdough and spread some guac and chili pepper flakes on it. Having breakfast together two days in a row is super rare, but it's very nice.

2 p.m.—We wrap on set and take an Uber back to the office. I buy the crew lunch, but will be reimbursed by work when I expense the meal. **$50.07** (expensed)

4 p.m.—My coworker and I brought back wine from Europe for our team, so we have a little happy hour.

7 p.m.—The work crew attends a special movie screening. B. comes as my plus-one. He buys us popcorn and a blue slushy. He's still wallet-less, but now has some cash. There's a Q&A with the cast after the screening, so we get home pretty late.

12 a.m.—My coworker stays over because she doesn't live in the city, and it's too late for her to get home. B. buys us sparkling water and pita chips because all we had for dinner was popcorn and we're still a bit hungry. Finally BED.

DAILY TOTAL: $0

| DAY TWO (B) |

8 a.m.—I canceled my credit card finally. Off the grid, baby! I'm going to round up these expenses now because I don't have a credit card statement to refer to, and I'll never remember cents. Who remembers cents? Who uses cents anyway?

9 a.m.—Break my hundred-dollar bill at the subway bodega so I have small enough bills to put in the MetroCard machine. Tic Tacs are $3 (highway robbery). I buy a MetroCard with cash ($27), which is a real punch in the dick because I had five weeks of unlimited time in my lost wallet. **$30**

10 a.m.—Morning coffee run. **$3**

12 p.m.—Lunch. **$10**

7 p.m.—After work, I venture uptown to a screening with my girlfriend. Popcorn, water, and a blue slushy. **$19.12**

12 a.m.—Realizing on the way home that dinner consisted of popcorn and a slushy, I buy more crap to eat before bed. Seltzer and pita chips. **$4.78**

DAILY TOTAL: $66.90

| DAY THREE (J) |

6:30 a.m.—It's a busy day. We have three small shoots and a happy hour. I make a smoothie with cucumber, pineapple, aloe vera, coconut water, and lemon juice.

8 a.m.—I get to work. I'm regretting having not meal prepped, but luckily the office kitchen is fully stocked. I have a bowl of cereal and a latte from the office coffee machine.

12 p.m.—My coworker brings back some snacks from her shoot, and I have half of my lunch from yesterday.

2 p.m.—I have a quick shoot at a wine bar. I try a sip of orange wine while I'm there, because I've never seen such a thing. It's pretty good and has a bit of a sour taste.

7 p.m.—A coworker and I go to a restaurant in Brooklyn for dinner; we were invited to try some items on their menu. We get a bunch of small plates and a "brooding" red wine—it's delicious.

10 p.m.—After dinner we decide to splurge on an Uber home since it's freezing, and our evening was free. **$11.38**

DAILY TOTAL: $11.38

DAY THREE (B)

10 a.m.—Morning coffee run. **$3.58**
12 p.m.—Lunch. **$9.75**

7 p.m.—Meet up with a buddy at this bar down the street, $5 drafts and $1 racks. Doesn't get much better than that. Also *Jeopardy* at 7 is a nice touch. **$34**

10 p.m.—Cheap falafel dinner on the way home. **$7.75**

DAILY TOTAL: $55.08

DAY FOUR (J)

7 a.m.—Snow! We have to push our shoot to this afternoon because of the snow. Cereal for breakfast again, plus a banana.

11:30 a.m.—It's a coworker's birthday, and we are having a fake meeting to surprise her with a celebration. They forgot to bring something to light the candle, so I run around looking for a lighter. I find some matches just in time!

1:30 p.m.—Good thing we pushed back our shoot because the lighting is beautiful.

3:30 p.m.—My coworker, who slept over the other night, brought me a sandwich from home for lunch. Mozzarella, red peppers, zucchini, and pesto on ciabatta bread. It's really good!

6:30 p.m.—I get home early tonight; it was a rough afternoon at the office. I call B. to remind him to pick up white wine and shrimp for our dinner. He cooks while I shower. Bless him. We are having baked shrimp scampi over zucchini noodles. We needed the white wine for the recipe, but it also pairs well with the meal. We finish the bottle.

8 p.m.—We get cozy and watch *About a Boy*. I fall asleep on the couch after the movie ends. I am exhausted.

DAILY TOTAL: $0

DAY FOUR (B)

10 a.m.—Morning coffee run. **$3.58**

12 p.m.—Lunch. **$11.92**

7 p.m.—Have to pick up some shrimp for dinner. **$15.79**

7:30 p.m.—Oddly enough, the bottle of wine is the same price as the shrimp. **$15.79**

DAILY TOTAL: $47.08

DAY FIVE (J)

8:30 a.m.—Free work breakfast on Fridays. I never get sick of it.

1 p.m.—I attend a seminar with some coworkers. They have lunch prepared, which means I did not eat my packed lunch one day this week.

Luckily, the burritos will last until next week and won't be wasted.

6:30 p.m.—I get home early after the seminar and have a glass of wine with B. He heads out to see the new *Star Wars* movie with his friends. I stay up doing some work. In bed by 11.

DAILY TOTAL: $0

DAY FIVE (B)

9 a.m.—Working from home today, and I'm too lazy to go out. Order some food for breakfast/lunch and coffee. **$23.16**

10 a.m.—Find out one of my favorite musicians has a new album out, but it's only available on vinyl or CD. Can't help myself. **$21.48**

7 p.m.—My friend is a *Star Wars* fanatic, and he bought me and some friends tickets to see *The Last Jedi*. He refused to be reimbursed for the tickets, so I get some popcorn and snacks. **$13.81**

10 p.m.—After the movie, we head to a bar. **$35**

12 a.m.—The subway is all out of whack, so I opt for an Uber. **$13.91**

DAILY TOTAL: $107.36

| DAY SIX (J) |

9 a.m.—I get up and start cleaning. B. is still asleep, he got back late from the movie. Our apartment is quite a mess, and I still haven't fully unpacked from my work trip.

10:30 a.m.—I'm done cleaning and pretty hungry. I decide to make us some blueberry pancakes, but I wake B. up first and send him out for coffee. Our order is always the same—he gets a black coffee and I get a latte. We eat the pancakes when he gets back.

12 p.m.—I hop in the shower, and B. cleans the floors. I usually end up doing all the cleaning (because I need to be organized and neat, and B. isn't bothered by messes), but I always leave the floors and the shower cleaning to B. He's also good at doing dishes.

1 p.m.—I Venmo B. $56 for our utilities this month (gas, electric, and Internet) and $100 for the new mattress we bought. It was an Amazon Prime deal. We are still a bit worried that our $200 mattress will be awful, but we figured we might as well try a cheap one before splurging. Worst case we are out $100 each, best case we saved $500 each. Fingers crossed. **$156**

4 p.m.—We watch an episode of *The Crown* while we eat a late lunch. We grabbed two bagel sandwiches from the shop below our apartment (very dangerous location) and have half of each for variety. B. buys.

7 p.m.—We're attending a friend's party tonight. He and his girlfriend are moving to LA. It's BYOB, so I grab two six-packs while we wait for the Uber. **$25.25**

10 p.m.—My group of girlfriends have been joking about taking an Art of the Blowjob class at Babeland since the summer. The joke becomes a reality when one friend signs us up. We each Venmo her for our ticket. **$40**

1 a.m.—Someone drank our last few beers, so we decide it's time to head home. It was a lot of fun, but we are beat. We also have to head out early tomorrow to celebrate my mom's birthday in New Jersey. I fall asleep in the Uber home. B. pays.

DAILY TOTAL: $221.25

| DAY SIX (B) |

11 a.m.—I start the day with a breakfast feast courtesy of my girlfriend. She sends me out to get coffee. **$8**

3 p.m.—I grab lunch at the bagel place downstairs. This time I have the courage to walk outside and order in person. **$11.15**

5 p.m.—For the third meal of the day, pizza. **$9.09**

7 p.m.—We go to our friend's party, and my girlfriend buys our beverages. Although I take care of the Uber there and back. **$20.02 + $19.56**

DAILY TOTAL: $67.82

| **DAY SEVEN (J)** |

8:30 a.m.—I wake up and gather all the things I need to take with me: my mom's present and a couple of things that need to be hand washed (thanks, Mom).

10 a.m.—I run downstairs to get an egg wrap with feta, peppers, and onions and two coffees. We split the wrap before heading to Penn Station. **$7.68**

11:07 a.m.—We're lucky to get a seat on the train, because it's packed with football fans. I buy a ticket on my phone for $14.75, but decide not to activate it. I know the conductor won't check for tickets until we get halfway there because of how crowded it is. I'll save the full-price ticket for the ride back and buy a new one for halfway through the trip for $7.50. I feel a little bad about cheating the system, but not really because of how often I use NJ Transit. **$22.25**

1:45 p.m.—We watch a movie with my parents. They buy the tickets and snacks. My favorite movie theater combo is popcorn, Sour Patch watermelon candy, and a blue slushy.

5 p.m.—We go for an early dinner at a Mexican restaurant, and my sister meets us there. We get margaritas, guac, and everything else you could imagine. Afterward, we are all stuffed. This always happens when I go home. My parents pay again.

8 p.m.—We get back into the city, but make a quick stop at Urban Outfitters so B. can get a Christmas present for my sister. He's a last-minute shopper, while I've had nearly everything purchased and wrapped since Thanksgiving weekend. I grab something to add on to my Secret Santa present that I am exchanging with my girlfriends next week. **$16.57**

9 p.m.—We watch *The Crown* before going to bed early.

DAILY TOTAL: $46.50

| DAY SEVEN (B) |

10 a.m.—Today, I find myself on NJ Transit once again. This time I buy my ticket first thing in the morning so I don't have to enter my credit card in on the train and my interim wallet (a rubber band) can reside safely in my pocket. **$14.75**

10:30 a.m.—Conveniently for the MTA, I only have $2.60 left on my MetroCard, which is just short of a ride, so I pick one of those random amounts the MTA presets on the screen (of course, it's not evenly divisible by the price of the ride, but I digress). **$26.25**

12 p.m.—A gift I ordered online has shipped and hit my credit card. **$33.99**

1:45 p.m.—Go to the movies for the third time this week. I've gone to the movies more this week than the entire past year. The movie was decent and I didn't have to pay for it, so I'd chalk it up as a win.

7 p.m.—My last expense of the week is ironically to NJ Transit for my ticket back to New York City. **$14.75**

DAILY TOTAL: $89.74

| THE BREAKDOWN |

J TOTAL SPENT: $321.63

FOOD AND DRINK: $131.43

ENTERTAINMENT: $40

HOME AND HEALTH: $100

CLOTHES AND BEAUTY: $0

TRANSPORTATION: $33.63

OTHER: $16.57

B TOTAL SPENT: $520.92

FOOD AND DRINK: $173.27

ENTERTAINMENT: $90.48

HOME AND HEALTH: $0

CLOTHES AND BEAUTY: $0

TRANSPORTATION: $136.24

OTHER: $120.93

| THE FOLLOW-UP |

When was the first time you two talked about salaries?
J: I first met B. when I was working at Enterprise Rent-a-Car and I wasn't making any money. I was making, like, $40,000. Then I got a nannying job that paid me $50,000, and I was like, *Woo!* I was excited.
B: You always told me how much you made hourly.

J: Yeah, and I always had an idea of how much B. was making, but I never asked about it until I had to. But I always knew I lived a very different adult money situation than he does.

B: I lived at home for a year and a half and saved a lot of money.

J: And I didn't. I remember one time I had to buy eye drops one night, and I really didn't want to buy them. I had a bachelorette party to go to that weekend, so I had already spent so much money. The eye drops were $11. I kept saying, "No, maybe I don't need them," as my eyes were tearing up. And he said something like, "It's only $11!" And I said, "I make $11 an hour! So it's a big deal."

Was that a surprise?

B: I don't remember how I felt then, but it was probably, *Oh, wow, damn. I should've just bought the eye drops for you.*

J: I think what you said to me was, "I didn't think of it that way."

How do you two split everyday expenses?

J: We typically split everything evenly.

B: Right, or like, she bought the beer and I got the Ubers. The diary did make me more aware of what each of us was spending. Because I'll run out and get everything the last minute. That kind of adds up.

J: Well, I also buy the groceries. Almost every time.

B: But it's your lunch stuff, too.

J: Yeah, that's why I buy it. I'll also get the dinner supplies. But he definitely gets all the coffees. Every time we make a big purchase, we split all that stuff evenly.

Do you two ever fight about money?

J: When we went to California, we splurged on a nice dinner, and I felt very much nervous, like, *Ah, okay, we're spending money!* And B. was just like, *Yeah, we're on vacation, we're splurging on this nice dinner.* It's not a fight, exactly. It's just that we have different reactions.

B: What was the splurge dinner?

J: The Lark? It wasn't even a huge splurge, it was maybe $100 a person. But it was still a lot of money to spend on one meal.

B: Yeah, we definitely said, "Fuck it, let's go all out."

J: It was worth it, but I always have that little buyer's remorse afterward. There's always a moment for me where it's like, *Okay, here comes the bill.* Whereas for you, it's just, *We had a nice time!*

Did doing this diary surprise you two?

J: I don't know if I learned anything new, except maybe you really are clueless in terms of how much I think about money. I really do think about money on a daily basis.

B: Well, now I know. And it should be on my mind more often. I don't think about it enough, even when I do buy things. I just buy some things impulsively. Honestly, now that you're saying it, I don't even think about it as much on a daily basis. And it sounds pretty shitty that I don't. So you gotta tell me if you're feeling that way so I can pick that up.

J: Well, in the past when I've been really vocal and stressed out about it, you'll say, *I got it.* That's really nice. One time I didn't want to go to brunch because I couldn't afford it, and you said you'd cover it. But also, sometimes you'll offer and then forget. That's happened a couple of times, and then we just split it.

B: Oh, just tell me.

J: I'm not going to be like, *Um, you said you were going to pay for this?*

When we started Money Diaries, we were thrilled that it inspired many conversations about salary and spending habits. But we were surprised that commenters also had strong opinions on one particular topic: men picking up the tab.

"Anyone else put off by the boyfriend chipping in to pay for things?" commenter Kate wrote about the diary of a product manager in New York City making $120,000. Then she called the diarist, "'50s AF."[3]

"This person is insufferable," another commenter wrote on Facebook. "You aren't saving money by mooching off your man at every chance."[4]

We were initially surprised by this criticism. After all, in long-term relationships, isn't there a little give-and-take when it comes to money? Money Diaries commenters were split—and very vocal about sharing their opinions. The copywriter in Queens was accused of "mooching off her boyfriend," but someone came to her defense, arguing that she should "absolutely never feel guilty about letting the bf pay, when he makes 3X your salary!"[5] What's a woman to do?

Though there have been endless conversations about gender equality in the workplace, the realm of dating seems murkier. So in the summer of 2016, we polled 656 millennial women who describe themselves as either straight or bisexual, in order to examine all the ways in which gender plays into dating expectations. What is expected of men and women on a first date? And does it still matter who pays the bill?

Romance or Coercion? The First-Date Conundrum

When Jessica Chou casually polled her friends about who pays for dates, they typically responded with another question: "Is this a first date?" They weren't the only ones to consider the first date an anomaly. Of the women we surveyed, 59 percent agreed that a man should always offer to pay for the first date. "If we split the bill, it's like, *What are we, buddies?*" one woman said.

A woman paying for her portion of the date signals her lack of interest in the man, many of the survey respondents argued. "On a first date, paying for myself indicates I'm not interested in another date," one wrote. And that makes some sense: picking up your half of a tab when hanging out with platonic male friends sends a clear message that we're not straying into "date" territory. "I feel like I'm getting friend-zoned if a girl pays for the date," one twenty-six-year-old man in Los Angeles said.

Many of the women surveyed had fairly traditional views on that subject. "For me, when he picks up the bill, I see it as an old-fashioned, chivalrous gesture," one woman wrote. "I think splitting the bill is a total romance killer," said another.

This isn't just a female thing, either; there are men who agree with this sentiment—and oftentimes not just on the first date. "My boyfriend won't even let me reach for the check. He always pays," one respondent noted. "On his birthday, he told me it was degrading to him for me to pay and has paid for everything ever since."

Still, there is a consequence to this first-date expectation. For all the talk of romance, paying for a meal is still a transactional situation—and treating someone can imply an expectation of something else. "I don't like men to pay for me, as I am afraid they will feel that I 'owe' them something in return (sex, another date, etc.)," one woman wrote.

Context and Location Matter

Here's an interesting contradiction: even though 48 percent of the women surveyed said they would let their dates pay for them and 54 percent of women said they "sometimes" or "always" expect their date to pay for them, 46 percent report feeling guilty when they don't pay.

That guilt probably explains why 36 percent of women we surveyed confessed to doing the "wallet reach." Many of our respondents noted that they always double-check, asking their dates, "Are you sure?" once or twice if their card is being waved off.

Beyond the first date, however, respondents rarely had one standard rule for figuring out money issues. "It depends" was the general response for most. As one woman put it, the bill question comes down to "How long you've been going out, who gets paid more, [and] who asked whom out."

But these discussions tend to occur after a few dates or even a few months, when the possibility of a long-term relationship becomes apparent.

"I am more inclined to split the bill once we've had the rela-tionship talk and are an official couple," one woman wrote. "If I am just casually dating someone, and he expects me to pay or split, I won't go out with him again."

What's Feminism Got to Do with It?

The issue of guilt that came up again and again seemed to have one common through line for most respondents: feminism. "I consider myself a modern, feminist woman, but, in the dating world, I at least need a sign the guy thinks I'm worth the effort, and money is the quickest way to do that," one survey respondent wrote, noting this applies only to first dates.

Another respondent shared a deal she has with her boyfriend: they take turns paying everyday expenses. "But if I say I want to go on a date night, he always pays," she said. "And I want him to, but I also feel bad. As a feminist, I know it's not what I should be doing, but I guess I am old-fashioned at heart."

To be clear here, there is absolutely nothing wrong about enjoying being treated. Who doesn't like free things, especially when in good company? But somehow, even in long-term situations in which couples agree and discuss the bill question, feminist guilt still creeps up.

When Should You Break the Rules?

There is, perhaps, a moment in a relationship when "romance" is no longer the reason men insist on paying and "feminism" is no longer the reason women pull out their wallets.

Maybe this is the world that we should be operating in, where money is just one aspect out of five billion inexplicable factors that make a relationship work or cause it to fail. One couple might adhere to traditional gender norms, while another might feel more comfortable dividing the bills based on income. But communication is key—and the first step is to start talking openly about money, how we spend it, and what exactly is feasible for every individual circumstance. Then, and only then, will the offer of treating someone come across less as a power play and more as a gesture of goodwill, something not to be expected in every situation but to be appreciated, always.

THIS IS A GOOD TIME TO:

Talk to your friends about money and dating. I know it might sound awkward, but if you're sharing the details of your hookup, why not mention if your date went south when you did the wallet reach? Talking about money and dating is important, and it's only going to get less weird if we do so.

While you're at it, save $7
Total saved so far: $28

When Priya showed me a list of forty money-related questions a Stash client asks potential boyfriends, I knew it was a good idea. Priya and I worked together to come up with our own list of twenty-one questions to help you navigate this sometimes awkward territory.

I like to talk about money away from home, over drinks or dinner. For others, drinking and talking about money can be a *terrible* combination. In the early stages of a relationship, you'll have some trial and error as you try to figure out the ideal time for these (sometimes) difficult conversations.

Don't feel bad if it makes you feel uncomfortable. We aren't saying it's easy, but it's necessary. Money powers your future, and there are few things more thrilling than planning a life with someone. So make a date, and start talking.

1. What do you do for a living? Do you like your job? Is this something you thought you would do when you were younger?

These questions are more than just simple "getting to know you" conversation starters, and your date's answers can reveal a lot.

2. Can we split the bill?

Establishing yourself as equals from the start can help you set expectations for money and your relationship.

3. Do you feel we have an equal relationship?

This is especially important if you date someone who makes significantly more or less than you do.

4. What do you think about marriage?

If you don't want to get married but your date's been planning the big day since they were five, it's better to learn that early.

5. Are you planning any major career changes in the foreseeable future?

Follow-up question: Will these career changes result in your moving and/or taking on debt?

6. How do you manage your money?

If you're a spender and the other person is a saver, things could be tricky (but not impossible). The key is to be clear about your habits early on.

7. If either of us gets a bonus/wins the lottery, what will I/you/we do with that money?

This is a good way to tackle the "yours, mine, ours" question. For more on combining incomes, see page 63.

For more on combining incomes, see page 63.

8. How much money do you make?

If you're going to be open about your salary with one person in the whole world, it should be the person you're in a committed relationship with.

9. How will we split the rent? How will we split the monthly bills? Fifty-fifty or based on our incomes?

This seems so simple, but if you don't have a conversation about it, resentment can build.

10. Do you have student loan debt? What are you doing about it?

It's important to know how your partner is tackling their debt.

11. Would you someday want a joint bank account?

You should definitely talk about the pros and cons before you make this kind of commitment.

12. I do/don't want you to go into debt to buy an engagement ring. How much do you think we should spend? Where will the money come from? Would you be upset if we both helped pay for the ring?

For many people, an engagement ring is the first major purchase they make together. Shouldn't you discuss the cost?

13. What are your feelings about a prenup? Does your family have any opinions?

This is another really scary conversation—and, some would argue, very unromantic.

14. Do you want to have children? When?

Because kids are expensive. More on that in chapter 6.

15. How much should be in our emergency fund?

Everyone has a different idea about this (more details in chapter 4), but it's a decision you should make together.

16. Who is going to pay for our wedding?

Weddings are expensive AF. Before you start planning (and going into debt), make sure you're clear on who's footing the bill.

17. Will an equal relationship mean the same thing now as it does in five years? ten years? etc.? How do you see us dividing responsibilities over the next five years?

This question should be brought up again, especially as your careers take off, you think about having kids, and so on.

18. If one of our parents, siblings, or friends was in dire straits, how would you want to help?

You and your partner should talk about this issue, so you're on the same page.

19. How do you see us raising our children?

Nanny or day care? Public or private school? Will we pay for their college? The expense of raising kids is constantly changing, so these conversations will keep bubbling back up.

20. What would we do if one of us got sick? Do you have life insurance?

This can be depressing to talk about—but if you're making big plans (house, kids, travel), you want to make sure you've got backup plans for a worst-case scenario. (See chapter 4 for more on this topic.)

21. How would we handle a career break?

Whether you or your partner are taking time off to have kids, to go back to school, or following an illness or a job loss, you'll need to consider the impact on your finances. This is a tough question, but it's important to be prepared, whatever life throws at you.

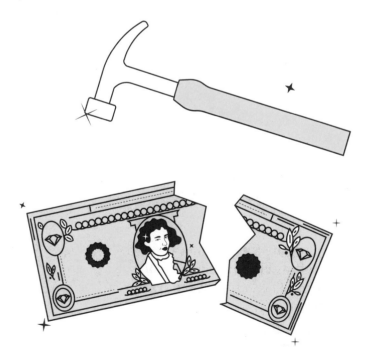

At my wedding, my matron of honor told a story about a list we had drawn up in high school describing our ideal man. I can't remember many of the particulars, except that my dream guy had to play guitar. It might be the smallest thing (nice eyes, a great laugh, cute butt) that initially attracts you to your partner, but when you start thinking about the long term, you need to find someone you're also financially compatible with. My financial deal breaker is someone who will feel threatened if I make more money. Below, seven millennial women share their own deal breakers.

LAURYN, 23 | BALTIMORE, MD | STRAIGHT | ANNUAL SALARY: $60,000

"I date ambitious men. I can't handle men who don't have, or are not trying to get, their shit together financially."

KELLY, 24 | ARLINGTON, VA | ANNUAL SALARY: $57,500 | S.O.'S ANNUAL SALARY: $175,000

"I need to date a guy I know can support himself financially. I don't make enough to support someone else and myself!"

JEN, 26 | BOSTON, MA | STRAIGHT | ANNUAL SALARY: $60,000 | S.O.'S ANNUAL SALARY: $65,000

"Don't go out to eat if you aren't going to tip properly."

AMANDA, 24 | NEW YORK, NY | BISEXUAL | ANNUAL SALARY: $75,000

"Anything other than splitting the bill with a man on the first few dates is a no. With women, I'm often more inclined to pick up a tab. If you don't even offer to pay, though, it's a hard pass."

BETH, 31 | LOS ANGELES, CA | STRAIGHT | ANNUAL SALARY: $280,000 | S.O.'S ANNUAL SALARY: $30,000

"I would never date a guy who didn't pay for dinner when he meets my parents."

"They can't have an illegal job! I will never date a weed messenger again!"

"I would never, ever date a man who wants us to merge our finances. My money is mine, and no one else's; even if I was married, I'd keep my money separate! You've got to take care of you, and sensible should trump sentiment when it comes to your own life savings."

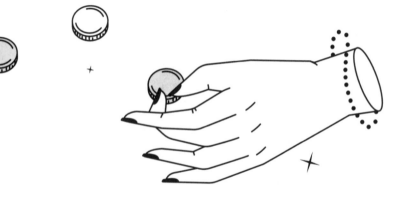

Discussing your finances with your S.O. gets a whole lot more complicated when they are set to inherit millions of dollars. Meghan, 30, shares the story of how she and her now husband navigated the stressful process of signing a prenuptial agreement on their way to finding their happily ever after.

I met my husband on a plain old dating site. I share this detail as proof that when I first set eyes on Mike, I had no way of knowing that his family was exceedingly wealthy. He lived in a normal apartment. We took turns paying for dinner. Eventually, when we moved in together, we split the rent and our furniture was secondhand. And so you can only imagine my shock when, five years into our relationship, Mike inherited millions of dollars.

Yet this windfall didn't really change our daily lives. In fact, the impact of Mike's fortune on our relationship didn't come into focus until after we got engaged, when I found myself in the office of a high-powered attorney, a 40-page prenuptial agreement staring me in the face.

I grew up in a middle-class family; both my parents worked, and I was raised with the understanding that nothing would be handed to me. I paid my own way through college, and later worked a full-time job and a part-time gig while going to graduate school at night.

This independence was a point of pride. Mike often told people that my "scrappy" spirit was one of the things that attracted him to me. I appreciated that he didn't try to water me down. He appreciated my fierce ability to fend for myself.

But I felt far from fierce sitting with my lawyer, who charged almost $900 an hour. (Mike, I'll admit, paid the fees.) "The way this contract stands, you can *never* stop working," she said. I had no plans to give up my career, but it was gutting to read the terms spelled out by Mike's attorneys. The agreement made it clear that even married, Mike and I would not build a financial future together.

I came home from that first meeting in tears. I wasn't initially upset about a prenup because I trusted it would be fair: If our marriage didn't work out, Mike would rightfully walk away with the bulk of his money. But I had assumed I would still have some piece of the life we were both invested in. Instead, what the contract spelled out was a flat fee for each year we were married, with my annual "value" increasing slightly if we had children. "That's what I call the 'breeder clause,'" my lawyer scoffed. If she meant to rile me up, it worked. I got angry thinking of my soon-to-be husband becoming the de facto CEO of our relationship.

Mike seemed genuinely concerned that I was upset. It was clear that my ability to contribute financially to our life together was limited compared to his, and to me, this meant that even if we discussed financial decisions, most final calls would be his.

The back-and-forth between our lawyers went on for months. But in the comfort of our home, Mike and I were doing our own negotiations. We had a lot of hard conversations about how we saw our marriage; what a real partnership looked like, both from a financial and nonfinancial perspective; and how our different upbringings shaped our views. There were a few tears, but also laughs, and ultimately so much excitement for our future. Unexpectedly, the process brought us closer.

Two weeks before our wedding, Mike and I signed the prenup. We took out the "breeder clause," and my earnings are protected. It's not perfect, but it was weirdly comforting to go into marriage knowing we could work as a team.

"That sucked. I love you," I told Mike after we put the prenup in a bin in the back of a closet, hoping to never see it again. He pulled me close. "That did suck. And I love you more."

It started with a check: to Ken and Lindsey Partridge. I might have married Ken, but I didn't take his last name. We didn't have a joint account in which to deposit the check (or the pile of others addressed to both of us), and I wasn't sure how I felt about combining accounts. I knew it would simplify things—but I was also a little worried that Ken would start looking more closely at my spending and give me a hard time about that $10 cheese I just bought at Whole Foods.

But both our parents had shared accounts, so without much discussion, we opened a joint checking account, dumped all our money into it, kept separate credit cards, and never looked back. Ken has never closely tracked my spending, I enjoy being able to watch exactly what goes in and out of our account, and we've lived happily ever after, never, ever fighting about money. (Yeah, right.)

I always kind of assumed that all married couples manage their money like me and Ken. How naïve! Just read a few Money Diaries, and you'll see the couples come up with a range of solutions for managing their finances. Some seem a little extreme to me (Venmo-ing your husband for half of the Netflix bill), but very few diarists go the traditional route of simply combining everything.

In many ways, we're dealing with the same gender politics issues here as picking up the tab on the first date—just with much higher stakes. Should each person in the relationship have an individual account to protect themselves in case a partner is unfaithful or bad with money? The debt you acquire while married is in both your names, and if one person has a bad credit score, you're both impacted. In many states, a judge will require an equal division of assets if you get divorced—so all that time you spent keeping a balance sheet of who owes what won't mean much.

I have to admit, I've always felt rather smug about the way Ken and I handle our money, especially after a friend's divorce attorney mother mentioned that the happiest couples she knows are ones who combine everything. I also think it sounds like a lot of work to track your money so carefully, especially if you have kids. Take Jen, 29, who is married with a toddler but doesn't share a bank account with her husband. They had an unorthodox courtship (her phrase), and five months after they met, they found out Jen was pregnant.

Jen and her husband have very different money philosophies—and a huge salary discrepancy. Jen was making a quarter of his salary. She describes him as superfrugal, while she believes money is for spending. Jen says she never carried credit card debt before she got married but also admits she lacked any real savings. When she moved into her husband's condo, he didn't ask her to contribute to his monthly mortgage payments, but they also decided not to combine bank accounts.

"It was organic to keep our finances separate when we first moved in together," Jen says. "But today it's a very conscious decision."

Jen covers the day-to-day expenses for their family of three, from groceries to diapers to dinners out. Her husband covers long-term expenses, including rent, utilities, and car payments. His savings account is for their future house, and hers goes to their child's college fund and short-term expenditures such as travel.

  Jen has access to her husband's account and he to hers, but they don't track each other's expenses.

Anna, 30, keeps an Excel document to manage her and her husband's spending. Every morning, she logs in and records the previous day's expenditures, and at the end of the month, she sends her husband the spreadsheet to review and the total he owes her for bills. They split shared expenses such as groceries and dinner out, but they each pay for their own wants and needs.

"I'm worried we'd judge each other's spending habits," she says. "I don't want to pay for his dinner out with friends."

The couple came up with this system when they moved in together and got a joint credit card. Anna doesn't ever see it changing even if they have kids; she imagines they will handle child-rearing costs the same way they manage pet expenses: a joint account that's just for the puppy (well, in this case, just for the baby, but you get the picture).

 All the financial advisers I've worked with over the years have thoughts on this topic, so I asked Manisha Thakor what she tells clients to do when they're getting married (or decide to make a long-term commitment). She recommends what she cheekily calls the "Financial Three Way."

It's not as kinky as it sounds; basically it means that a couple has three accounts: yours, mine, ours. You should discuss how much you will each contribute to the shared account and what expenses that account will cover, as well as what expenses will be paid for from your personal accounts. The same can go for credit. A joint credit card can be an easy way to manage shared expenses such as groceries and Netflix, while having your own personal card will allow you to have some discretionary funds to spend as you see fit (see my expensive cheese habit).

Arguably, when both people in the relationship are employed and make similar salaries, these conversations are much easier.

It gets more difficult if one partner ends up unemployed. If or when that comes up, how should you handle both shared and personal expenses? Is the one out of work no longer allowed to buy something personal?

Lisa, 34, found herself in that situation when she and her husband moved to Brazil for his job, and she wasn't able to work for a year. Where they once split everything fifty-fifty, Lisa now had to rely on her husband to support her.

"It was weird to have to ask him for money so I could go out with friends," Lisa said. "I stopped shopping for myself, I felt really uncomfortable buying anything that I wanted. Of course, my husband was able to go out and buy whatever he wanted.

"We took a trip to the north of Brazil, and I saw a pot I really wanted, and it wasn't necessarily expensive. I think it was $35. My husband was like, 'If you want that, then you have to use your savings, because I'm not buying that.'"

 Manisha recommends sitting down with your partner twice a year to have a thorough discussion of your personal finances. Get an aggregate look at your household picture: review what income has come in, as well as how much is going out. (We discussed this in depth in chapter 1.) It's also worth discussing your long-term goals (see chapter 9) and adjusting your savings and spending habits depending on what you're trying to achieve. Even with separate accounts, financial transparency is crucial to a successful relationship.

But that transparency isn't the only key to success. There's something about Anna's comment about not wanting to pay for her husband to have dinner with friends that rubs me the wrong way. Marriage is about becoming a team. When one team member is having a shit time (financial or otherwise), it's up to the other to support them. Isn't that the whole point of matrimony?

At the end of the day, the most important thing is to try to be open and honest about your finances and maintain some control over your long-term financial health. Because if you're having trouble talking about splitting your Seamless tab, how do you think you're going to navigate paying for a new couch or putting a down payment on a home? If your goal is to take ownership over how you spend and invest your money, you need a partner who is on the same page about what that looks like. Period.

THIS IS A GOOD TIME TO:

Decide on a long-term (or even midterm) savings goal with your S.O. together. Even if you're not at the stage of combining accounts, coming up with a shared plan can bring the two of you closer together (and give you a better sense of how you each manage money).

While you're at it, save $8
Total saved so far: $36

Make a Money Date with Your Partner

TIME: 1 hour plus
TOOLS: Your S.O., your account details

Every single financial adviser I spoke to while working on this book recommended couples do regular financial check-ins. Shannon suggests you do it quarterly; Ken and I don't have regularly scheduled reviews, but that doesn't mean we're not talking about it frequently.

The kinds of conversations you're going to have with your S.O. about money will vary depending on where you are in your relationship. In those heady early days, you might not worry about it too much. But as you get more serious, the sooner you have these conversations, the easier they are.

Of course, if you're battling big debt, it can be really stressful to share that with someone you like. It's important to remember that debt isn't a moral failing (see chapter 5 for more on that topic) and being vulnerable is a big part of being in a successful relationship. After all, this is someone you also sleep with; who, over the course of your relationship, will see you at both your very best and your very worst.

One more thought on money dates: don't go into them angry. Managing your money can be really stressful, but going into these conversations pointing fingers or assigning blame will only make things worse. That's why I really like to get out of the house when we have big money conversations. Ken and I come to our best decisions on long walks.

Not sure what to say? Early on, you can reference one of the twenty-one questions Priya and I shared earlier in this chapter. Later, you might want to have some dates that are purely administrative—such as taking time to open an investment account or discuss buying life insurance—and others that are more focused on planning for long-term goals.

While you're at it, save $9
Total saved so far: $45

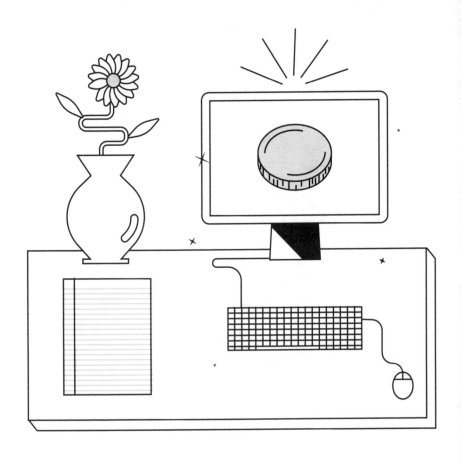

CHAPTER 3

Work & Money
(Or How to Make Bank)

There are many reasons why women should want to take control of their finances, but I would argue the most compelling is the fact that we make less money than men. You probably know the stats by heart by now: On average, women who work full-time make 80 cents to every dollar their male counterpart makes. Black women make just 64 cents, and Hispanic women make a measly 54 cents.[1] The data suggest we won't reach pay parity in the United States until 2152.[2] That's 134 fucking years.

Unequal pay is just one of many workplace problems we face. A 2017 Pew Research Center poll found that four in ten women have been discriminated against at work.[3] A *Wall Street Journal*/NBC poll found that nearly half of women have faced some kind of sexual harassment in the workplace.[4] Talk about an ambition killer.

Yes, there are a lot of systemic obstacles holding working women back—but lack of financial savvy should never be one of them. In this chapter, we want to arm you with the tools you need to navigate the financial side of the workplace, from understanding your whole compensation package to negotiating a raise.

Like all personal finance advice, there's no one-size-fits-all solution to work and money. Use the information in this chapter to improve your situation and remember to pay it forward. Because the only way we're going to destroy the glass ceiling is if we help each other out along the way.

A Week in Philadelphia, PA, on an **$88,000** Salary

OCCUPATION: Marketing manager
INDUSTRY: Telecom
AGE: 26
LOCATION: Philadelphia, PA
ANNUAL SALARY: $88,000 + $15,000 annual bonus. I also watch dogs ($2,000 per year) and freelance for wedding event company ($5,000 per year).
PAYCHECK AMOUNT (EVERY TWO WEEKS): $1,832.06

HUSBAND'S INDUSTRY: Health care
HUSBAND'S ANNUAL SALARY: $80,000 + about $5,000 in overtime
HUSBAND'S PAYCHECK AMOUNT (TWICE A MONTH): $1,892.97

GENERAL FINANCIAL INFORMATION:

Checking Account Balance: ~$13,000 total (My husband and I each contribute 85 percent of our paychecks into a joint account and 15 percent into our personal accounts.)
Savings Account Balance: ~$10,000 (We want to grow our emergency fund to have at least three months of expenses saved up.)

HOUSING:

Rent: $2,152 for a 700-square-foot studio (The cost includes one parking spot, renter's insurance, and pet rent.)
Utilities (including water, heat, electricity, and gas): ~$100 per month
HOA: $260
Cable: $40 (I get a discount through work.)
Phone: $137 (We pay for my husband's parents' service, too.)

TRANSPORTATION:
Car Payment: $400 (Almost done after three years!)
Car Insurance: $121

HEALTH & SELF-CARE:
Health and Dental Insurance: $127 for just me. (This is the last year my husband can be on his parents' plan.)
HSA: $10/paycheck
Prescriptions: $10 (I'm lucky that I have great health insurance. I have ankylosing spondylitis and need to take a shot every two weeks. Without insurance, the shots would cost about $24,000/month; my insurance covers most of it.)
Yoga: $260 for 20 classes (I use one pack every 1.5 months.)
Flywheel: $280 for 10 classes (I use one pack every 1.5 months.)

DEBT:
Student Loan Debt Total: $45,000 in combined student loans

Student Loan Payment: $72/month but I pay $150 (I worked full-time my last two years of college and applied for at least 10 scholarships per year) + $180/month for my husband's
Credit Card Debt Total: $8,000 (On a 0 percent APR card. We paid for our wedding ourselves, and this is what's left to pay off.)
Credit Card Payment: $1,000/month
Additional Mortgage Payment: $1,100 (We used to live in Atlanta and still own our condo down there, which we are renting out. Our tenants pay $1,400, and we put the little bit of excess in an account to help with taxes.)

RETIREMENT:
401(k) Contribution: $600/paycheck (I contribute 10 percent, and my company matches 7 percent.)
401(k) Total: ~$60,000

7 a.m.—I wake up groggy and grumpy. Last night, I flew home from Orlando, where I was supporting a friend in her first marathon. I catch up with my husband, D., for a bit this morning (winky face).

8 a.m.—I go through my morning routine: face mask, coffee, makeup, and walk the dog out. I pack leftovers (Israeli couscous-stuffed green peppers) and walk to work with D.

12 p.m.—There's a lot going at work. My manager was recently promoted and his old role (which is a director level) is being backfilled. I have my manager's blessing to apply for the position, and I know the next few months will be crazy as I try to prove myself. I know I'm young and inexperienced, but this role is exactly what I want to do professionally, and I know I'd kick myself if I didn't at least throw my hat in the ring. I heat up my leftovers and work through lunch at my desk.

3 p.m.—I take a midafternoon break to blow through a Talbots gift card from Christmas. They're having a great sale, and I end up with two dresses, a sweater, a shirt, and two pairs of shoes. After my gift card, I pay **$62.14**.

4 p.m.—I grab coffee with a colleague since there is a rumor he may become my new boss. He pays for my coffee, and we talk for an hour about the reorg, and how we can leverage it to fulfill both our career aspirations.

6 p.m.—I get home and change for yoga. I have a spinal condition called ankylosing spondylitis, which most people just call AS. Right now, I'm able to manage my disease with exercise and medication, so I still feel lucky. I head into a heated vinyasa class using a class credit from my account.

8 p.m.—I get home and start dinner: a lemony zucchini orzo with spicy pork sausage. D. helps. After dinner, I lay out clothes for work and the gym, and we watch *Beat Bobby Flay* and *The Challenge*. I head to bed before D. (per usual) around 10:30.

DAILY TOTAL: $62.14

| **DAY TWO** |

5 a.m.—I drag myself out of bed and head to a 6 a.m. Flywheel class. I buy the Flywheel classes in bulk, so I don't owe anything for this class.

8 a.m.—I get into the office and make a cup of shitty office coffee. Usually, I treat myself to a cup from Saxby's, but I spent *way* too much money this past weekend, and I'm feeling stressed about it. When D. and I went through our 2017 expenses, it was eye-opening how much money I spend on useless things. I'm trying really hard to be better with my spending (aka avoiding Target and buying coffee).

12 p.m.—My boss and I have a one-on-one to discuss my future at the company. I'm super prepared. I spent any downtime I had in Orlando working on a PowerPoint for our meeting. The "double jump" (going up two levels to director) is uncommon where I work, and my boss lets me know that HR/senior leadership is not super receptive. However, I think he's impressed with the work I've put in, and he tentatively agrees to give me a few big projects that would be responsibilities of this position. We discuss all of this over lunch and coffee that he expenses.

6:30 p.m.—I'm signed up to work a yoga class in exchange for a free class. I show up to the studio 30 minutes early to prep.

8:30 p.m.—Arrive home. I'm too tired to make dinner, so we eat leftovers while watching TV. I work on a freelance project and do a little design work on my friend's wedding invites. Head to bed around 11.

DAILY TOTAL: $0

| DAY THREE |

4 a.m.—I can't sleep (ugh), so I get up and do some work. Eventually, I get sleepy again and head back to bed for a bit.

7:30 a.m.—Go through my morning routine and a shower. I'm unsatisfied with every single outfit I put on, and so I have to hurry to take the dog out. I still have my lunch from yesterday, but I grab a grapefruit half for breakfast.

4 p.m.—Another manager heard I was interested in expanding my responsibilities and reaches out about a senior manager position on his team. I'm superflattered, but don't know what to think. I've only been in my role for seven months (although I've been with this company for three years), and I just got the opportunity to handle some more complex projects from my manager. On the other hand, I know I'd be really good at this senior manager role, even if it's not my dream job. Plus it would come with a title promotion and a higher salary. I text two of my mentors from Atlanta to crowdsource opinions. I work until 5 and head home.

5:15 p.m.—Time for a meeting with the wedding company I freelance for. I hop in the car and head on my way. I make sure to track my mileage for year-end write-offs. The company owner is really excited about my social media suggestions. She wants me to take on more responsibility and asks for my prices. Eek, I don't know what to charge! I tell her I'll get back to her and make a mental note to post in some of the Facebook marketing groups I'm in to get an idea what to charge.

7:30 p.m.—I get back and drag my feet to the gym. I'm training for a half marathon and really need to do my speed workout. When I was first diagnosed with AS, I was told I could never run again, which was incredibly hard for me because I've always been a runner. When I moved to Atlanta, my rheumatologist put me on a new type of medication. Although I have to inject myself with a needle every two weeks, it has improved my quality of life so much. Last March, I ran my first half marathon since my diagnosis and cried with emotion when I finished. Right now I'm training for another and am hoping to run a full marathon later this year.

8:30 p.m.—I heat up a Trader Joe's pizza and hop in the shower. I'm dog-sitting this weekend, so I pack a bag with some things I'll need. I talk about the career opportunities with D., who is super supportive of whatever I choose. I'm so lucky. We originally moved to Philly for my job, and he knows I'm superambitious. I head to bed around 10.

DAILY TOTAL: $0

| **DAY FOUR** |

6:50 a.m.—I head into work early since we have early release today. On my walk, I post in a couple of Women's Marketing groups to ask what I should charge for the additional work for the wedding company.

12 p.m.—I have a meeting with one of my mentors. I think I'm going to turn down the senior manager role. I know this director-level job would be a big jump, but it's something I'm really passionate about and know I'd be really good at. My mentor confirms my thoughts and lets me know she's impressed with my maturity. I leave her office feeling good and grab a poke sushi bowl from our company café. **$14.19**

2 p.m.—Our team is headed to a happy hour. I stay for about two Moscow mules (aka 90 minutes). (It goes on my boss' tab.) Then I head to dog-sit.

5:30 p.m.—Oops, I got sucked into some trashy shows, and I'm running late to dinner. I take an Uberpool and text D. that I'm going to be 5 minutes late. **$10.19**

6 p.m.—Tonight we're eating at a super snazzy Stephen Starr restaurant called Buddakan that a coworker recommended. Per our server's suggestion, we share lobster fried rice, lobster egg rolls, mushroom potstickers, spicy rock shrimp bao buns, and dim sum donuts. We both stick to water, and the bill isn't nearly as bad as I thought it would be ($70.80 +

$15 tip). We Lyft back to our place ($8.19). **$93.99**

8:30 p.m.—D. drops me off to spend the night dog-sitting. I walk the pup and then fall asleep watching *Law & Order: SVU*.

DAILY TOTAL: $118.37

| DAY FIVE |

6 a.m.—Get up and take the pup for a walk in the rain, clean the cat litter, and food for all. I walk to the yoga studio, where I'm assisting a class.

9 a.m.—Go home to shower and crawl in bed with D. and our pup. We cuddle for an hour and then get up for breakfast. We hang out for a bit until I leave to go meet another dog I may watch in a few weeks and D. leaves to help some friends move. I check in on my Facebook post from yesterday. The general consensus is that I should charge around $800/month.

11 a.m.—I meet the pup, and she's supersweet. From there, I head to the post office to mail back my Garmin GPS watch that's been acting up and drop off some model horses I sold online. I head back to the pup I'm dog-sitting to let him out. **$7.49**

78

5 p.m.—I order groceries for the week. There's not a lot of options for food shopping near us, so we order from Peapod. I've found its low prices justify the $6.99 delivery fee. I get cauliflower, mushrooms, onions, green peppers, jalapeños, beef chuck, ground pork, pork shoulder, Chobani Flips, corn starch, white vinegar, pulled pork slow cooker sauce, kidney beans, sweet potato chips, pretzels, and roasted red pepper hummus. **$94.96**

7 p.m.—We're watching our friends' two dogs while they move. We end up eating another frozen TJ's pizza since we don't trust all the dogs to behave if we run out to grab something.

9 p.m.—I Uber back to the puppy I'm watching for our last overnight. Because this is technically a "work" expense, I note it in my write-offs spreadsheet so I can deduct it at the end of the year. **$4.20**

DAILY TOTAL: $106.65

| **DAY SIX** |

7 a.m.—I wake up slowly. Eventually I get up and take out the dog. I start to clean and pack up since this is my last day with him!

8 a.m.—On my walk back home, I stop at Trader Joe's because (1) they have free samples and (2) it's warm in there. I buy Swedish fish, frozen waffles, more frozen pizzas, sparkling limeade, steak, and four-cheese blend. This should tide us over until our Peapod order comes through tomorrow. **$48.10**

12 p.m.—I head over to the dog's house for one last walk.

2 p.m.—D. and I are starving. I eat the leftover lobster fried rice, and he has leftover pizza. I clean up the house and then start on a few things for work.

6:30 p.m.—Our friends take us out to dinner for watching their dogs yesterday. We head to a nearby pub. There's a wait, so we hang out at the bar until a table is ready. A draft IPA for me and a hard cider for D. ($12.50 + $2 tip). For dinner, the table splits an order of fries, and I get a seasonal flatbread with fig jam, Brie, arugula, and bacon. We all order a couple more rounds of drinks. When the check comes, our friends graciously treat. We head to our apartment for more drinks and to watch *Making a Murderer*. They head home around 11, and I promptly pass out. **$14.50**

DAILY TOTAL: $62.60

| DAY SEVEN |

9 a.m.—I actually slept in today! I take our dog out and make coffee and waffles. I spend the morning finishing up my friend's wedding invites and updating some decks for my main job.

1 p.m.—D. and I have reservations at Butcher & Singer for Restaurant Week. I'm so excited! We accidentally order a bottle of fancy water and are terrified by how much it's going to cost (it ends up only being $7, but still WAY too much for water). For lunch, there's a prix fixe three-course menu for $20 per person. I order the crab cake, salmon, and a lemon tart, and D. gets the burger. The total comes out to $50.19 + $10 tip. As we pay, D. mentions how proud he is to be able to pay for a $60 lunch. He grew up poor, and he had never been to a non-fast-food restaurant until he went to college. **$60.19**

3 p.m.—For Christmas I got D. a $250 REI gift card so he can get a real winter coat. We go to Conshohocken to shop for one. Of course they don't have his size in the coat he wants, so we end up driving to King of Prussia. The coat costs $280, but the additional amount will come from D.'s personal account. On the way home, we get the car washed ($8) because there was a ton of salt from driving to Boston for the holidays. **$8**

6 p.m.—We finally make it home and watch an episode of *SNL* while I start on dinner. Tonight, D. has a soccer game, and I make dinner for my younger cousin who also lives in Philly. We hang out and talk for a bit and then he heads back to his apartment.

8 p.m.—Our Peapod grocery order is delivered, and for once, they actually had everything in stock! I put everything away and take the dog out one more time. I work on some projects for work until D. comes home. He heats up leftovers, and we chat for a bit. I head to bed around 10.

DAILY TOTAL: $68.19

79

WORK & MONEY

| THE BREAKDOWN |

TOTAL SPENT: $417.95

FOOD AND DRINK: $317.74

ENTERTAINMENT: $0

HOME AND HEALTH: $15.49

CLOTHES AND BEAUTY: $62.14

TRANSPORTATION: $22.58

OTHER: $0

| THE FOLLOW-UP |

Your hustle in this diary is impressive. What are some of your professional goals?
I was in fourth grade the first time I said I wanted to be a CEO, and my parents thought that was hilarious because they are very blue collar. My dad passed away when I was 15, and I think that's part of the reason I'm so driven and determined. It sounds funny, and it sounds unrealistic, but I really do want to be a CEO, and be someone who is powerful in my industry.

Has your illness impacted how you go after your career goals?
I feel that AS is a part of who I am, just like some people have diabetes. I'm never going to let it slow me down. I definitely do talk about it at work because I want to inspire people. There are so many dimensions to us as employees, and just honoring that and talking about it, that's important to me.

You mentioned in the diary that your husband grew up poor. How did his childhood experiences impact how you spend money as adults?
It's really hard for D. to spend money—he'll buy a pack of ten undershirts because it's 4 cents cheaper than the pack of five—even though he hates the quality of the ten-pack. Now that we both make good money, he's getting more comfortable with going to expensive dinners or buying nice work clothes, but it hasn't always been that way. I think my husband has some guilt around having money, and when we're around his parents or friends, he acts like we really don't have money and doesn't talk about money. His parents don't want to be a burden, so when we visit they want to take us out to dinner to a Wendy's. I never grew up eating fast food and I know I'm really lucky for that—but I'd prefer that we just pay and go somewhere that we'd all enjoy. I'm fortunate that my husband and I can have honest conversations around money, but sometimes I do get frustrated with his hesitation to spend money on things that we want/need.

Who do you talk to about money?
My parents were notoriously bad with money—they fell prey to the "keeping up with the Joneses" mentality. I primarily talk with my best friend or my mentor about money. My best friend really inspired me to say, "I don't have the funds right now"—not because my account is at $0 but because I have financial goals. My mentor (and another amazing friend) is in her mid-30s and seems to have it all together. She grew up blue collar and is a kick-ass lawyer. She's another example of someone who has money but doesn't flash it around (she drives a fifteen-year-old car!) and is completely happy. That's financially where I want to get to.

What surprised you most about doing a Money Diary?
I realized I need to get out more and make more friends! It's been tough to make friends since moving to Philadelphia.

My starting salary at my first job was $28,500, and my employer offered a 401(k) match, plus paid fully for my health care, which (being completely unfamiliar with the ways of the world) I didn't realize was a huge perk. I stayed at the company for almost seven years, got a few raises and promotions, some pretty sweet bonuses, and never once negotiated my salary. When I left to work at Martha Stewart, I technically got a $5,000 raise (to $55,000) but in reality took a pay cut because I didn't understand the monetary value of my whole compensation package.

This is how I've approached most of my job offers over the years: a company has offered me a job, and I've accepted it. I haven't tried to negotiate anything. Most of the time, I was just relieved that I'd gotten the job, either because I really wanted it or because I really needed it. And I didn't want to do anything that might result in the company rescinding the offer.

Don't be like me. Because here's the thing: it's not likely that a prospective employer will rescind a job offer because you try to negotiate or ask questions. In fact, it will probably make the company value you even more. To protect yourself, make sure you don't resign from your current gig until you have your accepted job offer in writing.

I asked Priya Malani to help me explain what you should look for when reviewing a compensation package. Even if you're not looking for a job right now, it's worth reading this section, as you can potentially use the information to negotiate a better package at your current gig.

Health care benefits: What kind of insurance does the company offer (HMO versus PPO)? What are the monthly premiums and yearly deductibles? Does the employer offer FSA and/or HSA? What about paid family leave? When will you become eligible for those benefits? Will your current doctor accept the plan? (See chapter 4 for even more on understanding your health care benefits.)

Retirement benefits: Does the company offer a retirement savings plan, and does it match? When will you become eligible? Is there a vesting schedule for the match? If you're leaving a big company that provides a great matching program for a small company that doesn't, it could be worth negotiating a raise or bonus to cover the lost money. (See chapter 9 for even more on understanding your 401(k).)

Bonus: Are you guaranteed a certain percentage? Will it be prorated? How is bonus size determined, and how is it awarded (annually, quarterly)? Is there a sign-on bonus? Are there any additional bonuses you can receive? (Don't forget, your bonus is often taxed at a much higher tax bracket—40 or even 50 percent, says Priya. While you'll get some of that back in the form of a tax refund, a $12,000 bonus looks more like $7,000 when it hits your bank account. Just something to keep in mind.)

Stock options: How does the company determine how much stock you will be allocated, and will you receive more each year you work for the company? What's the vesting schedule? What are the company's long-term plans, and how might they impact what the stock is worth?

Vacation time: Time off does have a monetary value—after all, if you don't get paid vacation, you lose money when you take time off. It's easy to do the math to see how much your time off is worth. First, figure out your hourly pay rate (annual salary divided by 2,000). If you make $50,000, your hourly rate is $25. If your job provides you eight paid holidays (Memorial Day, Christmas Day, etc.) and fifteen vacation days, your annual vacation compensation is $4,600. It's also worth asking if you can accrue vacation days over the years or if you have to use them or lose them each year. Many companies will pay you for vacation days if you leave before you've used them.

Additional perks: Are there commuter benefits? Can you make overtime? Does the company provide snacks or meals? Gym reimbursement? Fertility reimbursement? Does it offer day care discounts? Often these perks have real monetary value. Make sure you know about them.

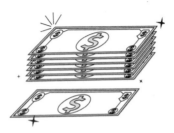

Besides salary and benefits, you should also consider quality of life. Does the company offer flexible schedules or a work-from-home option? You can make all the money in the world, but if you're doing a job you don't like, it might not be worth it.

Also, consider what kind of career path the job offers. Will taking the job enable you to grow your career in a new and exciting (and potentially lucrative) direction?

Every article on negotiating I've ever read recommends that you don't negotiate just salary but all benefits, from vacation time to stock options. I've only ever successfully negotiated a salary increase. That said, it can't hurt to ask for what you want. The worst a company can say is no. The best case is that you will get a yes. So go ahead and see if the company will guarantee you a year-end bonus as a percentage of your salary or let you have a flexible schedule. You might be pleasantly surprised.

Plan a vacation. I know that might not seem like a financially smart decision for some of you, but I didn't say you have to take a fancy trip. It's so important to use up your vacation days, even if you take a staycation—sleeping in every day, binge-watching Netflix, and improving your skin care game (sounds pretty good to me).

While you're at it, save $10
Total saved so far: $55

I really want to tackle all the weirdness that comes with negotiating your salary. I don't think it's an easy conversation to have—in fact, it's something I'm embarrassed to admit I've never done well. But not asking for a raise or negotiating your salary when you receive a job offer can have a huge impact on your overall earning potential.

Just how much, you ask? A 2009 study by Michelle Marks and Crystal Harold found that people who negotiate their first salary on average earn $5,000 more per year.[5] Assuming a 5 percent annual increase over a forty-year career, a twenty-five-year-old who negotiates an initial $55,000 salary will make over $600,000 more than her nonnegotiating colleague who starts out at $50,000.

I called up Sallie Krawcheck (the founder of Ellevest and general financial badass) and Fran Hauser (the author of *The Myth of the Nice Girl* and my go-to for career advice), two very smart and successful women who have been on both sides of the negotiating table, for their excellent advice. I also added a few of my own tips so you can learn from my mistakes.

A lot of the advice offered here is geared toward employees working in corporate America, but I'd argue that every woman across every industry should strive to become comfortable discussing salary and compensation. This might be one of the hardest conversations you'll ever have, but it's actually worth it in the most literal sense.

Know What's Up in Your Industry

It's important to be tuned in to what's happening at your company—and within your industry as a whole—before you begin any compensation talks. If your company just went through layoffs or some other kind of restructuring and you've seen a similar trend happening to your competitors, this might not be the best time to ask for a raise.

Don't Ask for a Raise During Your Year-End Review

Both Sallie and Fran told me that you should talk to your boss about compensation well before the end of the year, when budgets are already locked down and most bosses are trying to figure out how to split up their bonus budget.

So when should you ask? Sallie and Fran gave slightly different but still helpful answers. Fran suggested that you bring up the topic after you have a big professional win. Did you do something amazing that got your boss's attention? Now's the time to strike! Fran said that even if your boss isn't able to give you a bump right now, you'll be on her radar, and she'll know that you're expecting some kind of compensation increase come year-end.

 Sallie suggests bringing up your salary in January—not to ask for a raise but to have a clear conversation with your boss about your goals for the upcoming year. What do you want to accomplish, and what does your boss want you to accomplish? Get on the same page, and write it all down. During this conversation, it's worth saying, "By year-end, I'd like a promotion and comparable raise if I hit these milestones." There's nothing worse than getting to December and saying, "I accomplished this," when your boss was wanting you to do something else, Sallie says. By sitting down at the beginning of the year and laying out clear goals, you'll have a road map to a possible promotion and raise.

Make sure you catch your boss when she's in the right mood. Has she been out with a sick kid, is another staffer causing problems, are you all working under a crazy deadline, or did your boss have a stressful meeting with *her* boss? Now might not be the time to bring up your needs. Wait a beat until the mood around the office is happier to put in your ask so it doesn't totally backfire.

Another quick thought: Sallie and Fran's advice is great, but if you're unsure it will work with your boss, why not ask her? I know it sounds a little ballsy, but asking, "When and how would you like me to bring up compensation conversations?" could lead to an open and honest chat about how you can best ask for a raise.

You Have to Say What You Want

We've all got to stop assuming that our bosses and colleagues can read our minds. They cannot. We also need to stop thinking that they are thinking about us all the time. Most bosses manage more than one employee and their own crazy workload (and have personal lives). Yes, they should think about your compensation and career advancement, but they aren't focused in the same way you are. You have to voice what you want.

 "If you are silent, you are losing," Sallie says.

Ouch.

But it's true. The first time I got up the courage to ask my boss for a raise was when I was two beers buzzed at a holiday party. What was most surprising to me about that conversation (besides the fact that I've got shockingly bad timing) is that my boss couldn't believe that I hadn't asked earlier. And it turned out she wasn't even the one who managed compensation! If I had just asked her months earlier, I wouldn't have felt so undervalued, and I would probably have gotten the raise earlier.

This also goes for seeking out promotions. There have been a couple of times in my career when I missed out on an opportunity simply because I didn't ask. It's something that's gotten easier as I've gotten older, but I would definitely encourage you to apply internally for a job you want, even if your boss hasn't tapped you on the shoulder. Even if the answer is no, it gives your boss a sense that you're seeking out new challenges and opportunities.

Know How Much You're Worth

It can be really nerve-wracking to figure out how much of a raise to ask for, but I thought Fran had a good suggestion: talk to recruiters.

Nearly every industry has recruiters who help fill open roles. Even if you're not looking for a new job, it's good to connect and talk salary, Fran says. They can tell you if they think you're being paid fairly, what the market rate is, and how competitors are paying. And in some ways, it's much easier to talk salary with a recruiter because there's less emotion involved.

Of course, another option is to share your salary with people within your industry. Make sure you're asking not just women but men with comparable job titles at competing companies.

You can also talk with your colleagues, though this can be tricky. Most companies will tell you not to share your comp with coworkers, but it's not illegal. It can be a loaded question, though—if you make more or less than a colleague, it can stir up conflict.

You should be really careful how you use this info to get a raise. I don't recommend going to your boss and saying, "So-and-so makes more than me, and that's not fair." A better tactic? Expressing concern that your compensation might not fall within a salary band that's appropriate for your role and level of experience. It might even be worth asking HR if the company practices salary banding—the people there can often give you insight into your employer's compensation practices.

Also, unless you're part of a union, I don't recommend going to your boss as a team to ask for an increase. This usually backfires, and it really makes managers angry because they feel as though they're being ganged up on—and rightfully so.

A less invasive option is doing a search on a site such as PayScale or Glassdoor. Both companies compile salary data to help workers (and employers) know their true market value. The data they have can be incomplete, and if you have a very specific job or weird title, it can be hard to find the details you need. But if you're just starting out, it can be a great place to learn about entry-level salaries.

Having this information is important so you don't undervalue yourself but also so you don't overask. I've seen young women ask for salaries that are $30,000 more than the typical income for a certain role. You'll want to leave some room to negotiate but not so much that you automatically take yourself out of the running.

Make a List

I asked Sallie what her employees need to do in order to get a raise. "I want to see great performance," she replied.

That seems obvious, right? But we need to remember why a company would want to pay you more money, and it's because they want to keep you because you're valuable to the bottom line. So when you go in to ask for a raise, you need to show you're a fucking big deal.

Take a page from my friend Vanessa's playbook, and write down a list of your professional accomplishments. Really, you should be keeping this list all year round. Every time you have a win at work, write it down. (Even if you're not asking for a raise, this is a good thing to do, as you can use the info later to update your résumé.)

Pump Yourself Up

You want to go into this conversation feeling your absolute most confident, Fran says. Wear your favorite outfit. Go for a run or to your favorite workout class that morning, meditate, or take a walk. My friend Cristina used to do a little bathroom dancing (and once got caught in middance by her boss). Looking at cat memes before the interview might make you feel better, or rereading an email filled with positive feedback.

Stay Positive

When I was talking to Fran about asking for a raise, I mentioned that I'd never seen any advice about what to do if your boss is the one who gets emotional or acts surprised or upset that you're asking for a raise. Sometimes women are told they're supposed to be grateful for opportunities, but opportunities don't pay the bills—unless they come with some money attached.

"I'm not emotional," I whined to Fran, "so why do they make it so awkward? What can I do to make it less weird?"

Fran told me from her experience, the employees who were most successful in asking her for a raise came into the room exuding positive energy.

Huh, I thought, *I wonder if I do that?* Oftentimes, when I'm finally sitting down to have a comp conversation, I'm so mad that I have to do the asking that I'm resentful. *Why can't they just see that I'm worth it? Why do I even have to ask?*

Fran's feedback—that you can't go into a compensation conversation as though you're ready to do battle—really resonated with me. As a manager, I'm always more willing to help a team member who's superpositive.

She recommends starting the conversation off by talking about the things in your job that bring you joy. Then, after you've got everyone feeling good, go in with the ask. Stay friendly and positive throughout the whole thing.

THIS IS A GOOD TIME TO:

Research your worth. Take Fran's advice and talk to recruiters, ask friends in the industry (men and women) for salary ranges, and do research to figure out your market value. Use that information to either ask for a raise or find a new job.

While you're at it, save $11 **(maybe you'll want to use that money to quit your job one day)**
Total saved so far: $66

I had almost ten years of work experience before I first got up the guts to ask for a raise when I was 33. Looking back at my salary history, I have to wonder how much money I've missed out on because I was so passive. Here five women share their stories of asking for more money. Use their success as motivation to negotiate for yourself.

SAMANTHA, 33 | JERSEY CITY, NJ | COMPLIANCE | SALARY INCREASE: $8/HOUR

"I was working as a temp at an investment bank. I loved what I was doing, but when I checked Glassdoor, I realized I was very underpaid. Six months into the role, my manager relied on me for nearly everything, from training new analysts to conducting meetings. I knew I needed a raise. I emailed the temp company and told him I was offered a job somewhere else (sometimes you have to fib your way to happiness), and I was looking to leave unless I got at least $5 more an hour. He went back to the bank's HR, who went to my direct manager to get their feedback. After a couple of days (and my anxiety skyrocketing), I got a call that they were increasing my hourly wage by $8! So I went from making $22.50 an hour to $30.50 an hour!

A couple of months later, I was offered a full-time position with a salary of $85,000, plus a 15 percent yearly bonus. So in nine months, I went from making a little less than $50,000 a year to $97,000! I feel more confident than ever!"

"After two years in my job, I felt like I was ready to take on more responsibility. I wrote down a few key points on why I deserved both a raise and a management position. My boss seemed impressed by my preparation and the valid points I brought up. It took a lot of negotiating to agree on a final number, but we found a good compromise we were both happy with. Later, my boss said he had never had someone walk through his door with such determination and zero signs of fear. Little did he know I was actually crying/screaming/shaking inside. #fakeittillyoumakeit"

"I had been at my first job out of school for two years, and I was doing well. But when I started talking to other people in my field, I figured out that I was being underpaid. I had received a few calls from recruiters for similar jobs and ended up calling one back. They told me a starting salary would be a good $20,000 over my current salary. The next week, I mentioned to my boss that I was feeling underpaid and undervalued and there was a company in the area willing to pay more for me. He went to management, and they came back with options to keep me happy/engaged in the role. I ended up taking a promotion with a salary bump of $18,000."

"I was working an entry-level job with an entry-level salary. Not long after I started, the senior-level person left and I assumed all of his duties while management searched for his replacement. I excelled, and even when they hired someone, I kept many of the new duties. Because it was a public university, I knew that I was being paid $8,000 less than the next-lowest-paid person on my team. I made a full $40,000 less than the senior-level hire. I asked for a meeting, stated my case, and provided concrete, measurable proof of my work, and only received a $2,500 raise. Management also told me that I was too ambitious. I immediately started looking for new jobs after that meeting. The offer I accepted came with a $23,500 salary increase."

JESSICA, 38 | MOUNT LAUREL, NJ | SALES/
MANUFACTURING | SALARY INCREASE:
$15,700

About a year ago, I asked the new district manager for a much-needed increase. I was making about $30,000 and I used Glassdoor to see what someone in sales with my experience should be making. It was a real shock—I knew I was underpaid but not how much. I asked the DM for a meeting to discuss my compensation. I printed out the reports I found along with a detailed list of how my job responsibility had changed. I went in, ready to fight for myself. I asked for $44,000 and he lowballed me at $41,000. I said no, and he approved a raise to $45,700. I think he was testing me.

"I was working at my job for two years for what I consider to be a
pretty low rate despite always getting glowing reviews from my
boss. I talked to my therapist and my fiancé about how to go about
asking for a raise. They did a good job pumping up my confidence. I
researched average wages in my area, but my job is pretty unique,
so I kind of guessed. Once I had a number, I went into the performance review ready. The review went great, and at the end my
boss asked me if I wanted to talk about anything else. I made my
case and asked for a raise from $16.50 to $18.50 an hour. She said
she thought that was fair and that she would talk to our executive
director to confirm the amount. I was ecstatic! About a week later
she called me into her office and said she thought I had undersold
myself and offered me *double* the raise I had asked for. That raise
made me feel really valued, and it really helped me feel more motivated at work."

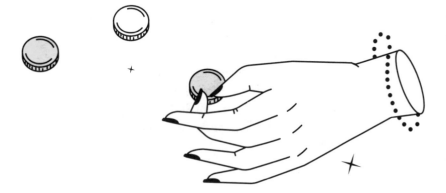

In the fall of 2011, I was laid off. My pride was wounded, but I was also relieved I didn't have to go back to that soul-sucking gig. But what was I going to do?

I started talking to anyone and everyone who'd meet with me. I met with book editors and agents, branding consultants and startup founders, ad execs and freelance writers. And more often than not, they told me my experience was all wrong and they couldn't hire me.

When you're looking to make a career change, that is the most soul-crushing news you can hear.

I began to wonder if I needed to go to grad school. I didn't want to be a lawyer, and at the time, I didn't even consider getting an MBA. (*I'm bad at math*, I thought.) But a master's degree sounded like an easy fix to my problem. That's how I found myself sitting in an NYU classroom one Tuesday night with a group of students getting their master's in communications.

The class was awful.

I realized that it really didn't make sense for me to go back to school. It was expensive, and even the best program wasn't really going to give me the real-world experience that most employers were looking for. I could easily spend $100,000 or more on tuition, only to see a small pay bump on the other side. Not to mention that it would be two more years out of the workforce. Financially, it just seemed like a really bad idea.

In the end, I took a $20,000 pay cut to work for a small startup so I could get some digital experience. It was one of the best decisions I ever made, as it eventually led to my job at Refinery29. And I'm relieved I'm not sitting on a pile of student loan debt right now.

I bring up my own experience because a lot of women hit a point when they wonder if they should make some kind of career change. Grad school is a solution if you're pursuing a career that does require a higher degree, but before you take on more debt, there are a few questions you should ask yourself:

Why am I thinking about going to graduate school in the first place?
Are you bored or unhappy at your current job? Do you want to put off real-world decisions for a couple of years? Or do you want to make a big career change that requires a graduate degree?

Is a graduate degree necessary to do the job I want?
Do you want to become a lawyer or a doctor, a nurse or a physical therapist? Or are you just hoping that having a graduate degree will help you get a salary bump at your current job or an intro into a new industry? Does anyone you know in the industry have a graduate degree? Do they think it was a worthwhile investment?

Will having an advanced degree increase my earning potential?
It's really important to do your research and actually talk to people who've gone through the programs and now have jobs. You should also reach out to hiring managers and recruiters to see if they consider graduate degrees when hiring and if candidates with graduate degrees earn higher salaries.

Will getting an advanced degree be cost-effective?

This is a question where a little research can take you a long way. There's a lot of data online that can help you determine whether it makes financial sense to get a master's degree. A 2016 PayScale study found that an MBA with a focus on IT was a slam dunk; a master's in graphic design, not so much.[6]

Considering that the average cost per year of getting a graduate degree at a public institution is $30,000,[7] you'll want to make sure you'll see a salary increase that's significant enough that you won't be bogged down paying off student loan debt for the rest of your life.

Would real-world experience be better?

Unless a graduate degree is essential to get professional credentials, you should think long and hard about whether you're better off just getting more real-world experience. Maybe you should take an internship or an entry-level job or focus more on your side hustle.

Calculate Your Total Compensation Package

TIME: *30–60 minutes*
TOOLS: *Paycheck, benefit details, calculator or spreadsheet*

We talked earlier in the chapter about the importance of looking at your total compensation package when shopping for a new job. But this is an exercise that can be useful at any time—and could potentially lead you to feel one of two ways. (1) You'll be impressed by just how much more you're earning than you thought. Or (2) you'll realize you're undervalued and it's time to start working on your plan to ask for a raise (go back to page 86 for more on that) or start looking for a new job.

For the most part, it's pretty easy to figure out your total compensation, with the exception of health care costs. Most HR departments won't tell you how much your company spends on health care. So we'll leave that off this list. But if you are comparing two job offers, you should find out how much you'll pay for insurance and the yearly deductible at the new job because you can compare that to your current out-of-pocket health care expenses, including your monthly premiums.

These are the easy numbers you can include (I threw in some sample numbers for reference):

Annual Salary: $50,000
Bonus (total, regardless of whether it's annual or quarterly): $2,500
Retirement Benefits (does your employer offer a match?): 100 percent up to 6 percent (so if you're maxing your match, that's an additional $3,000 per year)

Number of Vacation Days and Paid Holidays: 27 (making the monetary value $5,184—and this is why you should always take all your vacation; otherwise your hourly rate decreases)
Additional Perks (cell phone bill reimbursement, gym discounts, free snacks, meals, or coffee, day care discounts, etc.): Let's say that you get $60 per month for your cell phone, you're saving $100 per year on your gym thanks to a corporate discount, and your employer has great coffee, so you never have to buy a $5 latte. Total savings = ~ $2,125 per year

Add those up, and voilà, you've got your total comp package (minus health care) = **$62,809.**

While you're at it, save $12
Total saved so far: $78

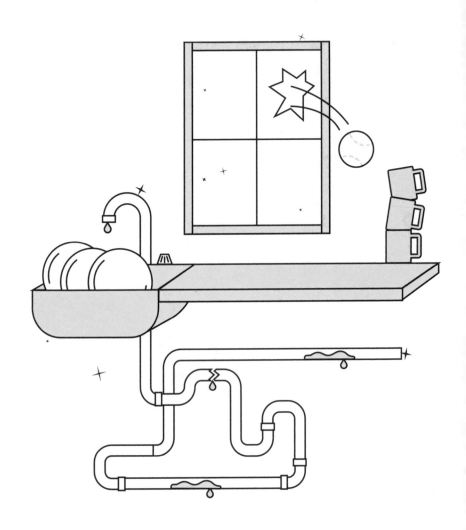

CHAPTER 4

Emergencies & Money
(Or What to Do When the Shit Hits the Fan)

A few years ago, the writer Paulette Perhach got a lot of attention for a story she wrote for the website The Billfold about the importance of what she termed a "fuck-off fund." She painted a picture of a young woman who had made some really bad financial decisions, ended up with a lot of debt, and was stuck in a really bad relationship and a really bad job. If she had saved her money and not wasted it on overpriced cocktails and party dresses, she could have walked away when shit got bad.

Though I wasn't personally a fan of Paulette's melodramatic tale—it feels like such a stereotypical portrayal of a young woman making dumb money mistakes—I do agree with the fundamental advice: *Every single person needs an emergency fund.* You can call it a "fuck-off fund" if you want or an escape plan or your rainy-day account. Whatever. You just have to have one. Because melodrama or not, I've found that in my life when it rains it fucking pours. Your car will break down in the exact same week that your neighbor floods your apartment, destroying your laptop, in the same month that you suddenly owe back taxes and your S.O. dumps you. *Fuck.*

In this chapter, we'll explore ways you can protect yourself in those times when everything seems to go wrong—from saving for an emergency fund to understanding your health insurance to building an escape plan. It's often in those most stressful moments that it just feels easier to throw a lot of money at the problem. But if you've got no money, the next option is credit cards, which just make an expensive problem even worse.

A Week in Charleston, SC, on a **$37,000** Salary

OCCUPATION: Content coordinator
INDUSTRY: Media
AGE: 25
LOCATION: Charleston, SC
ANNUAL SALARY: $37,000
PAYCHECK AMOUNT (TWICE A MONTH): $1,018

GENERAL FINANCIAL INFORMATION:
Checking Account Balance: $1,498
Savings Account Balance: ~$11,000 ($500/month)

HOUSING:
Rent: $500 (For my share of the rent in a three-bedroom/one-bath apartment. I share a bedroom and a small home office room with my partner. Our roommate covers the third bedroom.)
Electricity/Heat/Gas: $68 (for our share of the bill)
Water: $36 (for our share of the bill)
Internet: $45 (for our share of the bill)
Renter's Insurance: $8
Phone: $68

TRANSPORTATION:
Car Payment: $0 (I paid cash for my used car.)
Car Insurance: $100

HEALTH & SELF-CARE:
Health Insurance: $0 (I'm still on my parents' plan.)
Dental Insurance: $0 (covered by my employer)
Eye Insurance: $0 (covered by my employer)
FSA: $0 (My parents graciously let me use their shared FSA while on their plan.)
Yoga: $15 (I work-trade with a studio to cover the rest of my monthly membership)

SUBSCRIPTIONS:
Spotify: $11
Amazon Prime: $99/year
Daily Burn: $7.47
(I bum Netflix, Hulu, HBOGO off friends and family.)

DEBT:
Student Loan Debt Total: $0
Credit Card Debt Total: $0

RETIREMENT:
Roth IRA
Contribution: $5,500 annually, which breaks down to about $458 monthly
Roth IRA Total: ~$20,000
(I opened it shortly after graduation.)
401(k) Contribution: 5 to 8 percent of my paycheck
401(k) Total: ~$4,000

DAY ONE

7:30 a.m.—Read HuffPost and eat an RXBAR. Make a cup of pour-over coffee.

8:15 a.m.—I throw what's left of my coffee in a travel mug and drink it on my commute. There's traffic, and I'm late to work. Good thing it's Friday.

1 p.m.—I drive home for lunch. I fry two eggs and it eat over spinach and half an avocado, along with some blue corn chips. My partner, A., is home (he's in grad school), and we spend some quality time together. I make a salad, grab the beet hummus I made last night, and pack both into a cooler to take back to work since I have a dinner party right after.

4 p.m.—Cupcakes for an office birthday. I take one to go, I can't eat it because of an allergy but plan to take it home for A. as a nice treat. I make a cup of chamomile tea.

5:30 p.m.—Head to the dinner party. Enjoy the food and conversation, and it's a nice forced separation from my technology for a few hours.

10:30 p.m.—I head home. I make a cup of hot water with lemon and watch *Man in the High Castle* with A. before bed.

DAILY TOTAL: $0

DAY TWO

8 a.m.—My yoga studio sponsored me to go to an assistant training this weekend (saved me $400). I make a cup of coffee, pack snacks, plus a journal, yoga mat, water bottle, and change of clothes.

9 a.m.—Training starts. I'm going to smell so bad when this is over.

1 p.m.—Break for lunch. I volunteered to help at the merch table, so I eat the lunch I packed (green juice, leftover beet hummus, chips, and a salad) while I work.

6 p.m.—Training is over, but I have to work another merch table shift. I scarf down an RXBAR even though I'm meeting my grandmother for dinner. While packing up the table, I cave and buy a new tank top. **$35**

7:45 p.m.—Arrive at my grandmother's apartment for dinner. She got me a salmon quinoa bowl from her assisted living facility cafeteria. She lets me shower and change before we sit down to eat. We talk politics and watch *Abstract*.

9 p.m.—Home. I eat a couple of

medjool dates and tahini while we watch *Man in the High Castle*.

DAILY TOTAL: $35

DAY THREE

7:30 a.m.—I pack supplies for training and make a cup of coffee to go.
9 a.m.—Today, we practice a live class. I'm matched with a teacher visiting from Miami, and I assist my partner through an hour sequence. We switch, and she assists me through the next sequence.
1 p.m.—Break for lunch. I eat an RXBAR on the drive home. I shower on the short break because the day is only half over, and I've already sweated through my clothes. I throw on clean clothes, grab an apple, and rush back to training.
6 p.m.—Training is over, and I head home to shower and crash. A. makes me some eggs with vegetables. We're both trying to cut our expenses, and so we've been eating a lot of eggs. We watch more *Man in the High Castle*.
8:30 p.m.—I crawl into bed, I'm wiped.

DAILY TOTAL: $0

DAY FOUR

7:15 a.m.—I wake up feeling a little off, but I shake it off as being sore from yoga training. I make a smoothie and pour-over coffee. I leisurely drink my coffee, something I missed out on over the weekend. I wipe down my yoga mat, pack my yoga clothes, and get ready. There's a studio around the corner from my office, so I'll head to class after work.
12:30 p.m.—I notice a dull pain in my pelvis. I make a grocery run on my lunch break for organic spinach, baby carrots, goddess dressing, hummus quartets, guacamole, dark chocolate, sweet potato chips, root vegetable chips, trail mix, frozen cauliflower, sprouted bread, almond butter, a birthday card, tea, and a take-'n'-bake pizza. Since A. is in grad school and living off loans, I like getting him groceries that I know he wouldn't splurge for otherwise. I zip over the bridge to drop stuff at our house and make a quick to-go lunch of eggs, avocado, and lettuce. I grab an RXBAR and a green juice for a late-afternoon snack before rushing back to the office. **$43.57**
5:30 p.m.—I change at work and jump in the car. I'm at class by 5:40.

8:45 p.m.—I'm home and beeline for the shower. I'm disgusting after my weekly back-to-back class and work-trade shift. I notice my pelvic pain persists and decide to go to the doctor tomorrow if it's still bothering me in the morning.

9:15 p.m.—I make dinner and sit down to watch another *Man in the High Castle* episode before bed.

DAILY TOTAL: $43.57

| DAY FIVE |

7 a.m.—I get up a little early because it's my boss's birthday, and I plan to stop by a bakery on the way to work. I make a smoothie and drink it while getting ready for work and take my coffee to go.

8:10 a.m.—I stop at the bakery and browse the dessert choices. I land on a couple tarts. My co-worker pays me back for the tarts, since I got the card and a nice box of tea to accompany this gift (purchased on my grocery run). **$7.50** (expensed)

9 a.m.—I still feel my pelvic pain and decide I need to see my doctor. I'm worried my IUD might be out of place. Make an appointment for 3.

12:30 p.m.—After delivering the birthday treats we head to lunch. We pick a cute place that has outdoor seating, since it's a gorgeous day and my teammate has her pup in tow. I get a half sandwich, half salad with an iced tea. **$15.75**

2:45 p.m.—We're having a great time, but I have to leave to get to the doctor. I pay the co-pay with my FSA. An ultrasound confirms that my IUD is out of place and now in my cervix. It has to be removed immediately. **$35**

4 p.m.—Following the removal, my doctor discusses my options. Since the initial insertion experience was pretty painful, she recommends I wait to get a new IUD until the end of the month, after my next period, and I can take medication in advance for the pain. I ask her if I need to buy backup birth control since I was recently intimate and it's unclear how long my IUD has been dislodged. She says if it's stressing me out, I should go ahead and get it. She gives me a coupon.

4:30 p.m.—Back at the office, feeling distraught and frustrated that I'm going to have to go through the insertion process again and schedule a sick day to do it. Fortunately, I have the sick leave through my job.

7 p.m.—I stop at the grocery store after yoga since we're going on vacation this weekend and staying in a remote cabin. I grab baby wipes, smoked turkey, pepper jack cheese, discounted chicken thighs (to make for dinner tonight), and more baby carrots. **$19.56**

7:30 p.m.—I stop by the pharmacy for backup birth control and some CeraVe hand ointment since I'm also in the midst of an eczema flare-up. I give the pharmacist the coupon from my doctor and swipe my FSA card; it covers the ointment but not the Plan B. I give her my credit card for the rest. At least I had a $10-off coupon. **$50.43**

8 p.m.—I'm wiped out by the time I get home. I jump in the shower, and A. makes the chicken thighs. I make a salad, and we watch more *Man in the High Castle*.

DAILY TOTAL: $128.24

| DAY SIX |

7:45 a.m.—I give myself an extra 30 minutes of sleep, which means no time to waste this morning. I jump out of bed, make coffee and a smoothie to go. Pack clothes for yoga, get dressed, and I'm out the door by 8:20.

11 a.m.—I go to the restroom and notice some tenderness. Should this be a normal symptom from the removal procedure?

2 p.m.—I take a late lunch since I was stuck on a conference call. I zip home to eat and write a few postcards to my senators. On my way back to the office, I call my doctor to get a nurse's opinion on the swelling. They'll call me back.

4 p.m.—A nurse calls back. I shouldn't be having any symptoms, and she tells me to come in if it persists.

5:30 p.m.—I drive home after work and take a walk around the neighborhood with my friend and her dog. We walk to a dock and take in the sun setting over the marsh.

7 p.m.—A. made over-easy eggs, and I throw them on top of some spinach with goddess dressing and sriracha. We eat together on the couch and browse Netflix for something more upbeat to watch. We land on *Mind of a Chef*. I grab a handful (really two) of chocolate trail mix for dessert.

8:30 p.m.—I take a shower. I'm feeling overwhelmed and disconnected from my body. I read a book until I fall asleep.

DAILY TOTAL: $0

| DAY SEVEN |

7:25 a.m.—I'm up before my alarm and grab my phone before quietly leaving our room, I don't want to wake up A. In the bathroom, I notice that my symptoms from the IUD removal haven't gone down. I make coffee and a smoothie and pack a lunch with the hope I'll get to the doctor at lunchtime.

8:30 a.m.—I quickly call my doctor's office. They have an opening at 11:30. I take it and plan on an early lunch break.

11:30 a.m.—At the doctor's office I pay the co-pay, and a nurse takes me back to an exam room. My doctor examines the swelling and confirms it's nothing to worry about, but she recommends that I take it easy and prescribes a topical steroid. She says it looks more like a reaction to an irritant than anything else. So I guess going to hot yoga after my removal procedure on Tuesday and then running errands afterward in my sweaty clothes wasn't the best idea . . . **$35**

12:30 p.m.—Back at work, I eat an almond butter and apple sandwich. I check my email and have a new message in my doctor's portal online. It is a bill for my IUD removal for $237 after insurance. I'm surprised the bill is so high and decide to call my mom about it after work for her insight.

4 p.m.—I check how much it's going to be to get a new IUD. I log in to my insurance portal, and it will be close to $430 out of pocket. This doesn't change anything, because having an IUD is worth it, but it doesn't make me feel any less stressed. At least I can use my FSA, and it's not like that money can be used for anything else.

5:30 p.m.—Call my mom on my commute home. She tells me she's not surprised by those costs but says it's frustrating nonetheless. I yell about how it's expensive to not get pregnant and expensive to get pregnant and expensive once you're pregnant. A lose-lose. I feel grateful I have insurance and a mother who is health insurance savvy, but in that moment I want to scream, "Ugh this suuuuccckkkksssssss."

6 p.m.—There was a backup on the bridge, and my commute was longer than usual. Once home, I continue to chat with my mom and start making dinner. I make some eggs, and A. puts on some rice. I have another fried egg spinach salad with some sweet potato chips and hummus. We plow through a whole hummus quartet while our eggs and rice cook.

8 p.m.—I clean the kitchen and head upstairs to shower, read, and try to get to bed early again. Once in bed, I go ahead and pay the IUD removal bill. Ugh. **$237**

DAILY TOTAL: $272

| THE BREAKDOWN |

TOTAL SPENT: $489.31

FOOD AND DRINK: $96.88

ENTERTAINMENT: $0

HOME AND HEALTH: $357.43

CLOTHES AND BEAUTY: $35

TRANSPORTATION: $0

OTHER: $0

| THE FOLLOW-UP |

Was this your first time dealing with an unexpected medical expense?
It's not, but it was definitely the biggest in terms of costs. It was a big chunk of change, between having the removal procedure, getting the Plan B, and then having to get another IUD inserted. All that stuff adds up really fast.

Did the experience change how you prepare for unexpected expenses?
Dealing with all of this—understanding your insurance and your medical bills, calling your insurance provider or your doctor's office, trying to make sure you're not overpaying or getting double billed—all this stuff is so complicated and convoluted. If I didn't have my mom's help, I would have been totally lost.

Definitely ask questions before you pay the bill. I've had a few instances where I paid a co-pay that I didn't even owe. Make sure to call your insurance before you pay a $300 bill. It's inconvenient but totally worth it.

You're on your own insurance plan now. Are the costs different from what you experienced with your parents?

Since I've transitioned to my own insurance, I now realize how great theirs was. 'Cause now I'm paying for X-rays out of pocket until I meet my deductible, and I'm paying for the $5 urinalysis test when I have a UTI. Like that kind of stuff, I didn't realize wasn't standard to be covered under a company insurance plan.

Who do you talk to about money? Your parents? Your partner? Friends?

I talk to my mom a lot about money. My relationship with saving money is because of her—for better or worse—so I've always leaned on her for advice. I talk to my partner a lot about money, too. We're in it to win it, so we talk a lot about spending habits and finances. I'm really grateful that he and I randomly have very similar saving and spending habits so we are usually on the same page when it comes to priorities. Like right now, we're working together to cut expenses so we can start paying back his loans at a faster rate when he gets out of school.

What surprised you most about doing a Money Diary?

Living in a city, even a small one like Charleston, is expensive, and I'm really grateful for my parents. They made it possible for me to go to college, graduate without debt, and be able to both support myself and put money away, so when the unexpected happens, I can afford to deal with the costs without additional stress.

Also, everything adds up; a trip to the grocery store for what feels like just a few things quickly becomes $20 to $30. When I'm making a bunch of trips to the store over the week, that becomes a lot of $20 to $30 purchases.

It's easy to argue that an emergency fund isn't sexy—after all, it's money you're not supposed to spend unless things get really, really bad. Can we change that narrative, please? Start thinking of it as your ticket to freedom.

Freedom from staying awake at night worrying about an unexpected medical bill. Freedom to leave a terrible boss or relationship. Freedom to get up every day and move through this crazy, unpredictable world with the confidence that if things get really bad, you have the financial means to take care of yourself.

If that's not sexy, I'm not sure what is.

I tapped Manisha Thakor for her realistic (and doable) advice, so you can tackle this financial challenge once and for all.

How much should I have in my emergency fund?
The short answer is three to six months of fixed living expenses (rent, utilities, health care, etc.). If you were to lose your job and needed to access these funds while you looked for a new one, you'd seriously cut back on flex spending.

If you're making $60,000 and spend around $2,000 a month (maybe $3,000 if you live in a city), your fully funded emergency account would have between $12,000 and $18,000.

Hold up! I have debt! I live paycheck to paycheck. There's no way I can save $12,000. Ever.
Slow down. We don't expect you to have $12,000 right away. That's a *lot* of money to save. We're quite aware that you've got competing priorities, but Manisha is here to help.

Remember in chapter 1 when we talked about the importance of the 50/30/20 rule? Emergency funds fall into that 20 percent bucket, but oftentimes other expenses (your 401(k)), student loan or credit card debt) take priority. Don't get overwhelmed. Here's how Manisha suggests you prioritize:

1. Pay at least the absolute minimum on your debt on time every month.

2. Start saving for a $2,000 emergency fund. Until you have $2,000 in your savings account, do not prioritize any other saving—that includes near-term goals (travel, buying a new couch) and slightly longer-term goals (planning a wedding or buying a house), and your 401(k). The bottom line, Manisha says, is that you need a $2,000 emergency fund before you start spending on fun things.

3. Once you've hit $2,000, start participating in your 401(k) up to the match. (We'll explore this more in chapter 9.)

I know you might be thinking, *Wait, shouldn't I always be investing in my 401(k) if my employer matches? I don't want to lose that free money.* I asked Manisha the same question, and she admitted there's a lot of debate about this. The reason she recommends focusing on that $2,000 emergency fund first, and then investing in your 401(k), is that if you do have an emergency and you don't have the funds to cover it, it's likely you'll take on credit card debt. Which means any extra money you might have made with that 401(k) match will essentially be lost to the high interest rates you're paying on your credit card.

4. If you have $10,000 or more in debt (especially credit card debt with high interest rates), focus on paying it off next. (See chapter 5 for more advice on paying down debt.) When you finish paying off that debt, you can transfer the dollar amount you paid on those bills each month into your emergency account so it can grow even quicker.

5. Once you have a fully funded emergency account, start saving for longer-term goals, as well as increase the amount you're saving for retirement. It's even easier if you've already built in a savings routine.

Okay, so I really need only $2,000. I'm not even sure I can do that.

Think of it this way: $2,000 split over 365 days comes out to around $5.50 a day. It's easy to spend that much on a latte. In New York, $5.50 won't even get you a beer at most bars outside of happy hour. I promised I would never say, "Don't buy the latte" (or the beer, for that matter), but it's worth pointing out how quickly $5 a day can add up to a significant sum. If you don't have an emergency fund but you do find yourself giving in to impulse buys at the drugstore, remember, it's the small tweaks that can add up to something big.

I have an emergency fund, but I'm always dipping into it—and not usually for emergencies.

Do you start out each month with the good intentions of saving $200 toward your emergency fund? But as the month goes on and more and more unexpected expenses pop up, do you find yourself dipping into your savings account for a little extra cash? And it's so easy because your savings account is attached to your checking account, so one quick transfer and voilà, back in black.

Stop!

You need to make your savings account less accessible. Manisha suggests opening an online savings account that's not directly connected with your checking account. The good news is that such accounts often have higher interest rates than you get at traditional brick-and-mortar banks (see Ally Bank versus Chase), so you'll earn more in interest each month (cha-ching!).

Also, you can have the money for your emergency fund automatically deducted from your paycheck so you don't have a chance to miss it. And if you don't have a debit card connected to the account, it's easier to just pretend you can't access that money at all.

What qualifies as an emergency anyway?

I can tell you what's *not* an emergency: plane tickets to your best friend's destination wedding in Aruba; a leather tote for your upcoming job interview; or a new sofa for your apartment.

The definition of "emergency" is highly personal, but Manisha generally thinks that you should tap that account to buy an expensive plane ticket to see a loved one before they die or if your tires blow out and you need your car to get to work. Unexpected medical bills or essential home repairs also apply. I think of my emergency fund as my safety net in case I lose my job and I'm struggling to pay the mortgage.

If, God forbid, you do find yourself needing to tap into your emergency savings, stop, take a deep breath, and make sure you're spending smartly. And not, as Paulette suggested in her essay, staying in a luxury hotel and ordering champagne. You know better than that by now—and if you don't, you will shortly. If you do take money from the emergency account, your number one financial focus should be on building it back (and quickly!).

Open a high-yield savings account. Seriously, don't leave your emergency fund (or any savings, for that matter) in a savings account that's got a terrible interest rate. My Bank of America account has a ridiculously low APY (0.02 percent) compared to my Capital One account at 1.45 percent. If you have $2,000 in your emergency fund, that's a monthly interest earned difference of 4 cents versus $29.

While you're at it, save $13
Total saved so far: $91

I've always been healthy (knock on wood), and I've always had access to pretty good insurance through my job or Ken's. Usually, when open enrollment comes around, I choose the plan that gives me access to my regular roster of doctors, and I don't think too much about the monthly costs. That money comes straight out of my paycheck, so I never get a chance to miss it. (I am very grateful to have this privilege.)

It feels a little irresponsible, though—and I often wonder if I'm losing money by being so careless. So I asked Priya Malani to help me understand my health insurance a little better. I'm still struggling with it—and we can only just scratch the surface in this chapter—but I'm hoping the questions that follow will help you save money and make the most of your insurance policy.

If we don't answer your question here, can I suggest that you pick up the phone and call your insurance company? It can be awkward, and I've found that insurance reps can sometimes be frustratingly dismissive. Ignore them and keep asking questions until you get an explanation you understand.

What should I look for when reviewing a plan's summary of benefits and coverage?

Priya recommends you look at the premium (the amount you pay each month for coverage) and deductible (the amount you pay out of pocket before your insurance kicks in). You'll also want to see what kind of coverage your insurer has for in-network and out-of-network services. Is it an HMO plan, in which you can go to see doctors only within the insurer's network, or a PPO, in which you get more freedom to choose your doctors? Then you'll want to do some research to make sure your doctors accept the insurance. A little googling (or a call to your doctor's office) can answer that question.

Wait, I still don't really understand what a deductible is.
So say you have a $2,000 deductible; you pay the first $2,000 of *covered* services. In some cases, your plan might have an "in-network" deductible and an "out-of-network" deductible. Generally, co-pays don't count toward your deductible. So if you visit your doctor and your insurance company requires you to pay a $20 co-pay, your deductible isn't reduced to $1,980.

However, if you end up being billed $200 for any tests the doctor orders, that will count toward your deductible, reducing it to $1,800.

What will give me more bang for my buck? A plan with a low premium and a high deductible or one with a high premium and a low deductible?
Choosing a health care plan is highly personal, Priya says, so it's hard to give blanket advice. If you never, ever go to the doctor, it probably makes more sense to go with a high-deductible plan. But if you have a chronic illness or you tend to visit the doctor every time you get a cold (hey, no judgment!), you might want to consider a plan where you spend less out of pocket every time you visit.

If you do take the cheapest plan, you might want to automatically transfer the savings into an emergency account to pay for costs that aren't covered by your plan after you've spent all your FSA dollars.

Should I be putting money into an FSA?
This really depends on how much you normally spend on health care throughout the year—and if you're good about remembering to get reimbursed for those purchases. The maximum

amount you can put into the account varies from year to year (in 2018, it was $2,650). You can roll over only a small amount of your FSA savings, and then you have to use it by a specific date. If you don't use it, you lose it—and that sucks.

If you change jobs (or you're laid off), your FSA is impacted as well. Every health plan handles this a little differently, so if your job situation changes, be sure to contact your benefits department (and submit any outstanding claims) well before your last day.

What should I look for in an insurance plan if I'm considering infertility treatment?

Priya recommends picking up the phone and calling your plan provider to learn just how much it will pay for infertility treatment. If you're beginning to consider family planning, it's also worth looking at plans with higher premiums. Oftentimes, they come with lower deductibles and more access to different doctors. The monthly cost might be higher, but you could save money in the long run if you visit the doctor frequently.

Many insurance companies also offer coverage estimates online, so you can get a ballpark sense of how much you'll pay out of pocket to have dental surgery or see a physical therapist.

What's the bare-minimum plan I can sign up for?

If you're employed full-time and your employer offers insurance benefits, the bare minimum is usually a high-deductible plan. If you're a freelancer or an entrepreneur who can't afford traditional insurance, you might consider catastrophe insurance, which would offer coverage if the worst happened (e.g., you get hit by a car). If you decide to go this way, you definitely need a fully funded emergency account, okay?

Spend the money in your FSA. These pretax accounts are great if you spend the money. There's a limit to how much you can roll over each year (check on the IRS website, but it's usually around $500), and anything else you didn't use you lose—making all those tax savings null and void.

While you're at it, save $14
Total saved so far: $105

The Obama administration passed the Affordable Care Act in 2010 with the hope that every American could get access to high-quality health insurance. Unfortunately, by the end of 2017, 12.2 percent of Americans are still without coverage (and that number seems to be rising, according to the Gallup-Sharecare Index).[1] But even if you can afford insurance, it's not unusual to find yourself momentarily uninsured when you're unexpectedly unemployed. Alexis, 40, lost her job due to downsizing in the beginning of 2017. She decided to travel while she looked for a new job, but she didn't bother to sign up for insurance in the interim. Unfortunately, it was during that vulnerable time that she discovered she had breast cancer. Here is her story.

I was traveling to Mexico last March when I first felt a lump under my armpit. I started freaking out. I had a feeling at the time that it was bad. Because it was under my armpit my first thought was that it was lymphoma. Breast cancer didn't even occur to me.

At the end of 2016, my job (and department) were eliminated and I lost my health care coverage. In early 2017, I was employed full-time on a freelance project, but it didn't come with benefits. I was pretty sure I had a new job lined up, so I decided not to sign up for private insurance for just a few months. I had planned to travel for a few weeks after freelancing from January through March, but I came home early after I found the lump.

I went to my gynecologist of seventeen years. She knew that I was temporarily uninsured, and I paid for the appointment out of pocket. As soon as she saw me, she was like, *Something is wrong*. She sent me to get a mammogram and a biopsy immediately. I saw her on a Friday and had all the tests done on Monday.

I paid for all the testing (a mammogram and biopsies) out of pocket. I didn't even give it a second thought. The insurance part was obviously weighing on me. To be uninsured without something wrong is nerve-racking. It was also a new feeling to me; I'd lived a healthy life with few reasons to worry (knock wood) for nearly four decades. I felt really panicked, but I also knew that I wasn't going to let money stop me from finding out what the fuck was wrong with me. If the doctors had told me that a mammogram cost $20,000, I would have taken out a loan. I would have found a way.

A week after the biopsy, in late April, I found out I had breast cancer. The first thing I did—after telling my family—was start looking for insurance. I was fortunate enough to have a friend of a friend who's a cancer nurse. She immediately suggested I should work directly with the hospital instead of an insurance company.

She was a guardian angel. I hit pause on filling out insurance applications so I could learn more. I don't know what possessed me to do this, but I called up a social worker at Memorial Sloan Kettering Cancer Center to ask for advice. I'm in New York City, and that's supposedly the best place for cancer treatment. I simply said, "I was diagnosed yesterday. I have no insurance. I know this isn't your problem, but is there anything that you recommend I do?"

The social worker told me about New York State's Medicaid Cancer Treatment Program. One of the qualifications is that you've been diagnosed with one of four kinds of nonpreventative cancer (colorectal, breast, cervical, or prostate) and that you have no insurance at the time of diagnosis. I kept thinking, *Thank God I didn't submit any of those insurance applications.* It felt as though fate had intervened. That woman was another guardian angel. The next day, I was at the Medicaid office uptown, applying for the program.

The woman who helped with the Medicaid application back-dated it to March so the original tests (the mammogram and biopsy) were covered. It saved me a few thousand dollars in lab costs. My gynecologist doesn't accept Medicaid so I still paid for that out of pocket, but it was a few hundred dollars and an expense I'd budgeted for.

I was really worried there would be more expenses not covered by the Medicaid, so my friends set up a GoFundMe for me. It raised a lot of money, and I was beyond appreciative. But I haven't touched that money because I'm really nervous about what might happen a year from now or two years from now. Will I have trouble getting insurance because of my preexisting condition? What if I'm paying for mammograms out of pocket at some point? What if I'm not able to work? So I've kept that GoFundMe money in a separate account. God forbid I need it.

Even though my insurance covered all of my cancer treatments at Sloan Kettering, I've had a lot of other unexpected, outside expenses. I do acupuncture once or twice a week. I've had to go through physical therapy to learn how to drain my lymph nodes manually. Crazy shit like that. But I paid for that myself because I'm still working, pretty much full-time. The job I was waiting on came through, and I started there two weeks after my diagnosis.

Still, for most of the last year I didn't really spend money on myself. I was worried for so many reasons that I just kept working really hard, paying off debt and saving my money. I wasn't ordering Seamless or buying myself a new sweater as a treat. If anything, I spent a lot less money. I haven't been able to travel since I started treatment last summer. I lost all my hair, my eyelashes, and my eyebrows—so I wasn't spending money on haircuts, color, nails, waxing, et cetera. I wasn't spending money on makeup or skin stuff because I was basically using nothing but essential oils. I wasn't spending money on clothes, because I was wearing fucking sweatpants most days.

I wasn't drinking, so I didn't spend money on alcohol; I got a medical marijuana card, and I spent some money on pot. I didn't really look at it as a treat because I couldn't eat unless I smoked pot. In my case, pot was truly medicinal. In some ways, I spent more on food because I wanted to eat (even) healthier. It's quite expensive to eat healthfully, especially in New York City. There are dollar slices of pizza everywhere, but there aren't dollar green juices. But because I was barely going out to restaurants and not drinking at all, I still felt deprived.

Besides all the health stuff, I bought a lot of books. I supported a lot of West Village bookstores and the Strand. I had chemo on Fridays, and so I would spend all weekend lying around reading hardcover books. I used to wait until books came out in paperback. Not last year.

It's been the longest year. It's tough because I think what people want to hear from me is "It's over. It's done!" What I've learned is there's not a very definite ending for me. The cancer cells were very aggressive. Right now, in early 2018, I'm at a point where the cancer's out of my body and my doctors are very, very, very concentrated about it not coming back. For me, that means more chemo and possibly hormone therapy. I'm going to be spending another fucking year getting treated.

I just want it to be done. Every time I get through another hurdle with chemo and surgery and radiation, I'm like, Can I be done now? I want to feel better. I want to be off drugs. I want to be pain free. I want my life back.

I know that in some ways I'm lucky. I have amazing doctors. I'm not going into debt over this. I still sleep in the same bed. I've been able to work. I haven't had to uproot my life. Everything has changed, and nothing has changed. I hope that I can look back at this at some point like a blip on a radar. As a one- or two-year span that I spent 100 percent on treating my health.

Barbara Ginty, a Certified Financial Planner professional and the founder of Planancial, and I were talking one afternoon about the various financial projects women should tackle, and after the obvious—saving for an emergency, maxing your 401(k) match—she mentioned estate planning. *Ugh*, I thought, *one more thing I need to take care of (yesterday)*.

Barbara likes to call it *escape* planning, because, as she points out, most of us don't have estates. You might think you can skip over this section because you're single, without kids, and have just some student loan debt, but there are a few things to consider to protect both yourself and your family.

It's probably not a bad idea to have term life insurance.

If you have one kid (or more), both parents should absolutely have term life insurance, Barbara advises—even if one parent doesn't work. And if you both work in order to afford your lifestyle, you *really* need the insurance. This is the money that will help cover expenses—mortgage, child care, etc.—in the event that a parent dies.

Employer life insurance policies aren't enough.

Barbara admits that employer life insurance policies can be a great deal, but it is important to have your own policy. She points out that it's not likely you'll stay at your job your entire life. Say you leave after seven years, your work life insurance isn't always portable, she explains, which means you can't take it with you. Or, if you can, the rates will likely go up since you're no longer under a group plan.

It's great if your new employer does offer its own group plan, but if not, you'll have to get a new policy. You'll be seven years older, and your health could have changed (your rate is determined by your age, gender, and health). Barbara says to think of employer-provided life insurance policies as icing on the cake and not rely on them as your only financial backup plan.

Shop around for a policy.
Barbara recommends getting quotes from multiple companies—or you can work with an insurance broker who will shop around for you. You'll need to determine the length of time you think you'll need coverage (known as "term" in the insurance world). Common terms are ten, twenty, and thirty years. She recommends buying the longest term if you can afford it, as it gives you more options and control. When you sign up for the insurance, make sure you get a level-term policy, which means you'll pay the same premiums each year for the entire length of the insurance.

Barbara says it's also really important to check that the insurance is convertible into a permanent policy before it runs out, so if you choose a twenty-year policy, at year 19 you have the opportunity to extend it. Depending on the company, you can pay monthly, quarterly, or semiannually. Often it will be slightly cheaper if you pay annually.

Don't sign up for whole life insurance.
Period. Some insurance salesmen try to market this as an insurance policy *and* retirement account rolled into one. But the truth is it's very, very expensive, Barbara explains, and there are so many other things you could be doing with that money.

Understand how your debt impacts your cosigners.

I was shocked when Barbara told me that some private student loan debt sticks around *after you die* if there's more than one name on a loan. And, unlike a house, you can't sell a college degree.

In 2014, the Consumer Financial Protection Bureau (CFPB) released a report that showed that some private student loans go into auto-default when a cosigner dies.[2] Auto-default means the borrower is required to pay the entire balance *immediately*. Barbara had firsthand experience with this awful policy. One of her clients had to scramble to find $30,000 to pay off the remaining loan after her mother suddenly died.

Some student loan providers will allow you to remove a cosigner from a loan (often if you refinance the loan), but the same CFPB report outlined many bureaucratic barriers that slow the process. If you have a private student loan with a cosigner, take some time to research the company's policies. It's certainly buried in some boring fine print, but it's crucial information to understand.

If you have kids, you need a will.

Along with a life insurance policy, a will is essential for families. You need to decide who will care for your kids if you (and your partner) die. Barbara says you can add a guardianship provision that specifies who will care for your children and who will handle their finances and the financial decisions for the children—it doesn't have to be the same person. It is important to consult a lawyer on this one.

Double-check the beneficiaries on your accounts. It wasn't until I was chatting with Barbara that I realized my brother, not Ken, is still the beneficiary on my first 401(k) account. Not a huge deal, but it would be an unnecessary hassle if something bad ever did happen. Take a few minutes to update your accounts if your circumstances have changed.

While you're at it, save $15
Total saved so far: $120

131

FINANCIAL CHALLENGE

Try a Different Way to Save Every Day This Week

TIME: *Varies depending on the savings trick you choose*
TOOLS: *Again, depends on the savings trick you choose*

I'm not going to let you make any excuses that you can't save at least $2,000 for a bare-bones emergency fund. There are hundreds of ways to save money. Some of them are easy but annoying: Make coffee at home! Some of them are hard to do but more fruitful: Get a raise, but don't spend the extra income. Here are twenty ways you can save without too much heavy lifting to get you to $2,000 in savings faster.

1. Sell your unwanted gift cards.
2. Set up a system with your friends and/or family to share streaming service log-ins.
3. Go to matinee movies only.
4. Pack your lunch.
5. Bring a reusable water bottle with you everywhere.
6. Uninstall any car-sharing apps on your phone.
7. Sign up for your FSA (and use it!).
8. Open a no-fee checking account.
9. Open a high-interest savings account.
10. Sell your stuff (tech, clothes, etc.).
11. Don't drink for a week (or more!).
12. Take your spare change to the bank and deposit it into your savings account.
13. Sign up to get your regular prescriptions through your insurance company's mail-order service.
14. Hang up your work clothes in order to save on dry cleaning.
15. Download an app that will help you find cheaper gas.
16. Ask for free samples when you shop for beauty products.

17. Convince your employer to stock free pads and tampons.
18. Make dinner every night for a week (or longer).
19. Buy generic.
20. Renegotiate your phone or cable bill.

While you're at it, save $16
Total saved so far: $136

CHAPTER 5

Debt & Money
(Or How to Get Back into the Black)

I worry that being irresponsible with money has become something of a badge of honor. How often do we declare, "Ugh, I'm so broke," but we never, ever boast about our financial accomplishments. It's really not cool to share that you skipped brunch every Sunday for a month in order to pay an extra $200 toward your debt. (Admittedly, eggs Benedict *is* more photo-worthy than your student loan bill.)

My guess is that people don't talk about debt because there's still so much shame and confusion around it. While the media seem to assume that millennials aren't hitting milestones at the same rate as their parents because we're irresponsible with money, the truth is way more complicated. Sure, some of us carry credit card debt, and maybe we're sometimes guilty of overspending on dumb stuff or making some bad financial decisions. Many of us have a whole lot of student loan debt, earned in the process of trying to better ourselves. Combine that with stagnant wages and coming of age during a recession, and it's pretty damn easy to get into debt. What's maybe even more depressing is a recent survey suggesting that 68 percent of Americans who are in debt don't think they'll ever get out of it.[1]

Before we dive into all the ways you can work to pay off your debt, let's get onto the same page. Having debt isn't a moral failing. It doesn't make you a bad person. It also doesn't mean that you're hopelessly bad with money or that you're always going to be saddled with paying a premium for your past mistakes.

Keep this in mind as you work your way through this chapter. This is a safe space—no judgments, just solutions. What comes next might not be easy, but it will be okay.

Money Diary #5

A Week in Brooklyn, NY, on a **$65,000** Salary

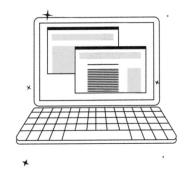

GENERAL FINANCIAL INFORMATION:

Checking Account Balance: $735.20

Savings Account Balance: $600 (I recently moved and spent $2,100 in moving costs (first month's rent/security deposit + furniture). I also recently paid down another $5,000 on my college loans, which depleted my savings.)

Digit Savings App: $306.31 (I typically use this to fund travel expenses. I recently bought tickets to Cuba and LA. Next I want to go to Milan.)

OCCUPATION: Associate account manager

INDUSTRY: Advertising technology

AGE: 24

LOCATION: Brooklyn, NY

ANNUAL SALARY: $65,000, plus a part-time job paying $15/hour, roughly $4,500 a year

PAYCHECK AMOUNT (TWICE A MONTH): $1,525 (full-time job) + ~$150 (every two weeks for part-time job as fitness studio coordinator)

HOUSING:

Rent: $850 (I have four roommates)

Electricity: $35.42

Gas: $24.13

Internet and Cable: $35.06

Renter's Insurance: $10

Phone: $0 (paid for by my mom)

TRANSPORTATION:
Monthly MetroCard:
$60 (pretax, employer pays for half)

HEALTH & SELF-CARE:
Health Insurance: $18.36/paycheck
Dental Insurance: $1.86/paycheck
Therapy: $40/session
Gym Membership: $20 (paid for by employer)

SUBSCRIPTIONS:
New York Times: $12.50
Spotify: $9.99
Netflix: $0 (I use my brother's ex-girlfriend's dad's Netflix. LOL.)
Amazon Prime: $99/year

DEBT:
Private Student Loan Debt Total: $52,399.33
Private Student Loan Payment: $652.86/month
Federal Student Loan Debt Total: $20,733.12
Federal Student Loan Payment: $186.46/month
Credit Card Debt Total: ~$3,900

RETIREMENT:
401(k) Contribution: $300/paycheck
401(k) Total: ~$1,800
(I just started contributing six months ago.)

DAY ONE

7 a.m.—I wake up to a text from Digit with my checking account balance: $735.20. I make a bet with myself to resist spending more than $35 before Friday (payday) to end the pay period with $700 that I can put toward my savings. I limit my chance of winning this bet by stopping to grab a small coffee with almond milk on my way into work. The barista gives me a free cookie because they're celebrating their anniversary. Anything to make a Monday easier. **$2.50**

10 a.m.—My best friend texts me to confirm that I want tickets to see our favorite Latin American pop star, Maluma, later in March. Despite the bet I made with myself just three hours ago, I throw in the towel and complete her Venmo request. **$96.70**

12:30 p.m.—Working in ad tech certainly has its perks, including daily catered lunch. I jump out of my desk to fix myself a plate of arugula, shredded beets, sweet potatoes, and cabbage.

7 p.m.—My therapist is located a ten-minute walk from Trader Joe's. I don't food shop in the traditional sense because I get free breakfast and lunch at work, but I do like to have a few snacks lying around to munch on while watching Netflix. TJ's is a madhouse. Shocker. I'm already hungry from talking about my feelings for the better part of an hour, so I buy two vegetarian tacos, scarf them down, and make my way to the subway home. **$7.62**

DAILY TOTAL: $106.82

DAY TWO

5:45 a.m.—I slept in my workout clothes with every intention of taking an early spin class. I work at Flywheel on the weekends, so I get classes free, which saves me $35/class. My alarm sounds. I avoid getting out of bed and check my email. I remember that my Italian class has been canceled tonight. I change my bike reservation for a 6:15 p.m. class close to my office and hit snooze. I wake up an hour later to make myself some Moon Juice Power Dust tea to sip while I read my first Italian novel, *Io Non Ho Paura* (I'm Not Afraid). I'm about eight years old in Italian-language years, so you better believe my Oxford Italian dictionary is close.

8:15 a.m.—In hopes of scoring another free cookie, I head to the coffee shop for a coffee with almond milk ($2.50). No free cookie. I make my way to the subway and find a horde of people waiting for the delayed train. I roll my eyes and start scrolling through my email. I get an email from St. Jude's asking for donations for #GivingTuesday. I gladly make a very small donation of $10. **$12.50**

12 p.m.—Not only is it #Giving Tuesday, it's Taco Tuesday! I take a break from answering emails to fix myself a veggie taco salad. I get a reminder from a friend to purchase tickets to a live podcast taping this Friday. I'm a subscriber, so I get 50 percent off the $30 ticket. **$16.74** (including fees)

3 p.m.—Head to an industry event with my team. Before heading out I grab a That's It fruit bar from the kitchen as well as a LaCroix. I'll have to head to Flywheel as soon as the meeting ends and want to make sure I have some preworkout fuel.

8 p.m.—I hurry out of Flywheel to meet my boyfriend, F., at Whole Foods. We decide to make a Mediterranean dish, and salmon is on sale for $9.99/lb. We buy salmon, orzo, feta cheese, assorted Greek olives, pita chips, and hummus. F. pays because I lent him cash last week. When we get home, we find that the cashier forgot to bag the feta and the hummus but still charged us for it. It's cold, and I don't want to walk fifteen minutes back to Whole Foods to retrieve the items. I call customer service, and they agree to refund us for the two missing items. F. runs to the corner supermarket to replace the missing items while I boil water for the orzo.

DAILY TOTAL: $29.24

DAY THREE

3 p.m.—After a recent failed attempt at fulfilling my dream to move to Italy to teach English, I have made travel a priority, even if that means I have to cut costs in other areas and work part time for extra cash. F. and I have been planning a trip to Paris for about five months, and he offered to buy tickets as a gift for our fifth anniversary. He gets an email from Scott's Cheap Flights announcing round-trip flights to Paris for $400 per person. HE BOOKS, HE SCORES! Au revoir, New York.

7:45 p.m.—I return to F.'s apartment after work and find him preparing dinner—scallops and linguine. Perhaps bœuf bourguignon would have been more appropriate, but I guess Italy is close enough to France. I'm on salad duty. We share a bottle of our favorite $12 wine.

DAILY TOTAL: $0

DAY FOUR

7 a.m.—F. and I forfeit an extra hour of sleep to take an early Flywheel class. I guest him into class. After class I grab a complimentary banana, which I scarf down on our walk home. Before I head upstairs to shower and get ready for work, I stop at the coffee shop on the corner to grab a small coffee with almond milk. **$2.45**

10 a.m.—It's payday! I get a text from Digit that my checking balance is over $2,000. I am rich. I move $400 into savings and pay $300 toward the $3,900 balance

on my credit card. I start scheming ways to save the world with all of this MONEY; then I remember that I must pay rent tomorrow. My dreams quickly die. Correction, I am poor. **$300**

12 p.m.—Today's vendor makes incredible sandwiches. I typically stay away from meat; however, the vegetarian sandwich choices are basically cheese sandwiches and not so healthy. I grab an arugula salad and half a turkey sandwich. I also grab a sandwich for dinner.

DAILY TOTAL: $302.45

DAY FIVE

8 a.m.—I resist picking up coffee on the way to the office. The first thing I do when I get to the office (after getting coffee) is check my inbox. Once it's cleared, I pay my rent online ($850). After paying rent, I'm left with $858 in my checking account.

6:30 p.m.—After work, I walk twelve blocks uptown to meet my friends for the podcast taping. After, we head to the Grey Dog for a bite to eat and a glass of wine. I order a Thai zoodles dish and a glass of nero d'avola. I head home shortly after we eat. I try to have an early night as I'm supertired Fridays after work. **$25**

DAILY TOTAL: $25

| **DAY SIX** |

10 a.m.—I get out of bed to make some coffee, then throw on my workout clothes. I love Saturdays because my favorite Flywheel instructor teaches a sixty-minute class. I usually drag F. to class with me, but he worked the night shift. I text a friend and ask her to take the class with me.

1:45 p.m.—I am always *famished* after Flywheel, so it seemed only appropriate to accept the brunch invitation from F. and some friends. We try this new place on the south side of Williamsburg. There's a forty-five-minute wait. We don't mind as long as we have booze. Bloody Mary for me, please! When we finally sit down, I order smoked salmon over eggs and another Bloody Mary. When we get our check, we notice that the waitress didn't charge us for our first round of drinks. Like the good patrons we are, we let her know. F. throws down his card for convenience and requests payment via Venmo from everyone. **$54**

5 p.m.—The gang heads out to another bar, but F. and I hang back. It's bedtime for him, and I'm already a little tipsy off of two Bloody Marys. We spend the remainder of the afternoon relaxing at home. I'm asleep by 10.

DAILY TOTAL: $54

| **DAY SEVEN** |

7 a.m.—I wake up and throw on a pair of leggings and my Flywheel tee. I have to be at work at the studio by 8:15 a.m. I buy coffee on my way to work, and when I get there we have to pick up fresh towels from the laundromat. My coworker and I frantically push four giant carts five blocks to the laundromat to pick up the towels before the riders start to arrive at the studio for the 9:30 class. Certainly did not need a cycling class to get my cardio in this morning. **$2.50**

2 p.m.—I promised my dad I would meet him in New Jersey to help him look at condos. After work, I jump on the L train and transfer to the PATH train to head to Hoboken. The PATH doesn't accept unlimited MetroCards, so I swipe another MetroCard that

I reserve for trips to New Jersey.
$2.75
5:30 p.m.—After looking at two properties, we head home. I decide to stay in Jersey for the evening, as it would be a pain getting back to Brooklyn and I can just commute to work from Jersey in the morning. My brothers, my dad, and I decide to order pizza. Because, New Jersey. I get an eggplant and a salad slice from our favorite local spot. My dad treats.

DAILY TOTAL: $5.25

| THE BREAKDOWN |

TOTAL SPENT: $522.76

FOOD AND DRINK: $96.57

ENTERTAINMENT: $113.44

HOME AND HEALTH: $0

CLOTHES AND BEAUTY: $0

TRANSPORTATION: $2.75

OTHER: $310

| THE FOLLOW-UP |

A year ago, you were planning to move to Italy to teach English. What happened with that?

Well, I got a job right out of college, but I wasn't really happy—I wasn't moving up, and it just wasn't the work that I wanted to be doing. During that time, I went to Italy with my dad, and it was a really incredible experience. I studied Italian in college, so I reached out to my professor and I asked her if she had any friends who could employ me, and she put me in contact with a woman who runs a toddler summer camp. So I signed up to be a teacher, committed to the trip, and bought my ticket. But then I just became really anxious about the whole thing.

What did you become anxious about?

I have a really high student loan payment every month, and I just started to think, *What if I can't make this payment?* I started looking for other full-time jobs because I thought, maybe this trip is just a reaction to me not liking my current situation.

When did you realize how much you had to pay back in student loans?

Three months after I decided to start saving for Italy. I had deferred my payment for a little while, so the first time my student loan debt hit me was when I started making payments the March after graduation, and that's when the anxiety kicked in. Every time I looked at the balance, I thought, *This is stupid, I need to be focusing on this.*

How much did you owe?

I owed around $150,000. Right now I'm paying roughly $830 a month in student loans, and my student loan debt total is about $120,000—and I went to a state school. It would be comical if it weren't so stressful. My private loan's interest rate is about 9 percent, which is extremely high, and I also pay a federal loan as well.

So you ended up canceling your move?

Yeah. I ended up finding a great job in ad tech and convincing myself not to go. It was a hard decision. I think it had to do with a lot of financial anxiety, and my boyfriend, who is very strategic and realistic, didn't think it was such a great idea. But I think the decision process was ongoing. Even though I had signed on to go, I was still looking for something, a sign that would tell me to make my decision. The sign was my getting a new job offer.

To cope with that dissatisfaction, I bought myself a pair of Italian sunglasses. If I couldn't go to Italy, I thought, I could at least support an Italian company. That was the biggest purchase I had made after saving like crazy for so long. They cost $177.

Is moving still a plan for your future?

I certainly am thinking about it, but I'm definitely doing it more strategically. I'm thinking about going to grad school there. I'm continuing to learn the language, and I'm also working on my dual citizenship. I'm telling myself that I'm going to do it on my own time.

It seems like you were able to pay down a good chunk of those loans.
I was in a cab accident five years ago, and right after I decided not to go to Italy, I got a settlement for $15,000. I was like, *Fuck, why didn't I go? I would've been able to lean back on this money.* But I put it all toward my loan. And it did feel good.

What surprised you the most about doing a Money Diary?
It's interesting how you can save—or think you're saving—but you can't really save for the unexpected. I often thought of a savings as permanent, but unforeseen things come up, which makes that money fluctuate. This, among other things, has made me more relaxed about my financial situation, and I'm more positive than I originally was about it. Maybe too positive.

There have been countless headlines about how student loan debt is a national crisis, but if you're facing huge monthly payments, it probably feels a lot more personal. The Federal Reserve reports that Americans owe $1.34 trillion in student loan debt,[2] and according to Pew Research Center, millennials on average owe $27,000.[3] It's likely that your friends, your coworkers, and the guy sitting across from you at Starbucks are all feeling overwhelmed by student loan debt.

It's downright depressing, and it can begin to feel as though you don't have a future because you're too busy paying for your past. But this debt isn't going anywhere. Shannon McLay told me a story of a client who ignored her student loan bill every month. The woman found out that she was in default only because her boss pulled her into his office one day to let her know that the federal government was going to start garnishing her wages.

This is a worst-case scenario. But even if you do make the minimum payments each month, there's a chance you could be paying even less if you took a little time to understand and manage your loans. Below, Priya Malani walks us through ten (fairly) easy things everyone should do to get their student loans under better control. Later in this chapter, we'll discuss how you can take some drastic steps to pay off your debt even faster.

***Know what kind of student loans you have and how much
you owe.***

Federal loans are issued by the government and typically have
a lower fixed-interest rate. Private loans are issued by a financial
institution and tend to have higher interest rates that might not
be fixed, which means the amount you pay for your loan can
fluctuate. Often, you have to begin paying back private loans
while you're still in school.

Once you know what kind of loan you have, write down the
total you owe. So many people just ignore this number because
it can be so intimidating. It's important to understand where
you are when considering your best repayment methods.

Automate your payment plan.

Set up a payment plan, and stick to it. Many loan providers
will cut your interest rate by 0.25 percent if you enroll in their
autopay programs. It doesn't sound like much, but it can add
up over the life of your loan. Plus, it's nice not to worry about
remembering to log in to make a payment each month.

Know your exact end date.

It can feel as though you're going to be paying off your student loans forever, but that's simply not true. Write down your
end date and keep it handy so you know the exact day you'll
become (student loan) debt free.

***Find out if you're eligible for an income-based repayment
plan or loan forgiveness.***

If you have a federal loan, you could qualify for an income-
based repayment (IBR) plan. If you do qualify, you have to
recertify your loan every year, showing proof of income and
including details such as the size of your family, your spouse's
income, and where you live. If you don't recertify annually,
you risk losing your IBR status and your monthly payment may
increase to the standard repayment amount. (You can find out
more on StudentLoans.gov.)

If you work in certain public service jobs, you might be eligible for loan forgiveness. The website Student Loan Hero has a fairly comprehensive list of jobs that qualify.[4] Hopefully, this program will still exist by the time you read this book, as the current presidential administration keeps threatening to end it.

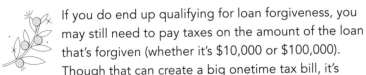 If you do end up qualifying for loan forgiveness, you may still need to pay taxes on the amount of the loan that's forgiven (whether it's $10,000 or $100,000). Though that can create a big onetime tax bill, it's still better than paying your full loan balance, but Priya recommends setting aside some savings to cover that cost.

Decide if you want to refinance your loans.

If your loans carry a high interest rate (6 percent or higher), refinancing allows you to obtain a new loan at a lower rate, which you then use to pay off your older, higher-interest-rate debt. Refinancing isn't right for everyone. Here are a few questions you should ask before you take the plunge:

1. Are you enrolled in a loan forgiveness program or an income-based repayment plan? If yes, you might not want to refinance, because you could lose these perks.
2. Are you struggling to make your minimum monthly payments?
3. Do you have a high variable interest rate? If you're paying 6 percent or higher in interest, and you have a good credit score, refinancing could help you.
4. Would you like to remove your cosigner from the loan? In some cases, refinancing will help you do that.

If you refinance, you'll want to do some research to find the best lender for your needs. There are several online calculators that can help you see just how much you'll save over the course of your loan. (At the writing of this book, many online refinancing options were promising savings of $20,000 to $30,000. That's no small change.)

Priya says lenders will do a hard credit pull if you do move forward with refinancing, and that can lower your score slightly. There are some easy ways to bump it back up (see page 29). But, she argues, the money you'll save when you refinance will more than make up for a short-term drop in your credit score.

If you only have federal loans, and you don't qualify for IBR or a loan forgiveness program, you might just want to consolidate your loans through the federal government. It's a fairly simple process that just involves filling out an e-form on StudentLoans.gov.

Never, ever miss a payment.
Being disciplined and paying on time and in full each month will guarantee that you pay off these loans in a manageable time frame. If you blow off the payments, you'll end up paying even more with penalties and late fees. Settle on a manageable plan, and stick with it.

Make payments more than once a month.
Instead of paying down your loan once a month, pay half your monthly payment every two weeks. That way, you'll sneak in a full extra payment every calendar year—lowering your principal faster and paying less interest over the course of the loan. Just make sure you ask the lender to apply the extra payments to the principal balance. This isn't always the default.

Unemployed? Look for deferment or forbearance options.
If you're unemployed and find yourself struggling to make the monthly minimum payment on your loan, you can defer your federal loans (meaning you don't make payments for a certain amount of time—and sometimes the government will cover the interest accrued during this period) or you can apply for forbearance (again, you get a reprieve, but for a shorter amount of time and no chance of the government covering the loan's interest).

Both require you to show proof of hardship, but they can definitely lessen the burden if you're in a tight spot. (Note: If you've refinanced your student loans, you may no longer qualify for deferment or forbearance.)

There's less flexibility for private loans, but you should check with your provider. Some companies allow out-of-work clients to delay payments for up to three months at a time (for twelve months total).

If you default, ask your lender to help you get back on track.

Environmental crimes, treason, murder, and student loan debt are the four things that have no statute of limitations in the United States. What's worse, if you have a parent or spouse who cosigned your loan, your loan will live on even after you die.

 There are a lot of bad things that can happen if you don't pay your student loans. The government can garnish your wages, Shannon says, or withhold your tax refund. It can threaten to sue you over your debt, and it can revoke your professional license.

If you do default, there's some good news: student loan lenders *want* to get you back on track, and there are loan rehabilitation programs in place to help you. Remember Shannon's client whose wages were being garnished? She got into a loan rehabilitation program and will be back on track within a year. Loan rehabilitation programs require nine months of reasonable and affordable payments over a ten-month period. And once your loan is rehabbed, the nonpayment blemish comes off your credit score.

You can rehabilitate your loan only once. Once you get back on track, it's really important to maintain that success. Skip ahead to page 160 for advice on tackling your debt head-on.

Don't forget: you still have to live.

I want to reframe the conversation around student loan debt a little bit. I get that it's awful to be paying back huge sums of money every month for what seems like a significant period of your adult life. And I understand why people are motivated to try to pay their loans as fast as possible. But please don't do this to the detriment of being young and having a life. This isn't a sprint, and for the most part, banks and other lenders consider student loan debt to be good debt, like a mortgage. It shows that you've invested in your future.

My best advice would be to get your monthly payments down to a manageable amount (with a low interest rate), so that you can actively be working to pay off your loans, while also having some disposable income to eat out, shop, travel, spend money on your present self—and in my opinion, that includes an occasional latte.

THIS IS A GOOD TIME TO:

Automate your student loan payment plan and write down the end date. This should take only fifteen minutes but will save you time (and a little money!) in the long run.

While you're at it, save $17
Total saved so far: $153

There are endless stats about student loan debt in the United States, but numbers on a page don't tell the whole story: the stress, the sadness, and the feelings of inadequacy and hopelessness that can come with being in your twenties and thirties, saddled with six-figure debt, and working a low-paying job. Here six women get real about their student loan debt.

BETTY, 28, LOS ANGELES, CA | ANNUAL SALARY: $113,000 | JOB: LAWYER | DEGREES: BA, JD | TOTAL LOAN AMOUNT: $230,000 | MONTHLY PAYMENT: $1,200

"I'm constantly depressed and anxious about every monetary decision that I make. I'm setting aside money for retirement, and I'm able to pay off all of my bills each month, but my student loans stop me from moving forward or enjoying life. I never had the money to travel when I was growing up or when I was in college and law school, but I had hoped that I'd be able to do that once I started working. Things are still exactly the same—I don't travel, I obsessively budget every penny, and I feel totally stuck in my life. In six years or so, when the loans are paid off or forgiven, I feel like it's going to be too late for me to do all the fun stuff I missed out on in my twenties."

ELLIE, 31, WASHINGTON, DC | ANNUAL SALARY: $57,200 | JOB: COMMUNICATIONS ASSOCIATE | DEGREES: BA (COMMUNICATIONS), MS (CORPORATE COMMUNICATION) | TOTAL LOAN AMOUNT: $120,000 (I HAD ONLY ABOUT $10,000 IN DEBT BEFORE I WENT TO GRAD SCHOOL SIX YEARS AGO.) | MONTHLY PAYMENT: $237

"I'm in the Public Service Loan Forgiveness program, but if that goes under, I'm pretty fucked. I'll just be paying them 'til I'm dead."

HANNAH, 34, BIRMINGHAM, AL | ANNUAL SALARY: $52,000 | JOB: LICENSED PROFESSIONAL COUNSELOR | DEGREE: MA (PROFESSIONAL COUNSELING) | TOTAL LOAN AMOUNT: $60,000 | MONTHLY PAYMENT: $280, BUT I USUALLY PAY MORE

"My husband and I had been living off one salary and putting the other toward my loans. But he lost his job of ten years, and we put the loan into forbearance. It's upsetting when I think about it. I got into my profession because I feel passionately about mental health treatment. But I feel like my loans keep us from other financial decisions, like having kids."

"Some days, I want to rip it off like a Band-Aid and just hustle as hard as I can to pay it off in one year. It really weighs on you when you see friends buying houses, paying for weddings, and having generally more expendable income because they have never had to deal with debt before or their parents pay for everything. Overall, though, if I am able to overpay my loans, go on vacations every so often, and still save a bit each month, it doesn't feel like so much of a burden. It's just when I overthink about the number that it really gets to me."

SARAH, 26, BROOKLYN, NY | ANNUAL
SALARY: $30,000 + MONTHLY COMMISSION
BONUS | JOB: PRODUCTION ASSISTANT |
DEGREE: BFA (FASHION DESIGN WITH MINOR
IN BUSINESS) | LOAN AMOUNT: A LITTLE
OVER $26,000 | MONTHLY PAYMENT: $152

"I know I'm lucky compared to some of my friends, so I can't imagine what would have happened if I'd gone to my dream school."

CAITLIN, 36, HOUSTON, TX | ANNUAL SALARY: $85,000 | JOB: ACCOUNTANT | DEGREES: BS (BIOLOGY AND MUSIC), MA (ACCOUNTING) | TOTAL LOAN AMOUNT: $56,000 ($53,000 FROM GRAD SCHOOL AND $3,000 FROM UNDERGRAD) | MONTHLY PAYMENT: $368.68

"Currently I am paying off credit card debt, which should be wiped out by mid-2018, and a personal loan from my credit union, which should be paid off by the end of 2019. Then my plan is to pay off my student loans, starting with making additional principal payments to the largest loan first. My loans are currently on the twenty-five-year standard repayment plan; I will be switching that to the ten-year standard repayment plan once my other debt is paid off. That will increase my payments, but it will help me pay the debt off faster, combined with reducing the principal with additional payments."

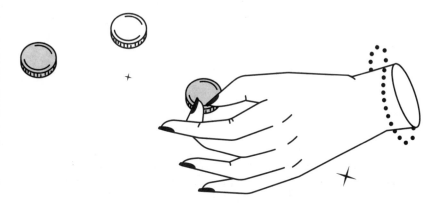

Create a Repayment Plan for Your Debt

TIME: 30+ minutes (depending on how much debt you have)
TOOLS: Details on your debt, including totals and interest rates

There are big financial benefits to paying off your debt quickly, even if it requires some sacrifice right now. But before we dig into all the ways you can throw more money at your debt, we need to come up with a repayment plan. Priya Malani suggests two popular methods:

Avalanche Method: Pay the minimum monthly payments on all your loans. If that total payment is less than 20 percent of your income, use the remaining money to pay more than the minimum on the loan with the highest interest rate, which will allow you to pay it down more quickly. Once you pay off that loan completely, you move on to the loan with the next-highest interest rate, and so on, until all your loans are paid.

Snowball Method: Focus on paying off the loan with the smallest balance first. So, as with the Avalanche Method, you'll make the minimum monthly payments on all your loans and then take anything left over to pay down the loan with the smallest balance.

The Snowball Method can be the most motivating repayment plan, as it quickly knocks out loans completely. But the Avalanche Method is the smartest from a financial standpoint, because you'll be paying the least interest in the long run.

Both methods can be applied to paying off all kinds of debt—not just your student loans. In fact, if you have considerable credit card debt, it's usually smarter to pay it off faster than your student loan debt, which likely has a much lower interest rate.

If you're thinking, *Whoa, there's no way I can put 20 percent of my income toward debt*, let's take a minute to reconsider that. Let's go back to the 50/30/20 rule we talked about in chapter 1. While you should be aiming to put aside 10 percent toward retirement, Priya also recommends setting aside 20 percent of your net income to paying down debt. You should do this even if 20 percent is more than the minimum monthly payments you owe on your debt.

Priya offered this example to show just how much you'll save if you achieve that 20 percent goal.

> Imagine you're making $55,000 a year (putting you in the 20 percent tax bracket), and you're paying off a $25,000 loan with a 5 percent interest rate.
> Your standard monthly payment would be $265 over ten years (which means you'll spend $6,819 on interest over the course of your loan).
> If you put 20 percent of your income toward the loan, your payment would increase to $733 a month. You'll pay down the loan in 3.1 years and pay only $2,021 in interest.
>
> That's nearly $5,000 in savings!

One thing to note: you should be putting 20 percent of your income toward debt repayment only if you have a fully funded emergency account and you're contributing 10 percent of your income to your retirement fund. For more on how to prioritize your financial responsibilities, see chapter 4.

While you're at it, save $18
Total saved so far: $171

Shannon McLay tells a story about a client who was $250,000 in debt. She's a lawyer and had taken out significant loans while in law school, working toward a degree that would ostensibly help her have a better life. Yet she was deeply embarrassed by that debt—and convinced that having a six-figure number attached to her name made it impossible for her to be in a long-term relationship.

So many millennials have debt—credit card, student loan, medical—yet we feel so alone carrying this burden that's preventing us from achieving our dreams, whether that's moving to a new city, traveling the world, or launching your own business. It can also have a huge impact on your romantic relationships. "Don't be afraid to get financially naked," Shannon says. I think it's okay to be a little afraid, but that shouldn't stop you from having that hard conversation.

For Refinery29's series "Not a Trophy Wife," Jessica Chou interviewed Sarah, a PhD candidate who made around $28,000 a year and had $100,000 in student loan debt. Her girlfriend, Alice, was making $175,000, with healthy savings and retirement accounts. Their first conversation about Sarah's debt was intense, to say the least.

"I rage cried the first time we talked about my student loans. One day, Alice came home with a financial book that tells you how to save and think about investments. I was like, 'I don't think you understand. I don't have positive income. I'm so terrified about how much debt I'm in, I can't even have this conversation.' I was worried to tell her that I have $100,000 in debt."

Shannon thinks that once a couple decides to get married and combine their finances, they should be committed to paying down debt together. After all, it's easier to tackle that debt when two people are paying it off. And that will allow you to get to your shared dreams faster.

That can be complicated when one partner makes significantly more money. Jill, 38, gave up her career to move across the country with her husband, John, who earns $500,000 a year. They didn't even talk about money until they got engaged—and that was only after Jill saw John's salary on a credit card application. At the time, she was making $95,000 a year and struggling to pay down credit card debt. One day, John offered to pay it off in full.

"I said, 'No, it's none of your business. It has nothing to do with you.' But that changed when we got married—he took all my credit cards and paid them off. It was, like, $15,000. He's crazy about that. He doesn't want to pay interest to these companies—not even a dollar."

It sounds good in theory, but when Jill tells the story, you can understand why she felt awkward. The prevailing school of thought is that we got ourselves into the debt, we need to get ourselves out of it. But John was right—that interest really adds up, and he had the means to pay off the debt. It made financial sense for him to do it for the family.

Paying off debt together—even if one of you accrued it before you met—can bring you closer together. Some of that goes back to the question of whether you consider this an equal relationship. That equality isn't about bringing in the same income but about valuing each other and giving equal weight to the decisions you make as a couple.

The average American with credit card debt pays over $900 in interest each year,[5] and those with federal student loans pay more than $6,000 in interest over the life of their loans[6] (even more if they have private loans). I can think of so many better ways to spend that money, and I'm sure you can, too. Priya helped me create a completely unsexy, totally tough-love guide to paying down your debt.

Even if you just pick a few of these tips to try, you'll put yourself on track to make bigger payments and become debt free faster. Once you settle on a debt repayment plan (see page 156), use this guide to make paying off your debt your number one financial priority.

Consolidate Your Debt

Before you start cutting out stuff, first make sure you're not overpaying on your debt. See page 148 for more details on refinancing your student loans.

Consolidating your credit cards is slightly more complicated. Look for a card that offers 0 percent APR on balance transfers. The catch is that these promotions usually last for only twelve to fifteen months, and then the interest rate can increase significantly, undoing all the good work you did consolidating in the first place if you are still carrying a balance. If you do consolidate your credit card debt, make sure you're committed to paying off that balance *in full* within the time frame.

A personal loan is another way to decrease your monthly payments so your credit card debt repayment is more manageable.

Read the fine print, though, and make sure you won't be paying crazy fees.

Cut Out Nonessentials

It's time to try Manisha's joy-based spending process from chapter 1 and go one step further: highlight everything that doesn't bring you joy *and* anything that's not essential.

That coffee you bought on the way to work? Non-essential. Netflix. ClassPass. Spotify. All nonessential. That stupid expensive group birthday dinner for your old college buddy you see only once a year? Completely nonessential. (And completely annoying!) It's time to cut those out of your life.

You don't want your life to become all debt payoff and no fun. Keep a few treats in the mix. Find cheaper alternatives to favorite splurges, such as doing your own nails, practicing yoga at home, hosting friends for drinks (and making the evening BYOB), or seeking out free activities in your area.

Ask for a Raise or Get Another Job

According to PayScale, 75 percent of people who ask for a raise get one, but less than half of Americans have initiated the conversation with their managers.[7] Sure, you might not get one if you ask, but if you *don't* ask, you have an even lower chance. (See chapter 3 for advice on how to prepare for that conversation.)

Once you negotiate the raise, *don't spend it.* (Sorry.) Put at least some (if not all) of the extra money toward repaying your debt.

Another option is to find a new (higher-paying) job. Research suggests you're losing significant money if you don't change jobs every three years.[8]

If finding a new job isn't an option, consider taking on a side hustle (or two) to earn some extra cash. There are countless ways to make a little extra money: bartending on the weekends (comes with free drinks), working the front desk at a gym (comes with free classes), I've heard it all. (See page 166 for more ideas.)

Change Your Living Situation

Priya estimates that most people spend between 25 percent and 35 percent of their monthly take-home pay on housing costs. That's a big bill that can hold you back from paying off your debt. If you're in aggressive debt-paying mode, spending less on rent can be a huge help.

How to do this? You could move home. If that's an option, it's a game changer, especially if your mom and dad won't charge you rent. Take that monthly payment (I'm talking 25 percent of your paycheck) and put it directly toward paying down your debt. If you've already been spending 20 percent of your monthly income toward debt repayment, you've just upped it to 40 percent or more, which means you can hit your goal considerably faster.

If you can't move home, look for a less expensive living situation, whether that means moving into a cheaper apartment (maybe with roommates) or taking on a roommate in your current place. (If you do consider moving, take a moment to make sure that you won't be spending more just to move. See chapter 7 for more thoughts on housing expenses.)

If you own, you can always consider subletting, refinancing your mortgage, or even Airbnb-ing a room in your home.

Sell Your Stuff

If you have a car and you find that you don't need it, getting rid of it can make a huge impact on your monthly expenses. If you do need your car, explore renegotiating your car insurance (Shannon says you shouldn't be spending more than $150 per month) or getting more aggressive about your gas budget. You might even consider trading in an expensive car for a cheaper model. Obviously, this isn't realistic for everyone, but getting out of extreme debt means considering extreme solutions.

If you don't have a car, look for other things you might reasonably be able to unload. These days, it's pretty easy to make some cash selling your clothes online, as well as all those unnecessary kitchen appliances your grandma keeps sending you or the old smartphones you don't use anymore. That could be worth at least a few hundred bucks.

You can use this to pay down your debt, or maybe just give yourself a break and spend it on something fun. You've been making a lot of sacrifices lately; we won't judge if you splurge on a nice dinner. Just don't fall off the debt-paying bandwagon. You're doing *so* well.

Live on One Salary

For a long time (before baby and child care costs), Ken and I lived (mostly) on one salary and saved the other. It allowed us to do some aggressive saving so we could upgrade to a bigger apartment when the baby did come along.

If you're going this route, it's important to have a frank conversation with your S.O. about how you'll make it work. Maybe you live on one and a half salaries. Maybe there's another version that works for you. But if you are in a relationship and you want to aggressively pay down debt or save for something big, teamwork makes the dream work, as they say.

Go on a Shopping Break

Can you go a month without buying anything new? What about two or three or a whole six months? Before you hit "Check out" at Zara or Sephora or wherever, pause to decide if you really, really, *really* need that shirt/lipstick/etc.

Make it a bit easier by getting rid of temptation. Unsubscribe from any store newsletters you get. Delete your credit card info from your favorite online stores. Spend the time you might be dropping things into an online cart doing something more productive (such as consolidating your loans!).

Get Rid of Your Credit Cards

This is a bit controversial, because having a credit card does help you build a strong credit score. And a good credit score is essential for everything from getting a mortgage to getting a job (yes, employers may look at your credit score before hiring you).

But for some people, credit cards offer too much temptation to spend outside of their means. If you are one of those people, you might just need to get rid of your credit cards altogether and use cash for *everything*.

There is a middle ground, of course. You could have one credit card and use it to make a monthly recurring payment, such as your phone bill. Don't carry that card with you, so there's zero temptation to use it.

Use Found Money

If your grandma sends you $25 for your birthday, if you get a sweet tax refund, if you're rewarded with a year-end bonus—put at least some of it toward paying down your loans. Priya recommends an 80/20 split—80 percent toward the loan, 20 percent for fun.

Don't Be Ashamed to Ask for Help

If you do find yourself in a situation where you can't get your finances together by yourself, consider seeing a financial adviser or even a therapist to get the professional support you need. It can be very helpful to get an outside perspective from someone who isn't so emotionally invested in your life and money, and who can provide you with the tools you need for success. Just make sure your financial planner follows fiduciary standards (more on that on page 287).

THIS IS A GOOD TIME TO:

Pay more on your debt. If you've started putting into practice some of our suggestions for paying off extreme debt, go ahead and use that extra cash to pay a little more than your minimum this month.

While you're at it, save $19
Total saved so far: $190

Find a Side Hustle

TIME: *Varies depending on your side hustle*
TOOLS: *Again, varies depending on the hustle*

When my dad first heard the phrase "side hustle," he laughed and rolled his eyes. Taking on part-time work to make extra cash is not a new concept. Leave it to millennials to give it a fancy name. Whatever you want to call the extra gig you take on in order to make some extra money, you're not alone: a 2017 study from Bankrate found that one in four millennials has some kind of additional income stream.[9] And if you're reading this chapter, I'm going to guess that you need the cash to pay off some debts. That's cool—it's easier than ever to get a side hustle to help with those pesky student loans.

Something to keep in mind when looking for a part-time gig: your best bet is to tap skills you already have. So if you're an English teacher, you might want to consider, for example, teaching English via Skype. Here are twenty-five ideas to get you started.

1. Airbnb your apartment (whether one room or the whole place; just make sure your landlord or building management is okay with it)
2. Become a personal trainer (requires certification)
3. Do online language tutoring
4. Dog walk
5. Babysit
6. Do photo editing
7. Do graphic design work
8. Write marketing copy
9. Do proofreading
10. Become a recreational league umpire or referee (requires certification)

11. Open an Etsy/eBay/Amazon store
12. Teach music classes
13. Provide translation services
14. Become a virtual assistant
15. House sit
16. Work as a bartender/server
17. Work as a front-desk receptionist
18. Work as a personal stylist
19. Work as a professional organizer
20. Become a brand ambassador
21. Become a career coach/résumé writer
22. Become a local tour guide
23. Take on handyman jobs
24. Become a ride-share driver
25. Become a secret shopper

While you're at it, save $20
Total saved so far: $210

CHAPTER 6

Kids & Money
(Or How the Hell Do People Afford Babies?)

I

If having kids changes your life, their impact on your finances is more like a seismic shift. A 2015 USDA report found that it costs the average American family $233,610 to raise a child from birth to age 18.[1] At the same time, when mothers return to work they face a wage gap and diminishing career opportunities. According to a study by Michelle Budig, a sociologist at the University of Massachusetts, women see a 4 percent salary decrease after the birth of their first child, while men see a 6 percent increase.[2]

That's an alarming statistic, when you consider that 70 percent of all women with children under 18 are in the workforce. But it's not just the "motherhood penalty" that's hurting our bottom line. Child care is grossly expensive. Paid family leave is minimal. When men are offered leave, it's usually far fewer weeks. Working mothers still do more housework than working fathers, and let's not even get started with the mental load we carry. It's no wonder that women find themselves making dramatic career choices when they reach childbearing age: leaving the workforce to raise kids or forgoing having children altogether (research shows the most educated women are the most likely never to have a child[3]).

We could do a lot of hand-wringing in this chapter about all the systemic reasons why it's so costly to raise a child in the United States and how it's so detrimental to a woman's career. It really sucks. But this book is about taking personal steps to gain control of your money right this minute, and entering parenthood with open eyes and a clear financial plan can help ease some of the burden. In the end, maybe having this foresight will help us change the culture as a whole. It's definitely a cause worth fighting for.

Money Diary #6

A Week in Columbus, OH, on a **$60,000** Salary

 OCCUPATION: Associate merchant
INDUSTRY: Corporate retail
AGE: 32
LOCATION: Columbus, OH
ANNUAL SALARY: $60,0000
PAYCHECK AMOUNT (EVERY TWO WEEKS): $1,554 + $228 a month in child support

 GENERAL FINANCIAL INFORMATION:
Checking Account Balance: $1,472
Savings Account Balance: ~$3,000 (I deposit $200 a month into my savings, and consider $2,000 of it my emergency fund.)

 HOUSING:
Rent: $930 (for a two-bedroom/one-bath two-story town house in a six-unit building)
Electricity and Heat: $100
Internet and Cable: $60
Water: $35
Renter's Insurance: $160/year
Phone: $150 for two lines with un-limited data (It's a lifesaver when I need some "mom" time.)

 TRANSPORTATION:
Car Payment: $0 (Paid for!)
Car Insurance: $69

 HEALTH & SELF-CARE:
Health and Dental Insurance: $95/paycheck
Eye Insurance: $4.34/paycheck
FSA: $1,100/year
HSA: $1,100/year
Gym: $75 for family Y membership
Before- and After-School Program: $275/month

SUBSCRIPTIONS:
CBS All Access: $9.99
Netflix: $11.81
HBO: $14.99
Amazon Prime: $13.81
Cloud Storage: $0.99

DEBT:
Student Loan Debt
Total: ~$85,000
Student Loan Payment: $470
Credit Card Debt Total: $640
Credit Card Payment: $100/month

RETIREMENT:
401(k) Contribution:
I invest 5 percent of my salary into my 401(k) each paycheck, which my company matches at 100 percent (10 percent total).
401(k) Total: ~$10,000

| DAY ONE |

9 a.m.—I wake up because it is very hot. I realize my daughter, the cat, and the kitten are all lying on me. I get up and make myself coffee.

1 p.m.—We are bingeing *Star Trek: Discovery.* We love all Trek, so I signed up for the free trial last week. I'm going to go ahead and pay for it monthly because I like the content. **$10**

5 p.m.—We are *finally* headed to the grocery store. I pick up apples, pineapple, spinach, bananas, grapefruit, tofu, pasta, spaghetti sauce, LaCroix (grapefruit is our favorite), Ben & Jerry's Fudge Brownie ice cream, Morning Star Farms veggie bacon, a few Amy's frozen meals, Parmesan cheese, whole wheat bread, milk, and a bottle of pinot noir. **$83.05**

8 p.m.—Eat some spaghetti and garlic bread with my daughter. I open the pinot, and she has some LaCroix in a wineglass. We each wind down with a book and call it a night.

DAILY TOTAL: $93.05

| DAY TWO |

6:30 a.m.—Wake up and get ready. My job is very casual, so I throw on some jeans and a T-shirt, fill in my brows, add some blush, and I am set. My daughter attends public school and grabs breakfast with her spending account at school.

7:30 a.m.—My daughter is signed in to morning Latchkey (a pre- and after-school program she does every day), and I am off to work.

8:45 a.m.—Traffic wasn't too bad this morning! I make myself coffee and instant oatmeal and read through Monday emails.

12 p.m.—The team heads to our café, but I packed, so today will be a no-spend day! I have Amy's cheese enchiladas, an apple, and a LaCroix.

3 p.m.—After two hours of IT testing . . . I want to either run for the hills or eat my weight in chocolate. I find some snacks and a soda in my snack drawer and eat those instead.

5 p.m.—Time to leave work and pick up my daughter.

6 p.m.—We are home! My daughter feeds the cats, while I get started on dinner. Fried tofu and spinach with brown rice. Another glass of pinot for me and LaCroix for my daughter.

9 p.m.—I am exhausted and head for bed. Very proud of myself. I set a goal of ten no-spend days for the month, and today was my tenth day!!! This is great because I know I have overscheduled myself this weekend, and it will be spendy.

DAILY TOTAL: $0

DAY THREE

7 a.m.—I am so late. Scramble to get myself and my daughter out the door. Not sure what either one of us is wearing today. It's all clean, so I'm satisfied.

9 a.m.—Slip into my desk and get straight to work. Skip coffee and breakfast because I am late.

12 p.m.—I have been buried with a crisis since I got here, but I force myself to stop and eat my leftover tofu and spinach. It's good, and I feel much better after I eat.

3 p.m.—Another two hours of IT testing. I am feeling stabby again,

so I stop by the cafeteria for a Cherry Coke and a chocolate chip cookie. I feel absolutely no shame eating my feelings. **$3.50**

5 p.m.—Thank GOD this day is over. I am out the door to get my daughter.

6 p.m.—She's so excited she got a perfect score on her photography homework. I'm so proud of her! I knew she nailed this one. We call my mom to let her know, since she was the subject of the photo.

7 p.m.—I went to lie down after we got home because I was exhausted. I wake up to find my daughter has made mac and cheese and green beans. She might make me cry tonight with her sweetness. We eat together cuddled on the couch while we watch some silly Disney Channel show.

9:30 p.m.—I wind down by writing in my journal and call it a night.

DAILY TOTAL: $3.50

DAY FOUR

7:30 a.m.—By some miracle we are both out the door and off to school on time.

8:35 a.m.—Make it to work on time and make my usual breakfast. I realize I have been very unfocused the past few days and, duh, I forgot to take my ADD medicine. (Yes, both my daughter and I are ADD. Talk about the blind leading the blind.) I take my medicine and call in a refill.

11:45 a.m.—My medication makes me not hungry, but I eat my Amy's tortellini anyway.

3 p.m.—Testing. Again. I need another Cherry Coke and cookie. **$3.50**

5 p.m.—Leave to pick up the kiddo.

6 p.m.—Pick her up and get a call: our prescriptions are ready. We stop by Kroger to grab them. **$20** (this will be reimbursed by my HSA)

DAILY TOTAL: $23.50

| DAY FIVE |

7:30 a.m.—Miracle. I get her to school on time. I'm not sure why I'm having so much trouble waking up. I'm going to bed at a reasonable time . . . might be time for a checkup.

8:45 a.m.—I make it to work, but I'm out of creamer and instant oatmeal, so I head to the café for coffee and tater tots. **$5**

11:31 a.m.—I've been watching the clock since 10 to see when lunch is, so I'm immediately ready. There isn't a whole lot exciting today, so I settle on a veggie burger, fries, and a Cherry Coke. **$9**

12:45 p.m.—I call the doctor to schedule an annual exam. They inform me I haven't had one in three years. Whoops! I can't get in until June, but at least it's on the books.

1:15 p.m.—I have *nothing* to wear to the Spice Girls party on Saturday. My friend (who will be Ginger Spice) lets me know I need to be Scary Spice. I am always Scary (duh, I'm biracial and have wild curly hair), but I really identified more with Posh! Oh well. Hop on to Amazon and find a leopard-print bodysuit. It's ridiculous, but it's $20 with free two-day shipping. I will pair it with an equally ridiculous faux fur jacket and knee-high boots I already own. **$20**

6 p.m.—I pick up my daughter from school and head to drop her off at my mother's house. Tonight is restaurant week with my girlfriends!

8:30 p.m.—Dinner was so much fun! My friend brought her new baby, and we caught up. I sprang for a vodka cocktail called a "Pink Elephant," and it added $8 to

the prix fixe menu. I had loaded potato soup, a delicious pot roast with veggies over mashed potatoes, and a sumptuous brownie with ice cream. **$36.18 (with tip)**
9:30 p.m.—Cats are fed, kiddo and I are in bed.

DAILY TOTAL: $70.18

| DAY SIX |

6:30 a.m.—I slept well last night and get up with no trouble.
7:30 a.m.—Drop the kiddo off at school and head into the office.
8:30 a.m.—Still don't have creamer, so I head to the café for a quick coffee and breakfast smoothie. **$6.50**
12:30 p.m.—Vegetarian tacos in the café today! Boca crumbles are so good! I get myself three and a Cherry Coke. **$7.50**
4 p.m.—There was no IT testing today!!! AND we get to leave early for our holiday happy hour.
6 p.m.—After picking up my kiddo from school, dropping her off at my mom's, and getting an Uber ($20.30) downtown, I finally arrive at our department's holiday happy hour. (Working in retail, even the corporate offices, means you don't really celebrate the holidays with

the rest of the world.) We head to an amazing wine-tasting bar. There are basically soda machines of various wines available to taste. We're all given a $20 card, but of course my favorite wine of the night is $15 a glass. I reload my card with another $30. **$50.30**
9 p.m.—We decide to keep the night going and head to another local spot. Three vodka sodas later, I get a text from the guy I'm seeing asking if I'm still out. I pay my tab and walk with my friend to the next bar of the evening to meet up with my guy. **$30**
1 a.m.—My guy is ready to head to another bar. At this point, he is bankrolling the tab, but I'm done drinking. He grabs an Uber, and we call it a night.

DAILY TOTAL: $94.30

| DAY SEVEN |

9 a.m.—I wake up, and I want to die. I'd rather die at my mother's house, so I have my guy drive me home.
2 p.m.—I finally feel alive again and watch some TV with my kiddo while munching on a late lunch.
6 p.m.—My daughter has a game night at our church, so I drop her

off and head home to get ready for the Spice Girls night!

9 p.m.—Pick up my daughter from church and drop her back off at my mom's. Put on the rest of my ridiculous outfit and grab a Lyft to head to the movie theater. **$22.37**

10 p.m.—We are the ONLY people dressed up. I buy a round of vodka sodas for the girls to get the night started. **$30**

10:15 p.m.—I take one sip . . . and my body says, "Don't you dare!" I hand my vodka soda to a friend, and she offers to get me a Coke.

12:30 a.m.—The movie was so fun! We decide to meet up with friends and head to a local gay bar, where our outfits are a HIT!

2 a.m.—I end my night waiting in line for pizza with Posh Spice ($7). One more Uber and I am home ($21.92), and I know that I will not have another weekend like this for a long, long time. **$28.92**

DAILY TOTAL: $81.29

| THE BREAKDOWN |

TOTAL SPENT: $365.82

FOOD AND DRINK: $168.18

ENTERTAINMENT: $10

HOME AND HEALTH: $20

CLOTHES AND BEAUTY: $20

TRANSPORTATION: $64.59

OTHER: $0

| THE FOLLOW-UP |

How did you determine how much your ex-husband would pay in child support?
The state of Ohio has a calculator to determine child support based on both parents' incomes and the expenses associated with the child. At the time of my divorce, my ex-husband had just been laid off, and so I was the breadwinner. That's why I ended up with a very small child support payment.

Can it be adjusted if/when he gets a new job?
It can, but sometimes it works against you. He has two other children now, and I also make significantly more than I did at the time of our divorce, so you kind of have to weigh your options. Is it worth it to pay the attorney fees and the court filing fees to go back and even potentially lose some support?

Does he ever give more than $228? Say, if your daughter wanted to go to summer camp or something?
I think we have a pretty decent relationship, and he does contribute more occasionally. Last year, he gave me $400 for summer camp. If he takes her to the doctor, he'll pay the co-pay, things like that. But the contributions aren't so significant that I plan on adding to my budget. I basically go into every expense expecting to pay the full amount myself.

Do you also support your mother financially?
Not consistently, but there will be times where she'll ask to borrow a couple hundred dollars or if I can pick up a prescription. I expect those instances will increase as she gets older. It can be kind of stressful, just balancing everything, especially considering that I have some pretty significant student loan debt, too. I'm trying to get myself and my daughter to a place where we're secure financially, but then at the same time you feel like your parents sacrificed so much for you, you can't tell them no. It's a delicate balance. My mom definitely helps me out a lot, too, with child care and things like that.

How do you balance your daughter's wants with the needs of your household?
I use a budgeting app, but I also do a budget written out on paper, where I basically list all of my expenses for the month and when the due dates fall, so I know which paycheck needs to pay for what. Then I make decisions from there. I do my best not to put anything on a credit card ever. If there's something above and beyond that my daughter wants to do, I have to weigh it against the other expenses. So, like, if I don't eat out that week, then she can go on this field trip. There are definitely things I have to say no to sometimes.

I'm also really honest with her about it. I'm very clear that all the bills are paid and because all the bills are paid and we have groceries in our refrigerator, we're not going to go to the mall and blow a hundred dollars on junk.

I don't think my parents were always very transparent with me. It was either "We don't have any money" or I thought that the money was like magic. Like, *Oh, you just sign your name on a piece of paper, you get stuff, cool.* I'm trying to educate her, because I don't want her to make bad financial decisions. She's 11, so she's gonna start making decisions in the not so distant future. She's starting to talk about what colleges she'd like to attend and what that will look like. She's also starting to be interested in things like mission trips and sports and is aware that those cost money.

It's incredibly difficult to discuss the financial aspect of fertility. How much are you willing to spend to have a child? I know many women who've gone to great lengths and spent tens of thousands of dollars trying to conceive. Their stories are often inspiring and heartbreaking, and I've been amazed how generous women can be in sharing their experience in the hope of helping others.

Cat, 32, and Jen, 30, a lesbian couple living in Brooklyn, knew from the start they'd have to spend money in order to have a child. But that hasn't made the process any easier.

In 2015, we got really serious about starting a family and decided to start saving. But at some point, we realized we couldn't save up enough on our own because at the time we were both making just a little bit more than minimum wage.

Our families didn't come to our wedding. But they've felt guilty about it ever since, and they wanted to make it up to us. They threw us a big fifth anniversary party, but instead of presents we asked for cash so we could start a family. We would have just accepted an apology, but the money didn't hurt.

We saved $5,000. Now that we're in it, we realize how low that number is.

When we started doing research—looking for a sperm donor online and a midwife who could do the procedure—we were shocked by how much it cost. All said, it was looking to be $2,200 per try. And the success rate was only 9 percent. So we had a 9 percent chance of getting pregnant for every $2,200 we spent. With our savings, we'd only get two tries.

 We had lowballed it initially because when you go on the sperm donor website, the price they list is just per vial. So it was, like, $500 to $800 per vial. We were thinking that our $5,000 would cover at least four or five tries.

Of course, there were so many more expenses. You have to rent a nitrogen tank to hold the frozen sperm. You have to hire a midwife to do the IUI, because you can't turkey baste, so to speak, with frozen sperm. And then our midwife would only agree to do the procedure if we did two inseminations per cycle.

So that was, like, a minimum of $1,200 for sperm alone. The tank was $250, plus $50 a day to keep it. We'd need it for a minimum of two days. Then if you kept it over the weekend, you were fucked. Then it was another $250 per insemination with the midwives, so that's another $500.

Of course, this isn't including sales tax and other fees.

We freaked out when we realized how much it was going to cost, because that meant our savings would only cover the procedure twice.

Luckily for us, we found a friend who would donate the sperm. When we realized it was going to be so expensive to get sperm through a bank, we decided to ask. It's not ideal, legally, to have a friend donate the sperm. But we realized there was probably no way we were going to get pregnant if we went through the sperm bank.

Our friend thought about it for three months—it was very stressful—but he ultimately agreed to donate monthly for a year. We paid for legal fees to have a document drawn up, which ended up being about $1,000.

We're now in our fifth month of trying. But if we'd used the sperm bank, we would be broke already. Not to mention the stress. So now when a cycle doesn't take, we don't feel like we've wasted $2,000. Which is more than our rent. Otherwise, that would be too much pressure.

We do have a brand-new cost this month: we're going to go see an acupuncturist. We're going to pay a $300 consultation fee, then another $200 a week for the acupuncture. This month, we'll be paying $900 just for the acupuncture.

Cat is 32. She's not at the age when it's supposed to be hard to get pregnant. So the advice we got before we started trying was, *This is going to be extremely easy for you. Don't even bother trying to ask for advice right now.* We're a little bitter about that.

We're not sure what we'll do if Cat doesn't get pregnant within a year. Most insurance companies won't fund fertility treatments until you've been trying for six months or a year. But by definition "trying" is sex between a heterosexual couple. So we'd have to pay out of pocket for any fertility treatments, and we can't afford that.

We're beginning to feel a little desperate. It's the feast of Saint Brigid tonight, and we're lighting candles and praying. It's the midpoint between the winter and summer solstices, so it's a fertility holiday. We kind of believe, but also we're, like, *Let's not take a chance.*

It doesn't cost us anything to light a fucking candle.

MY BABY IS DESTROYING MY SAVINGS, ONE $7 ORGANIC YOGURT AT A TIME

It's Saturday morning, and Ken and I are standing in Trader Joe's fighting about money—again. Today, the argument is over $3 juice boxes. Last time, we fought about $6 almond butter. We have a seventeen-month-old picky eater with a peanut allergy, and I feel as though all we do these days is waste money on food the kid won't eat.

It's really annoying.

It's been almost a decade since Ken and I combined our bank accounts, and I'll admit that even before the baby we didn't always see eye to eye on grocery expenditures. In our prekid days, I'd leave Ken at home whenever I shopped at the specialty grocer, so he wouldn't freak if I spent $10 on a pint of fancy ice cream.

These days, we bicker over $7 organic yogurt for a baby who may or may not eat it. More likely than not, the yogurt will go straight into the trash. Prebaby, I didn't think much of splurging from time to time because we lived below our means. Whenever I paid a little more for some special pint or fancy cheese, I always thought about what my grandfather used to say: spending money on food isn't a waste if you eat it. And you better believe we ate every bite of that raspberry chip ice cream. Plus we'd save in other ways, buying generic peanut butter or whatever laundry detergent was on sale. We drank PBR instead of craft beer. The splurges were, for the most part, few and far between.

Postbaby, we have so many more expenses (no surprise), and as a result, I think about money in a whole different way. This new addition to our family takes up more than his fair share of space, demanding not only our full attention but most of our money. Most of the time I'm okay with that, but I have to admit I feel so annoyed and wasteful when he refuses to eat the yogurt or I fail to pack lunch once again because I was (happily) preoccupied with the baby.

When I first started talking with Ken about having a baby, he scoffed and declared we couldn't afford it. Ken's frugality is well documented—and he's never been the biggest fan of kids anyway—so his response didn't come as a big surprise. But I also wasn't going to let his financial hang-ups stop me. You don't have to be rich to have kids, I argued, and we had plenty of friends with babies to prove my point. We'll figure out a way to make the money work, I thought. No big deal.

For the most part, we have figured out the big stuff. Our annual spending has increased significantly—I'd estimate we spend close to $3,000 more a month—but we make that work. But with so many new expenses, there's a whole lot less disposable income burning a hole in my pocket. Yet because my time has become so precious, I spend more money than ever in the name of convenience. Last week, I spent $12 on a cab so I wouldn't be late to day care after subway delays held me up. Last month, I spent an extra $3 so I could preorder movie tickets.

These days, I rarely think twice about throwing money at a problem. If we run out of whole milk for the kid, I'll just spend an extra $1 at the convenience store around the corner. I know it might seem silly, but we wouldn't have dreamed of wasting a buck like that prebaby. I attribute that hypermindfulness as being one of the reasons we were able to buy an apartment in NYC. Now I reason that it's worth wasting that money if it means we don't have to deal with a fussy baby or take a long walk in the cold when we're tired. And because I work full-time, it feels as though every minute I'm not in the office or commuting should be quality time spent with the baby, not standing in line at the grocery store. Time *is* money, and I've got more money than time these days. I know I'm lucky: many working mothers don't enjoy this same money-to-time ratio. Some have neither time or money, and then what do they do?

But I'm not just bleeding money because I lack time. Like many parents, I also want our kid to have the very best of everything (or is this just a Brooklyn problem?). Scent-free, dermatologist-recommended laundry detergent, organic food (even the hot dogs), $50 for a box of name-brand diapers. I can only imagine what's it going to cost when he's outgrowing sneakers every six months.

My insistence that my kid have the very best plus my willingness to let little expenses slide in the name of saving time has become a tricky combination. People talk so much about the lifestyle creep, but for what my kid has done to my financial habits, I'm going to call it the baby bougie. It might sound like champagne problems, but I can't help but wonder if it's all made worse by the systemic problems and societal pressures that always ding parents (working mothers especially): lack of affordable, high-quality child care and education, the 24/7 on-call nature of our jobs, the high cost of healthful food, and the ridiculously high standards mothers are held to. (Why do we have the expectation that we can work sixty hours a week and also make our own baby food? Not this mother.)

I don't have a solution except maybe making more money. Because that's the other thing I've learned from all of this: I might be exhausted, cash-strapped, and time poor, but I'm still ambitious. And with this wonderful baby to take care of, I have more reason to earn than ever.

HOW TO BABY-PROOF YOUR CAREER

I got twelve fully paid weeks of maternity leave—practically a luxury in this country—and though I'm so grateful I had time to recover from childbirth and bond with my baby, I wish it had been longer. I wasn't ready to go back to work. My baby wasn't sleeping through the night, and I was absolutely exhausted. Most days I went into the office feeling like a shell of my former self— my work clothes didn't fit right, I was distracted all the time, and I wasn't sure I'd ever have a good idea again. I'd regularly come home from work and tell Ken I wanted to quit my job.

Thankfully, I had a wonderful support system both at home and at work, and I got through that rough patch. A year in, I still have days when it's a struggle, but for the most part I love my work and I love my baby. No judgment about women who stay home, but it's definitely not the right decision for me.

That rough patch was also a real eye-opener. It's *hard* to go back to work when you have a new baby, and if you don't have a good support system in place, it can make it downright miserable.

In *Lean In*, Sheryl Sandberg implored women not to step back from their careers when they start thinking about having kids. I think that advice is too simple. If you want to juggle a high-powered career and kids, it can't hurt to start planning a few years before you even start trying for those babies and thinking strategically about how you can manage it all. And that might include some leaning out.

Sound daunting? Here are a few ways to get started:

Find out what your company's paid leave policy is. And find out how much your partner will get.

In my dream world, every single person—regardless of age, gender, or sexuality—would bring up paid leave during job interviews in order to remove the stigma around the question. I have a friend who asked about maternity leave benefits during a job interview, and she never got a call back. It could be that she wasn't right for the job, or it could be that the company didn't want to deal with a worker who could be (or might become) pregnant. (It's illegal to discriminate in that way.)

It's really important to know your employer's paid leave policy *before* you get pregnant. Sometimes you have to work at a company for a certain length of time before you become eligible. [This is also true of the Family and Medical Leave Act (FMLA), which provides unpaid leave if you work full-time for a year for a company with more than fifty employees.] In some cases, employers require you to take out short-term disability insurance[4] to cover your salary while on leave—often it doesn't cover your full pay—and you have to sign up for it during open enrollment.

It's also important for your partner to find out if they will have access to paid leave. A study by the advocacy group PL+US found that less than 25 percent of the United States' largest employers provide equal family leave to all new parents, regardless of whether they are the birth parent.[5]

Look around and see if the mothers and fathers you work with are actually taking that leave.

It's pretty great if your company offers paid leave benefits for both moms and dads. But take a closer look: Are men *and* women actually taking full advantage of these benefits?

A paid leave policy is useful only if you won't get dinged for taking it. Once you know the policy, start talking to women and men who've taken advantage of it. How was their experience after returning to work? Did they feel supported? Would they have done something different?

Look around to see if there are any mothers in leadership roles at your company.
Company culture is vital to women's success in the workplace, but it's doubly important for working moms. Just because you become a mom doesn't mean your ambition dries up, and it's awful to feel as though you've been moved to the so-called mommy track if you still have your sights set on the C-suite. Read *Fortune*'s annual list of the Most Powerful Women in Business—the majority are also mothers.

If you're seriously considering having a kid, take a look at your company's exec team and note how many are parents. If the answer is none, you might want to consider how that could impact your own career aspirations.

It's also worth looking to your own boss. If they are a parent, how do they approach the work/life juggle? And if they don't have kids, how do they treat the parents on the team?

Commit to stay at your job for a while.
This is imperfect advice, but I'm going to throw it out here anyway. As we explored in chapter 3, the easiest way to get a raise is to change jobs. But there are perks to staying put in your current gig, especially if you work for a family-friendly company where you have some seniority or flexibility.

If you're thinking of having a baby and you have a good job that offers fantastic paid leave and promotes working mothers, stay in that job. Commit to the company, and (hopefully, in theory) your employer will commit to you.

There are plenty of awful examples when this hasn't played out the way it should and hard workers/new moms are fired upon returning from maternity leave, so this isn't ironclad.

If you do change jobs, make sure to negotiate leave.
Don't be scared to talk with your new employer about the kind
of maternity leave you'll need. I know this sounds risky—it is!—
and it's not something every woman will want or be able to do.
But like the earlier advice, I'm going to throw it out here for you
to consider.

If you do get an amazing job offer, and you're pregnant, you
should make sure the company will agree to give you time
off—ideally with your full salary—even if you don't yet qualify
for its standard benefits. I have a friend who negotiated twelve
weeks of unpaid leave plus a signing bonus that would essentially cover her salary while she was out. Plus she had the added
benefit of knowing her new boss really wanted her to join the
team and would be supportive when she returned to work.

Talk to your boss about what success looks like.
Funny story about me: I told my boss I was pregnant before I told
my mom. I was very scared I was going to have a miscarriage, and
I was having a really hard time concentrating at work, so I told her
what was up. I'm not suggesting that you go into such intimate
details, but when you do share the happy news, it's really important to also talk about how pregnancy, maternity leave, and new
motherhood will impact your career. Because it will.

This is another place where it might be good to
have a script—baby brain is real, and it can be
hard to advocate for yourself when all you want to
do is think about onesies (which is totally okay!).
This is a good time to connect with other working
mothers to get their thoughts, as well as reconnect with your
mentors. Also, despite what Sheryl Sandberg says, it's also okay
to lean out for a bit. Careers are marathons, not sprints, and
most of us aren't going to make a 40 Under 40 list.

Consider what a flexible schedule would look like for you.
More and more companies offer flexible work schedules and
job-sharing programs, and technology makes it easier to do
your job from just about anywhere. But you need to figure out
what flexible means to you and if it would work in your current
situation. Maybe it's as simple as working from home once a
week or shifting your hours so you start earlier and leave earlier.

Then start talking with your boss. And remember, there might
be a limit to how much flexibility the company can offer you. It
might not be popular to give the advice that you have to prove
yourself—and work really hard—in order to get more flexibility
after you have kids, but that's often the reality.

If you're worried your boss will be completely unreceptive (or
how it might impact your career), there's another route you can
take, which is to just go ahead and tweak your schedule without
making a formal request. Again, I recommend this only for
employees who've already proven their worth.

Discuss division of labor with your partner.
Before we had a kid, Ken and I split household chores pretty
evenly. But he was a reluctant parent, and I was really nervous
to talk with him about how things would change once the baby
came. At some point in my pregnancy, Ken declared he wasn't
going to change diapers. Cue record screech.

The good news: Ken changes diapers.

It might seem silly—or worse, uncomfortable—to talk about the
division of household chores, but just because you're a woman
doesn't mean you have to be the admin in your family. If you
made a decision to have a baby together, your partner needs to
know that you'll be raising the baby together, too. And if you're
a single mom taking on childcare on your own, make sure that
anyone in your circle you'll be leaning on for support knows
exactly what you need from them.

Make sure you have a solid support system.
I'm part of a very active moms' group, and from time to time there's a fantastic chain of advice giving support to a working mother who is struggling. I don't know most of the moms in real life, but I get a lot of comfort knowing I'm not the only one trying to figure things out.

That's an important note to end on: you aren't alone in this. I've really enjoyed making friends with other working mothers, and I try to be really open about how difficult the juggle can be. They are the ones who will truly understand the pain, joy, and frustration of trying to juggle it all, and they will be there when the balls drop (because they will). Chances are they will have a great hack for making things a little bit better. And if they can't fix it, at least they can offer you a glass of wine and a shoulder to cry on.

THIS IS A GOOD TIME TO:

Start saving! Day care, or big changes to budget if one parent is going to stay home, are likely to be the biggest expenses you'll incur as a new parent. Do some research, and start setting aside that amount each month into the high-yield savings account you opened in chapter 4. You'll get a sense of how the baby will impact your budget while saving a tidy sum for future expenses (braces, anyone?).

**While you're at it, save $21
Total saved so far: $231**

Open a 529 Account

TIME: *Less than 30 minutes*
TOOLS: *Routing number, account info, money!*

In an effort to one day pay for our kid's college education, Ken and I set up a 529 account shortly after he was born. No student loan debt for my baby (at least that's what I hope).

I got a lot of help from Priya Malani (and Rob Kovalesky, her cofounder of Stash Wealth) when Ken and I set up our account, and I wanted to share their advice on the topic because I do think it's a little complicated. You should think of your 529 as a 401(k) for college.

How much money should I put into a 529?
The IRS doesn't set a limit to how much you can put into a 529, but if you contribute more than $15,000 a year, you have to report it on your taxes. Priya also recommends that you check to see if your state offers a tax deduction for any 529 contributions. In New York, it's around $10,000 per couple, which can be a good savings goal.

Will having a 529 impact how much financial aid my kid might receive?
Because the funds in a 529 are owned by the parent(s), not the child, only 5.6 percent of the plan value can be used in the calculation of estimated family contribution (EFC) on student aid forms.

Can I use the money I save in a 529 for anything other than college tuition?
Under the new tax code that rolled out in 2018, parents can spend up to $10,000 a year from their 529 on private elementary or high school tuition expenses, including fees, books, supplies, and room and board.

What else should I know?

You don't have to open up a 529 in the state where you live, and you don't have to go to school in the state where you have a 529, so you can shop around for the best plan for your needs (i.e., lower fees and/or better investment options). You don't have to have a child to open an account. You can use the money to pay for education outside the US as long as the institution qualifies. If your kid doesn't go to college, you can transfer the money to another family member (a sibling, cousin, even yourself!), but the money does have to be used for education expenses.

While you're at it, save $22
Total saved so far: $253

CHAPTER 7

Home & Money
(Or Will I Ever Be Able to Buy a House?)

W. hen I first moved to New York City, my biweekly paycheck barely covered the $900 a month I paid for a tiny room in a three-bedroom apartment on the Lower East Side. In the years since, my monthly housing costs have always been my biggest expense, and I'm not alone. The average American spends more than $17,000 a year on housing.[1] Your rent or mortgage falls into the "fixed expense" bucket because we all need a place to live, but there are so many factors that impact how much you pay.

Things get more complicated when you explore the idea of homeownership. Buying a home has long been the ultimate American dream, but it's a dream that comes with a lot of baggage. A home is also likely to be the most expensive purchase you'll ever make.

Ken and I went the traditional route, buying an apartment as a couple. But you don't need to be coupled to take the plunge. Single women are the fastest-growing group of home buyers in the United States.[2] In this area, we're blowing men out of the water and proving that you don't need a partner to achieve this goal.

That said, it's also okay to say no to homeownership without feeling as though you're missing an important milestone. Being saddled with a mortgage isn't worth it for everyone.

This chapter starts with everything you've ever wanted to know about renting. If and when you decide you want to buy a home, you'll be ahead of the curve if you make some small savings tweaks ahead of time. And if you decide your version of the American dream looks a little different, you can always use that money to invest in another long-term goal. Who wouldn't want that kind of freedom?

A Week in North Carolina on a **$38,500** Salary

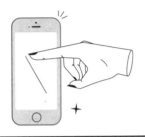

Utilities: $200
Internet: $70 (split with my fiancé)
Phone: $70

TRANSPORTATION:
Car Payment: $233
Car Insurance: $99

OCCUPATION: Social media and marketing manager
INDUSTRY: Advertising
AGE: 27
LOCATION: North Carolina
ANNUAL SALARY: $38,500
PAYCHECK (ONCE A MONTH): $2,512 + whatever I make freelancing (~$300/month)

FIANCÉ'S INDUSTRY: Public health
FIANCÉ'S ANNUAL SALARY: $47,878

GENERAL FINANCIAL INFORMATION:
Checking Account Balance: $2,373
Savings Account Balance: $9,773

HOUSING:
Rent: $1,150 (two-bedroom house that I split with my fiancé)

HEALTH & SELF-CARE:
Health Insurance: $190 (I'm not insured through work.)

MISCELLANEOUS:
Charitable Contributions: $40

SUBSCRIPTIONS:
Netflix and HBO Go: I use my fiancé's account

DEBT:
Student Loan Debt Total: $0 (My grandparents very graciously paid for school.)
Credit Card Debt: $0

RETIREMENT:
Roth IRA Contribution: $200/month
Roth IRA Total: $6,393

DAY ONE

8:30 a.m.—Wake up and drive my fiancé to a conference at the nearby university. Normally he'd walk, but he's running late.

8:45 a.m.—Back home, where I munch on watermelon and make a pot of coffee in the French press. I'm partially paid in trade for my job, and most of the agency's clients are in food and beverage. I get one bag of locally roasted coffee per week as part of my compensation. It's delicious, and I barely ever buy coffee anymore.

9:50 a.m.—I walk the two blocks to work. We're lucky enough to live in one of the only areas of the South where you can feasibly walk/bike everywhere. We use our cars so infrequently that we're planning on going down to a one-car household once my lease is up at the end of June.

10 a.m.—I answer some emails and get to work. My bosses used to own a record company and got used to starting work on the late side, thank God.

1:30 p.m.—I'm starving, so I walk home for lunch. I have leftover pasta and do the dishes from this morning. I get a call from an old friend in Dublin, so we catch up and make plans for me to visit.

2:30 p.m.—I chat for *waaay* too long. Oh well. Right before I leave, I take stock of our groceries to plan for dinner. I don't want to go grocery shopping until I know what we're getting in our CSA (community-supported agriculture) box tomorrow. I pull out some frozen leek and potato soup and rush back to work.

3 p.m.—I Venmo my brother-in-law my portion of the phone bill. **$70**

6:30 p.m.—I walk home and find my fiancé on the couch with one hell of a stomachache. Tums aren't helping, so I walk to CVS to get him some Pepto. **$4.29**

7:30 p.m.—I eat baguette slices with Brie while I make dinner. I heat up the soup and roast some broccoli. Our strawberries are about to go bad, so I make a quick shrub with lime zest and mint from the garden.

9 p.m.—Fiancé is still pretty miserable, so we watch a few episodes of *30 Rock* before turning in early.

DAILY TOTAL: $74.29

| DAY TWO |

8:15 a.m.—I wake up to find a bunch of beautiful turnips on our front porch. My fiancé's parents live nearby and have kick-ass vegetable gardens. They're always sharing their extras. I wash the turnips, snack on some more watermelon, and get ready.

9:50 a.m.—Pour myself some coffee and walk to work. I drop off our rent check on the way.

1 p.m.—It's gorgeous outside, but I'm stuck in meetings all morning, so I'm practically clawing at the walls by the time I leave for lunch. I walk home and eat baguette slices with Brie and some breakfast radishes. We're having dinner with friends, so I pick up some chips and salsa on my way back to work. **$6.11**

5:50 p.m.—After what feels like a thousand more meetings, I rush to the farmers' market to pick up our CSA before it closes. We prepay for 20 weeks of produce from a friend's farm (about $17 a week). This week's haul: cabbage, broccoli, bok choy, spinach, baby lettuce, and more strawberries.

6:30 p.m.—We head to our friends' for dinner. The food is incredible (holy shit, these braised chuck roast tacos). I feel bad about our piddly chips and salsa contribution.

9 p.m.—Our bellies are full of tacos and margaritas. Before we head home, our friends give us a giant bag full of fresh carrots and green garlic. I promise to bring a bag of coffee the next time we see them.

DAILY TOTAL: $6.11

| DAY THREE |

8:15 a.m.—Wake up and have some coffee and strawberries. We're supposed to have crazy thunderstorms, so I decide to drive to work.

11 a.m.—I'm already crashing, but I don't want any more coffee. A client dropped off chocolate truffles as part of a payment, so I grab one.

11:30 a.m.—I give up. Office coffee it is.

12:45 p.m.—I'm essentially curled up in a ball in my desk chair as I watch the House debate the ACA. I'm insured under the Affordable Care Act, and if it goes away, I'm pretty much screwed. Even though I've lost my appetite, I pull myself away for my lunch break. My rep is voting "No," but I call anyway. I pick at a salad at home.

1:15 p.m.—On my way back to work, I pick up a bottle of my favorite locally distilled gin. Regardless of how the vote goes, I'm going to need a strong-ass drink when this day is over. **$42.75**

2:15 p.m.—I watch the bill pass the House. I have a good ol' bathroom cry.

6 p.m.—Let's not even pretend this was a productive workday. My fiancé and I spend the afternoon Gchatting about how we could feasibly afford to add me to his insurance plan if this passes the Senate. It would cost us a little over $400 a month for just my coverage.

7:15 p.m.—I make myself a gin and watermelon shrub cocktail and start dinner—pesto made with turnip greens, carrot greens, and spinach mixed with some ricotta and served over pasta.

8:15 p.m.—I make another cocktail, throw in some laundry, watch *Friends*, and work on some freelance projects until bed.

DAILY TOTAL: $42.75

| DAY FOUR |

8:15 a.m.—Coffee and strawberries; I give my senators a call.

9:50 a.m.—Yesterday's rain left me a little stir-crazy, so I'm happy to see the skies have cleared. I pour some coffee and walk to work.

10:30 a.m.—Our real estate attorney billed us for the previous month's hours. We're buying an adorable 1940s fixer-upper, and we're getting a crash course in all of the additional costs that come with buying property. My fiancé covered the inspections, so I write the attorney a check. **$450**

11 a.m.—I spend the rest of the morning jumping between work projects and emails from our real estate agent. I'm starving when my boss suggests team lunch. The whole office goes out (there's only six of us) to a Mediterranean place. I get hummus, pita, and a roasted vegetable salad. The restaurant is a client, so they comp our meal.

6:30 p.m.—Enjoy a leisurely walk home. I head to Trader Joe's and get garlic, onions, milk, cereal, soy sauce, spicy chicken sausage, Kalamata olives, chicken stock, tortillas, mushrooms, ginger, trail mix, banana chips, and a tiny succulent because I'm a crazy plant lady. **$44.63**

7:15 p.m.—Pour myself a glass of rosé while I wait for the fiancé to get home.

7:45 p.m.—Some friends stop by, and we have an impromptu dinner party. I make a riff on moo shu pork with spicy sausage, cabbage, bok choy, mushrooms, and tortillas.

11 p.m.—I can barely keep my eyes open after dinner, so we call it a night.

DAILY TOTAL: $494.63

DAY FIVE

9:30 a.m.—Friends from out of town stop by for breakfast. We walk to the co-op, and I get a croissant, fruit, and a latte. Fiancé pays.

12:30 p.m.—Fiancé leaves to help some friends fix their fence. As much as I want to be outside, I have some work I have to get done first. I make another pot of coffee, put on a face mask, and make some headway on my freelance projects.

1:30 p.m.—I take a break for lunch. I microwave some leftover pesto pasta and top it with a fried egg and Tabasco. It's way better this way.

3:45 p.m.—I walk to the garden supply store and buy a cilantro plant. **$4.07**

7:15 p.m.—My fiancé's mother takes us to our favorite French place to celebrate his birthday. We do it up big—wine, oysters, paté, soft-shell crabs, the works. She treats.

10:15 p.m.—We're not quite ready to call it a night, so we head to a bar around the corner. Fiancé gets a local spicy ginger ale (he doesn't drink), and I get a dirty martini. **$17.85**

DAILY TOTAL: $21.92

DAY SIX

9:30 a.m.—Wake up, make coffee, and lounge with the fiancé.

11 a.m.—We head to his dad's house for his birthday brunch, only to find out that his sister went into early labor! We speed through brunch and head to the hospital to meet the baby!

3 p.m.—Mama and baby are doing great! I buy a really bad cup of hospital coffee and marvel at how tiny the baby is. **$1.25**

5:30 p.m.—Home. I'm looking for a shower curtain for the new house. I find one on Target's website that we both like, and it's on sale! **$22.52**

6:30 p.m.—Fiancé fixes dinner. Pesto pasta again, with poached eggs and Sriracha hollandaise sauce. I make a salad.

9 p.m.—I grab some mint from the garden and toss it with blackberries and a little balsamic vinegar for dessert. We talk about home improvement projects until we pass out around 11.

DAILY TOTAL: $23.77

DAY SEVEN

8:30 a.m.—I make coffee and eat some blackberries while I scroll through my phone.

9:15 a.m.—Shit. My fiancé made an appointment with a waterproofer to look at the new house and totally forgot about it. Our real estate agent won't be around until later, so we can't get in. I hightail it over to the house to explain the mix-up. He's pretty pissed. I write him a check to compensate him for gas since he drove over an hour to get here. My fiancé is normally pretty responsible, but we'll definitely have a talk about this later. **$20**

10:15 a.m.—Roll into work a bit late. I grab a cup of coffee.

11 a.m.—A local butcher we work with brings a huge box of sausages as part of a payment. I grab some chorizo and soppressata.

1 p.m.—Our due diligence period is up on the house, so I get a cashier's check and drop it off at our real estate agent's office. My fiancé will reimburse me for his half later. We've done all of our inspections, gotten quotes from contractors, and done some intense negotiating with the sellers. It'll be a ton of work to get it fixed up, but definitely a worthwhile investment. (*Knocks on wood*.) We're officially closing on Friday! **$2,000**

1:30 p.m.—I finish off the last of the pesto pasta for lunch.

6:15 p.m.—It's supposed to rain the rest of the week, so I leisurely walk home and enjoy the sunshine while I can. Fiancé feels terrible about the mix-up and apologizes as soon as I walk in. We kiss and make up, and he promises to reimburse me for the gas money.

6:30 p.m.—Our next-door neighbors invite us to grill out, so I grab a few beers. We enjoy brats and s'mores over the fire and head to bed around 11 p.m.

DAILY TOTAL: $2,020

| THE BREAKDOWN |

TOTAL SPENT: $2,683.47

FOOD AND DRINK: $112.59

ENTERTAINMENT: $0

HOME AND HEALTH: $2,030.88

CLOTHES AND BEAUTY: $0

TRANSPORTATION: $0

OTHER: $540

| THE FOLLOW-UP |

When did you and your fiancé decide to buy a home? And how did you prepare financially?
My fiancé was definitely way more ready than I was to take this step. He's a little bit older than I am, and he's been champing at the bit to get it done for a while. Before we bought the house, I moved every year for a decade, and I really wanted to stay put for a while and actually renew a lease. I also wanted a little more time to save up more money. But then my fiancé's parents gifted us the down payment, so that pushed up the timeline. It was an incredible present.

How much was your down payment?
We put $30,000 down. We got $20,000 from his parents, and the rest came from our savings.

What surprised you most about the home-buying process?
I didn't realize all the different kinds of people that we were going to have to pay. We paid a general home inspector to look at the whole house, a separate guy to look at the basement, and another guy to look

for termites. We had to get a real estate attorney to review all the contracts. I had no idea there were so many moving parts.

How do you and your fiancé manage your finances? Did it change any after you bought the house together?
We haven't combined our finances, but we've always practiced radical transparency with each other when it comes to money. After we bought the house, we had a shared financial goal for the first time. On top of our own savings goals, we're even more accountable to each other now that we're trying to pay off our mortgage as quickly as possible.

What surprised you the most about doing a Money Diary?
How privileged I sound! And how privileged I am, really. My fiancé and I do our absolute best to be responsible, but we've gotten *so much* help. Seeing it all in one place really put it into perspective for me, and it will likely affect the way that I make financial decisions in the future.

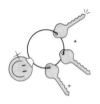

Renting your first apartment is one of those big adult moments that's incredibly stressful but probably doesn't have to be. Yes, rent is likely to be your biggest monthly expense. And yes, you want to like where you live. But a little prep work can make the whole process way easier. Below, Priya Malani and I have outlined everything we wish we had known about renting an apartment—from preparing the paperwork to making sure you have renter's insurance. Some of this info is big-city specific, but regardless of where you live, it's good advice to keep in mind when you're on the hunt.

Set a Budget

As we mentioned in chapter 1, most financial advisers suggest you spend no more than 30 percent of your net income (that's the money you bring home *after* taxes) on rent, but that can be pretty tight depending on the housing market.

Priya suggests the 80/20 rule: Live off of 80 percent of your income (this includes rent, any debt repayment, and utilities, as well as expenses such as your gym membership and Netflix), and save 20 percent. That gives you more wiggle room for rent, but it also means less money for other things. For some, paying higher rent is worth it to live in a better neighborhood, doorman building, whatever. Consider what's most important to you when deciding how much you can afford to spend on rent.

Many landlords require your annual salary to be 40 to 50 times the monthly rent. So if you're making $50,000, they'd be willing to rent you an apartment for $1,250. If you have roommates, you can obviously go higher—if the two of you make $100,000 a year combined, you can rent a place for $2,500. If you bring in a guarantor, landlords typically require that person to have an annual salary of 80 to 90 times the monthly rent.

You should also consider how much you'll spend on a broker's fee (in New York City, it can be as much as 15 percent of your first year's rent), as well as all the money you'll need to put down before you move in (first and last months' rent, security deposit, move-in and application fees). These can add up fast. If you're renting a $3,000 apartment, your move-in expenses can be as much as $15,000 if you have to pay a broker's fee. That breaks down to an additional $1,250 a month you'll be paying for the apartment over the next year.

Not sure you can afford a higher rent? There's a practical way to see how the increase will impact your budget. If your rent is $1,000 right now, but a new place would cost $1,500, spend a few months setting aside that extra $500 in savings so you can see what it's like to live without that extra cash. (Bonus points because you're saving extra money, too, which you could use later for the broker's fee.)

Decide Where You Want to Live and What Amenities You Can't Live Without

There are lots of personal preferences to consider when apartment hunting. Everyone should think about the following:

- Is there adequate parking and/or convenient public transportation?
- Do you feel safe?
- Are you close to a grocery store? Drugstore? Gym? Bank?
- Does the apartment check all boxes in terms of amenities (closets, dishwasher, elevator, etc.)?

No home is perfect (as anyone who watches *House Hunters* knows); it just needs to be *practically* perfect for you.

Prepare Your Paperwork

Have all your paperwork ready before you start looking. Depending on where you live, you'll likely need (some if not all) of the following handy before you start the hunt:

- Proof of employment letter, on company letterhead and signed by a company representative, stating your position, start date, length of employment, and salary
- If you're self-employed, a letter from a CPA stating annual income and source of income
- Your two most recent pay stubs
- Your two most recent tax returns
- Your two most recent W2s
- Your two most recent bank statements (including checking and savings)
- Reference letters from or contact information for previous landlords
- A photo ID (driver's license, passport, etc.)

Have a List of Questions to Ask the Leasing Agent/Landlord

This is where you're going to be living; it's important to know as much as you can about the apartment. Some examples:

- What utilities are covered in the rent?
- Do I have to pay for my own heat and hot water?
- Can I have a pet? Does it require an extra deposit?
- Is there a limit to the number of people who can live in the apartment?
- What are the building rules?
- Can I paint? Put nails in the walls?
- Who handles maintenance problems or emergencies?

- How much money is required to move in? (First month's rent, last month's rent, security deposit?)
- What's the penalty if I break my lease?
- Do you require a certificate of insurance from my moving company?

Inspect the Apartment

I've gotten better at inspecting potential apartments after a bunch of mistakes over the years. I've battled everything from low water pressure to a fridge door that wouldn't open all the way because it bumped into the stove. Don't spend all your time admiring the light pouring in through the big windows or debating where you'd put the sofa. Look for the following things before you rent an apartment:

- Run the water in the kitchen and bathroom and flush the toilet(s) to make sure everything works and there's adequate water pressure.
- If there's a dishwasher and/or washer/dryer, make sure they work. Same goes for the oven.
- Count the number of electrical outlets, and make sure they're in good locations. Bring a hair dryer to make sure the fuse doesn't blow every time you use it, or at least plug in your phone charger to make sure the outlets work.
- Make sure there are enough closets for your needs.
- Open the windows and check that the screens are in good repair.
- Check for any obvious damage that you might get charged for later (dinged countertops, scratched floors, etc.).
- Find out what the heat source is.
- Check that all doors and cabinets open and close properly.
- Make sure there is a working smoke and carbon monoxide detector.
- Look for signs of mildew in the bathroom and mold throughout the apartment.

Review the Lease and Know Your Rights

A quick Google search will pull up the standard lease agreements and tenant rights in your area. Your lease should include answers to some of those questions you asked earlier: Can you have pets? Whom do you call in an emergency? It will probably include other details, too, such as who's liable if the pipes burst or you set the kitchen on fire.

A few key things to look for when reviewing your lease:

- What's the length of the lease?
- Who's on the lease? (This is especially important if you have multiple roommates. The names on the lease are the people who are financially responsible for the apartment—including covering any expenses if there's damage when you move out.)
- Does the lease include everything you agreed upon? If your landlord said it was okay to have a cat but the lease says no pets, you'll want to revise it before you sign (which can be as simple as crossing out the section and putting your initials and your landlord's initials next to it).
- What happens at the end of the lease? Can you renew automatically?
- What happens if you need to break the lease? Will you be hit with a big fee?
- Are rent increases built in?

Many cities and states have strict laws that protect renters, but it's up to you to know your rights.

Sign Up for Renter's Insurance

It's so cheap, there's no reason *not* to sign up for it. We're talking around $30 a month, sometimes less. It will protect you from all the stuff your landlord won't cover. Typically, they are only required to take care only of building-related damages (for example, if a pipe bursts and floods your kitchen).

Consider buying. This is a complicated question, but something to think about. If you're getting ready to move and pay the first and last months' rent plus a security deposit, not to mention a broker's fee and moving expenses, you could easily be out $10,000 or more. The *New York Times* has a fantastic rent-versus-buy calculator[3] that's worth playing with if you're even beginning to consider homeownership. Buying is definitely not for everyone, but each time you begin the apartment hunt again, it's worth taking a moment to step back and consider whether you might be able to actually buy a place—and if it makes good financial sense.

**While you're at it, save $23
(you'll need it for that down payment)
Total saved so far: $276**

While most financial advisers recommend you spend no more than 30 percent of your posttax income on rent that can be tough to do in areas with a high cost of living. We asked women from across the country to share their monthly housing costs compared to their annual salaries and how that expense made them feel.

EMILY, 22 | MINNEAPOLIS, MN | ANNUAL SALARY: $50,000 (25 PERCENT TAX BRACKET) | MONTHLY RENT: $650 ($1,850 SPLIT AMONG THREE ROOMMATES; I PAY THE MOST FOR THE BIGGEST BEDROOM WITH A BALCONY.) | HOME SIZE: 3-BEDROOM TOWN HOUSE | PERCENTAGE OF ANNUAL SALARY: ~20 PERCENT

"I know people who pay a lot more for just as nice of a place. We live in a town house outside of the 'ideal' neighborhood, but we are still close to a lot of good restaurants, and my commute is very reasonable."

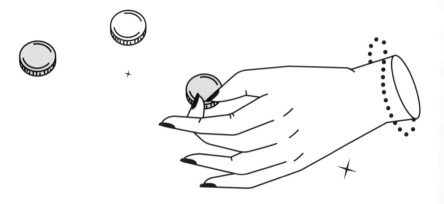

AMY, 22 | BENTONVILLE, AR | ANNUAL SALARY: $35,000 (15 PERCENT TAX BRACKET) | MONTHLY RENT: $600 (I LIVE WITH MY BOYFRIEND.) | HOME SIZE: TWO-BEDROOM DUPLEX | PERCENTAGE OF ANNUAL SALARY: ~24 PERCENT

"Love it because it's cheap! We have a huge backyard and pay about $300 less than all our friends."

AMANDA, 23 | NEW YORK, NY | ANNUAL SALARY: $45,000 (25 PERCENT TAX BRACKET) | MONTHLY RENT: $1,150 ($3,550 SPLIT AMONG THREE ROOMMATES) | HOME SIZE: THREE-BEDROOM, TWO-BATH APARTMENT | PERCENTAGE OF ANNUAL SALARY: ~40 PERCENT

"**It pains me on a daily basis to think that I am putting about 40 percent of my taxed income toward my rent. I am actually considering moving back in with my crazy family.**"

SHELBY, 24 | WASHINGTON, DC | ANNUAL SALARY: $65,000 (25 PERCENT TAX BRACKET) | MONTHLY RENT: $975 ($1,950 SPLIT WITH BOYFRIEND) | HOME SIZE: 500-SQUARE-FOOT STUDIO | PERCENTAGE: ~24 PERCENT

"Once my boyfriend moved in, it definitely lessened the burden, but sometimes it is ridiculous to think about how we pay $2,000 for about 500 square feet. I justify it by thinking about the money I would spend on transportation if I moved somewhere else in the city that might be a cheaper neighborhood."

ANNA, 25 | PITTSBURGH, PA | ANNUAL SALARY: $38,500 (25 PERCENT TAX BRACKET) | MONTHLY RENT: $500 ($1,475 SPLIT WITH PARTNER) | HOME SIZE: THREE-BEDROOM DUPLEX | PERCENTAGE: ~20 PERCENT

"Our rent is more than I would have wanted, but my partner makes double what I do, so we split rent proportionally based on our incomes. We're definitely getting a great deal—we live in a three-bedroom duplex with free parking, a washer/dryer in unit, and our landlord allows dogs."

ERIN, 27 | ANN ARBOR, MI
| ANNUAL SALARY: $120,000
(28 PERCENT TAX BRACKET)
| MONTHLY RENT: $301.50
($1,200 SPLIT AMONG TWO
COUPLES) | HOME SIZE:
TWO-BEDROOM TOWN HOUSE
| PERCENTAGE: ~4 PERCENT

"AMAZING! I have been able to destroy my student debt in 1.5 years due to how much I'm saving on rent. Does it suck to have three roommates and one bathroom? Absolutely. Would I give it up? Absolutely not."

ALLISON, 24 | EL MONTE, CA (LA SUBURB)
| ANNUAL SALARY: $44,000 (25 PERCENT TAX
BRACKET) | MONTHLY RENT: $1,600 (NO
ROOMMATES) | HOME SIZE: 450-SQUARE-
FOOT STUDIO | PERCENTAGE: ~58 PERCENT

"It's outlandish. Since I moved in (seven months ago), the monthly rent has already gone up $50 and the pet rent by another $10. I wouldn't mind paying so much for somewhere I loved, but my apartment is not that great. Not only is it small, but there is no laundry, no dishwasher, and it's not in a particularly great location. I have to live on a very strict spending budget and have plenty of credit card debt."

It's a hot summer afternoon in July 2009. I'm standing in an empty apartment holding a can of Pabst Blue Ribbon. Ken stands with me as we survey our new home. Earlier in the day, we were sitting in a dingy law office, signing a towering stack of legal documents, before handing over a very, very big check. I felt a little dizzy when the lawyer gave us the keys. It's official: we're the proud owners of a 700-square-foot, one-bedroom apartment in Park Slope, Brooklyn. How the hell did we get here?

Well, PBR had something to do with it. And peanut butter sandwiches.

Ken and I aren't millionaires. We're not Wall Street bankers or trust fund babies. We didn't win the lottery, and we're far from financial geniuses. We're savers. *Frugal* may be one of the least sexy words in the English language, but there are some benefits of being penny-pinchers (another ugly phrase). Because of our careful spending, Ken and I were able to save close to $100,000 in six years. It was enough to snag a piece of the American dream—in New York City, no less.

New York isn't exactly known for embracing its middle class. According to Zillow, in March 2018 the median home value was $773,770,[4] while census data revealed that the median household income in Brooklyn in 2016 was $50,640.[5] Beyond an outrageous real estate market, there's the high cost of living: food, entertainment, clothing, and general "keeping up with the Joneses." This is not a town for savers.

Couple the expenses of living in New York with the fact that Ken and I work in creative fields—industries not known for paying six-figure salaries—and saving money gets even tougher. When we bought our apartment, I was an associate editor at a book packager. Ken worked for an educational publisher and spent much of his downtime growing his freelance writing career. Though we made decent salaries, we weren't exactly rolling in money. After rent, groceries, and bills, there wasn't a ton left over. We managed to save by cutting corners: we don't have cable or gym memberships; we rarely eat out; and we really think about every single purchase we make. Sure, there were times we ended up missing out on some things I kind of regret. But in the end, we're homeowners. And for us it was worth every sacrifice.

As a couple who are incredibly careful with our money, buying an apartment made a lot of fiscal sense. Instead of wasting $1,600-plus a month on a rental, we're building equity. I wasn't totally sure what that meant at the time, but everyone I knew reassured me it was a smart decision. It was more than just a financial decision for us, though. Owning our apartment is a commitment—to our relationship, to this city, to building our future here.

Ken and I didn't sit down at twenty-two, when we started dating, and decide to save $100,000 to buy an apartment one day. We were like most postgrad twentysomethings: Ken had student loans; we didn't make a lot of money. Even in those salad days, though, we were pretty thrifty, saving what we could, when we could, never carrying credit card debt. We wanted to have some extra funds should we ever lose our jobs. After all, we work in media. We know plenty of people who have been laid off—both of us included.

Ken is definitely more frugal than I am. The man will go out of his way to avoid a service charge, bridge toll, or full-priced beer. For years, he ate a peanut butter sandwich every single day for lunch, skipping the jelly because it was an "unnecessary expense." But his dedication to that simple meal has saved us thousands over the years. Takeout lunch in Manhattan easily costs $10 to $15 if you're ordering from Seamless and adding a tip. Click "Place Order" five days a week, fifty weeks a year, and you're spending $3,750 annually for limp salad and bland sushi.

I'm not so strict with my spending. I have a weakness for expensive cheeses. I take my lunch to work a lot, but I usually indulge once a week and go out for lunch. I'm guilty of spending $7 for a half pound of Brussels sprouts at the farmers' market. And every once in a while, I will take a coffee break with a friend and have a $5 latte.

But despite our different saving styles, at the end of the day, we're pretty much on the same page. And I like to think that over the course of our relationship we've balanced each other out some. I've come around to many generic brands (aren't Target dryer sheets pretty much the same as Downy?). On the other hand, I've gotten Ken to agree that Hellmann's is the only brand of mayo worth buying.

 Okay, I realize that it still sounds nuts that we were able to save all that money in a relatively manageable amount of time, but there are a million little ways your spending can add up. Ken makes us coffee every morning (from a $3 can of Café Bustelo), and since we always eat breakfast at home (generic raisin bran for him), neither of us buys it on the way to work (easily $5 to $10 per day right there). If we want to go out for a drink with friends, we choose the $3 draft over the $14 cocktail. We cook dinner at home nearly seven days a week. And you can forget about brunch.

I read somewhere that most restaurant critics define a "cheap eat" as dinner for two for $50, not including alcohol. I'm sorry, but that's expensive. And let's be realistic: everyone wants wine. Say that brings the bill to $75 (and that's a cheap bottle you've ordered). Drop that on one dinner a week for an entire year, and you've spent nearly $4,000. Save it, and you're 4 percent of the way to your end goal of $100K. Every little bit really does count.

In eight hundred words, I've already saved you $10,000.

In our early days in NYC, we rarely said no to a chance to make extra cash. It was both a way to save and a way to grow our careers. From 2004 to 2008, Ken wrote hundreds of features and album and concert reviews for the *Hartford Courant*, and we crisscrossed the state of Connecticut, seeing everyone from GWAR to Christina Aguilera. The pay was okay, not great—Ken had to keep his day job. And he developed an attitude toward spending that still drives me crazy: he thinks about every purchase in terms of how much freelance work he did to earn the money. Want to go to the movies? Tickets for two come to $30, and that's the cost of a record review. Thinking about buying those running shoes? At $150, that's two concert reviews. You get the idea. That attitude keeps him from buying stuff he doesn't need (and some stuff he does). I know it's one of the reasons we were able to buy our apartment, but I still kind of hate it.

I didn't have a freelance income that I could save in the same way. I worked long hours for a book packager, frequently staying 'til midnight or later and working a lot of weekends. I was very lucky, though, to be rewarded with very generous year-end bonuses. I didn't use those (low) five-figure checks to go on vacation; I saved them, thinking one day maybe I could use the money for something bigger, just not sure what that would be.

All of this working and saving might make us seem sad or boring, but I assure you that's not the case. We have friends. We take advantage of so much that this city has to offer. We don't dine out, but our dinners at home are one of the best parts of the day. We cook something simple, set the table with cloth napkins and a candle, and Ken picks a record to play. Sitting at our kitchen table eating dinner, we finally get a few minutes away from our phones and computers. It's not just a way to save money but a chance to reconnect and really talk to each other, even if some days it's just to gripe about work or rehash whatever show we're watching on Netflix.

It wasn't until we moved in together in mid-2007 that it became clear we could combine our savings and buy an apartment. Before that, I had never asked Ken how much money he made or how much he saved. Maybe other couples have those conversations sooner? When we filled out a rental application and laid it all on the line, it was a little bit shocking. Between the two of us, we had one heck of a healthy savings account.

Ken and I are never quick to do anything. We dated seven years before we got engaged. So it took several discussions over the course of a year to determine that we might be able to buy an apartment. I insisted that we could; he was reluctant. We started playing around with a mortgage calculator online, and it seemed a little crazy. In order to make it a reality, we would have to spend nearly every penny we had. But when we crunched the numbers, it made more financial sense than renting.

Buying an apartment in NYC is weird. The rules are completely and totally different in other parts of the country, and the whole process is crazy, complicated, and stressful. You have to navigate the weird world of brokers who have their own agendas. You have to understand the difference between a co-op and a condo. And if you decide to make an offer, you learn quickly that it costs a whole lot more than just the 20 percent down payment. There are lawyer fees, broker fees, inspector fees, closing costs. We had to take all of that into account when deciding how much we could actually afford. But once we made the decision to go for it, there was no turning back. We told our landlord we wanted to go month to month on our lease, and house hunting practically became a second job—a third if you count the freelancing. Good thing Bustelo is so strong.

After months of house hunting, the process of putting in an offer goes fast. We saw the apartment we wanted for the first time on a Sunday. We got preapproval for a loan on Monday. We dragged my parents in for a second opinion on Wednesday. We made an offer Thursday morning. And, after a little negotiating, our offer was accepted by the end of the week.

That week was intense, but it was just the beginning.

The months leading up to the closing date were rough. Ken and I were planning our wedding at the same time, and the pressure was a lot to deal with. Nothing went smoothly; everything dragged. I knew we wanted to do this, but the process was miserable, and many days I just wanted to pull the covers over my head and stay put.

The funny thing about becoming an adult is that most of the time, you don't feel like a grown-up. And then, all of a sudden, bang, you are one. You have a lawyer. You write a check for $40,000. But that doesn't mean you always act like one. During those stressful weeks I didn't always handle things well, but somehow we muddled through. Spring turned to summer, and suddenly everything was coming together.

The day before we closed, our lawyer sent me an email with a list of the closing costs and a note to bring "a lot of extra personal checks," on top of the $40,000 cashier's check we were giving the seller. The email included a list of all the various closing costs, which we had known about in vague terms (she had warned us we would spend close to an additional $5,000 all told), but until then we had never seen any hard-and-fast numbers. It's crazy that Ken and I agonize over spending $40 on concert tickets, but that day in July we didn't think twice about writing a check for $1,700 for our lawyer (the remainder of the $3,000 total fee), $250 for signing fees, and close to $4,000 in bank fees. Needless to say, when the check writing was all done, the lawyer gave us the keys, and I managed not to swoon on the hot streets of Park Slope, we didn't exactly feel like toasting our success with Veuve Clicquot. We were gonna stick with the cheap stuff that had gotten us here.

And that's how we ended up in the empty apartment, raising a toast with cans of PBR, already arguing about where to put the sofa. But we were happy. Over-the-moon happy. At 28, we had accomplished a huge life goal. If we could do this, we could do anything.

Our frugal habits didn't disappear after we became homeowners, and we continued to save. In the winter of 2016, when we found out I was pregnant, we decided it was time to move into a bigger place. One-bedroom apartments in our building were going for around $600,000, and we found a really great real estate agent to help sell ours. The process was a lot less scary the second time around, but not without a few hiccups perfect for a whole new story. Thanks to careful saving and getting damn lucky with the market, we had enough to upgrade to a two-bedroom we love.

I might never dine at Per Se or buy a pair of Gucci loafers, but I've never once regretted the sacrifices we made to be homeowners. I'm more than happy to trade those luxuries for the simple pleasure of stepping across the threshold of my apartment each evening. After all, home is where my heart (and the PBR) is.

When Ken and I bought our first apartment, I was totally over-whelmed—and I think it would have been slightly less stressful if I had been more knowledgeable about the whole process. The second time around it was definitely a lot less scary.

I asked Barbara Ginty to help me put together the kind of home-buying guide I wish had existed when I first started attending open houses way back in 2009. Read on so you won't feel panicked when your mortgage broker starts asking you about points.

How do I know I'm ready to buy a house?
Quite simply: You have the money for the down payment. And that money doesn't come from your 401(k) or your emergency fund. Saving money for a down payment, on top of your fully funded emergency account, shows that you have the discipline necessary to buy a house, Barbara says.

How much house can I afford?
If we go back to Manisha's advice in chapter 1, you really shouldn't spend more than 30 percent of your income on housing. In theory, if you make $75,000 a year, your monthly mortgage payments should be around $1,400.

Maybe you already spend more than that on rent. Fair enough. As we mentioned earlier in this chapter, Priya argues that an 80/20 split on fixed expenses versus future expenses is an easier goal to achieve than the more rigid 50/30/20. But your increased housing costs shouldn't decrease your monthly savings and debt repayment contributions.

Play with an online affordability calculator. If you want to spend more on rent than you do now, it's worth doing a test run for a few months to see how the increased cost will impact your cash flow. Automatically transfer the difference into a savings account each month. Later, you can use that money to help cover closing costs or moving expenses.

Monthly mortgage payments aren't the only number you'll need to consider. There's also the down payment. While Barbara recommends putting down at least 20 percent, it is possible to put down less (though that will increase your monthly mortgage payments). There are also taxes and maintenance or homeowners' association (HOA) fees to consider.

Barbara also recommends thinking about what other expenses might arise in the near future. If you're having a baby, consider child care costs. Set aside money for repairs—home improvement costs can vary significantly depending on your renovation plans, your timeline, where you live, and so forth. If you're dreaming of doing gut renovation à la Chip and Joanna Gaines, you might want to bring along a contractor to offer some estimates as you house hunt. Then build in a cushion, because it always costs more than the estimate.

I've got the down payment; now what?
The home-buying process varies from state to state, but here are three things everyone should do:

1. **Comparison shop for a mortgage:** Barbara suggests looking at the rates offered at different banks, as well as credit unions. You can also work with an independent mortgage broker who will shop around for the best interest rate. Seek out a recommendation and make sure you like the broker—you'll be working with them a lot!

2. **Organize your paperwork:** I recommend having at least two hard copies as well as a digital copy available. Depending on your situation (and the state where you're buying the home), you'll need some or all of these documents:

- Tax returns
- Bank statements
- Credit card statements
- Retirement and investment account statements
- Student loan statements
- Statements from any other debt (personal loans, car loans, etc.)
- Credit score
- Pay stubs
- Letter verifying employment status

3. **Preapproval letter:** This letter from your lender states how much home you can afford and shows sellers that you're serious about your offer. In order to get this letter, the lender will run your credit score and ask for some (if not all) of the above documents.

What do lenders look at when they decide to give people a mortgage?

Barbara says there are three main things lenders consider:

1. **Income:** Banks don't just care about your savings account balance; they want you to have a steady income stream. If you're in a relationship and both parties are on the loan, the bank often wants you both to have jobs. Barbara worked with a family where one partner had to get a job in order for the couple to secure a mortgage. It can also be difficult to get a mortgage if you're a freelancer without a steady income stream. (This is where that high savings account balance can be a big plus.)

Also, lenders don't like applicants to change jobs during the mortgage application process. So your best bet is to sit tight at your current job until you close.

2. **Debt-to-income ratio:** You should already have a loose sense of your debt-to-income ratio because you know your monthly take-home pay and your recurring monthly expenditures thanks to all the prep you did earlier in the book! (Haven't done that work? Go back to chapter 1.) When deciding whether and how much mortgage to give you, lenders run a calculation to evaluate whether you can meet your monthly financial obligations including mortgage payments.

3. **Credit score:** The higher your score, the better your mortgage options will be, and it will ultimately help you save money in the long run.

Do I really need a 20 percent down payment?

Barbara recommends having a 20 percent down payment, but that's not always required. Depending on the type of loan, you may be able to put less money down. But remember, the bigger the down payment, the smaller your monthly mortgage payments will be. If you don't put 20 percent down, you might be required to take out primary mortgage insurance (PMI), which can add to your overall monthly payments. (It can be dropped if you refinance your loan.)

In very competitive markets, a bigger down payment makes you more appealing to sellers reviewing several offers.

How does a mortgage work?

There are basically two types of mortgages: fixed rate and variable rate. Barbara recommends a fixed-rate mortgage, and first-time home buyers should look at twenty- or thirty-year loans. (There are fifteen-year loans, but the monthly payments are much higher, which might make them too expensive for first-time buyers.)

As of the writing of this book, interest rates were
at an all-time low, which makes fixed-rate mortgages even more appealing. Also, many of us
remember the 2008 housing crash, and we know
how crazy-bad things can get when you take out a variable-rate
mortgage. There's no real reason to take that risk, so let's pass
on that, shall we?

A mortgage, Barbara explains, is made up of two components:
the principal, which is the amount you borrow, and the interest rate, which is what the lender charges you to borrow the
money. At the beginning of a mortgage loan, you pay primarily
interest, and as you get closer to the end of the loan, you pay
primarily principal. That's why you might want to consider
principal-only payments if you have a twenty- or thirty-year
fixed mortgage. Barbara is a big fan of principal-only payments,
and she gave us an example of how it can save you money:

> You have a thirty-year fixed mortgage
> The mortgage amount is $120,000
> Interest rate = 4.5 percent
> Monthly mortgage payments = $608
> Total interest paid = $100,000

By making an additional $100-a-month principal-only payment,
you'll save $27,943 in interest and knock 7.5 years off your
mortgage. You can set up principal-only payments through the
financial institution that holds your mortgage.

The other word you'll hear a lot when applying for a loan is
points. Basically, it's industry speak for percentage. Points are
a onetime fee the bank charges you in order to get a lower
interest rate. A point is 1 percent of the loan.

There are two ways points can be added to your mortgage.
First, they can be used to reduce the interest rate. Say, for
example, the bank has offered you a 4.4 percent interest rate
with 2 points for your $300,000 mortgage. If you pay an extra

$6,000 at closing, your interest rate would drop to 3.4 percent, lowering your monthly payments by $150. If you're planning on staying in the home for more than three years, this is a good deal; for a shorter period, it's not really worth the extra $6,000.

Points might also be added to a mortgage depending on your credit score, your down payment, or the type of property you're buying.

What does equity mean? And why should I care about it?

Equity refers to the amount of the house that you own versus the amount of the house the lender owns. One of the reasons Barbara recommends a 20 percent down payment is that you own more of the home from the start. Each month that you make a mortgage payment, you own a little bit more of your apartment or house.

Ken and I bought our apartment for $405,000 in 2009. We put down 20 percent, and each month we paid $1,500 toward our $320,000 mortgage. We lived in that apartment for almost seven years, which means we made close to eighty-four mortgage payments. When we sold, we had already paid close to $125,000 for the apartment on top of that initial $80,000 investment. Even if we'd sold the apartment for the same amount we paid for it, we would have gotten a check for $205,000 on closing (minus closing costs and real estate agent fees).

Any other unexpected surprises I should consider when buying a home?

Perhaps the craziest thing about buying a home is how many checks you'll write over a very short period of time. Barbara encourages first-time home buyers to be aware of closing costs *before* they start the process. Do your research, ask a real estate agent, and speak to friends who have previous home-buying experience. Then make sure you have that money earmarked in the bank (and again, don't dip into your emergency fund for this, please!).

Though real estate laws vary by state, one big cost first-time home buyers often aren't aware of is escrowing taxes. If you don't put down a 20 percent down payment, you'll likely be required to escrow taxes, which means you'll need a year's worth of taxes at closing. That can be a big check.

Other closing costs include appraisal, inspection, and application fees. Some homeowners' associations or co-ops also require you to have a year's worth of fees saved. So if you're paying a monthly maintenance fee of $600, you need to have an additional $7,200 in the bank.

THIS IS A GOOD TIME TO:

Pack your lunch. Okay, okay, I know it's pretty smug to suggest that if you just pack your lunch every day, one day you'll become a homeowner. There's a lot more to it than that. But little savings do add up, and if it's your dream, small tweaks can help.

While you're at it, save $24
Total saved so far: $300
And then do a little dance—you've saved $300

Try a Zero-Dollar Day

TIME: *24 hours*
TOOLS: *An empty wallet!*

In chapter 4, I provided a list of easy savings tricks so you can pay off more debts. In this challenge, I want you to go more extreme—try a zero-dollar day. I first learned about this concept from a freelancer, and I loved it. It's easy to fall into the habit of mindless spending: dropping $5 for coffee and a bagel on your way to work, ordering in lunch because you forgot (or didn't want to eat!) the one you packed, swinging by the drugstore to buy toilet paper and leaving with nail polish and chapstick, too. All of a sudden you've spent $50, and you don't even have much to show for it.

Not spending money for a day can take a little bit of preparation. You have to know what you'll be doing for breakfast, lunch, and dinner (plus snacks), your gas tank needs to be full, and it can't be the day when you pay all your bills. But there's something really satisfying about not cracking your wallet for twenty-four hours.

If not spending at all is impossible, you can just take a day off from unnecessary purchases. Skip buying breakfast, lunch, and dinner out of the house. But don't give up on the challenge if you have to swing by the grocery store to buy food. Sometimes, when you set out to have a zero-dollar day and you have an unexpected expense, it's easy to use that as an excuse to just buy whatever, because you're already spending money. Don't fall for that!

If you do a zero-dollar day on a Tuesday, take a few minutes to see what you spent last Tuesday. Take that total (as long as it doesn't include a huge expense, such as your rent) and transfer it to your savings. Nice work!

While you're at it, save $25
Total saved so far: $325

CHAPTER 8

Parents & Money
(Or When It's Okay to Lean on Mom and Dad— and When It's Not)

I have a joke with my colleague Judi that I don't know how to spell the word *privilege*. Yet I openly admit that I have a lot of it. My parents sent me to private school, paid for college, and supported me when I moved to New York City without a job. It's a lot less scary to take risks when you know you can always move back in with your mom and dad if shit hits the fan.

You can't write a book about millennial women and money without talking about our relationships with our parents. Thanks to a slew of negative statistics, most media coverage paints our generation as leeches sucking our parents dry. According to a 2015 study, 40 percent of millennials get some kind of support from their parents.[1] Pew Research Center found that it's more common for young adults to live at home than live with roommates.[2] And there's a lot of concern that baby boomers won't be able to retire because they spend all their money on their kids.[3]

Of course, the problem with headlines is they never paint a complete picture. You could argue that moving home to save money is a responsible decision. Or that if your parents have the means to help you, it makes sense to take advantage of it. And then there are the millions of millennials who provide financial assistance to their families.

In this chapter, we'll explore both the privilege of having parental support and the privilege of being able to support our parents. We'll also touch on the conversations you should have with your mom and dad about their future. It might seem awkward, but just think of how impressed your parents will be when you broach these tough subjects. Talk about acting like a grown-up.

Money Diary #8

A Week in Los Angeles, CA, on a **$26,300** Salary

OCCUPATION:
Planning assistant (full-time), contract naturalist, student
INDUSTRY: Parks and outdoor education
AGE: 27
LOCATION: Los Angeles, CA
ANNUAL SALARY: $26,300
PAYCHECK AMOUNT (EVERY TWO WEEKS): $821.33 + an additional $200–$300 a month for contract work

GENERAL FINANCIAL INFORMATION:
Checking Account Balance: $2,300 (I try to keep $1,000–$1,500 at all times.)
Savings Account Balance: $1,200 (I generally contribute $0–$200 per month.)

HOUSING:
Rent: $400 (In 2017, I converted my parents' garage into a very small studio (less than 200 square feet). This allows me to help them out.)
Utilities: $30
Internet: $10
Phone: $88

TRANSPORTATION:
Car Payment: $0 (I drive a 20-year-old used car.)
Car Insurance: $67

HEALTH & SELF-CARE:
Health Insurance: $0 (includes dental and eye; covered by my job)
FSA: $10/paycheck
Gym: $0 (Parks are my gym)

SUBSCRIPTIONS:
Hulu: $0 (thanks to my phone plan)
Cloud Storage: $0.99
Spotify: $4.99
Netflix: $11.99

DEBT:
Student Loan Debt
Total: $9,000 (but in deferment while I'm back in school)

 RETIREMENT:
457 Contribution:
$45/paycheck (+ 6.5 percent company match)
457 Total: ~$1,000
CalPERS Total: ~$3,579

5:20 a.m.—I'm normally up at 6:30, but I'm trying to wake up earlier. I get up and do yoga, then take my time making coffee in my Chemex. I get so much satisfaction out of making coffee; it's almost therapeutic.

6:25 a.m.—I make oatmeal with half a banana, flaxseeds, chia seeds, almond milk, frozen pineapple, and almond butter. I pack it into my eco lunch box to eat at work.

10:45 a.m.—I'm tasked with developing presentation ideas for an upcoming conference. I'm a bit nervous, but I'll do the best I can!

12:33 p.m.—I have homemade tostadas with beans, zucchini, corn, salsa, and avocado. I love leftovers!

5:15 p.m.—Home! Time to feed my cat and guinea pig.

6:45 p.m.—Dinner! I make fettuccine with lentil-and-mushroom "meatballs" and cover it with a garlic-tomato-basil sauce.

8:30 p.m.—I make a sushi burrito for lunch tomorrow. I add jasmine rice (made sticky with rice vinegar), peppers, carrots, avocados, cucumber, tofu, mushrooms, ginger, garlic, and honey to two nori sheets. I resist the temptation to take a bite!

10 p.m.—My boyfriend, D. got me into *Seinfeld*, and I LOVE it! I knock out after three episodes.

DAILY TOTAL: $0

| **DAY TWO** |

6:11 a.m.—I make oatmeal and add pear while it's cooking. I heat up yesterday's leftover coffee and refill my hydroflask. Out the door by 7:45.

11:25 a.m.—It's a boring day at work filled with invoices and contract requests. Thankfully, I have a side job as a naturalist where I get to actually go out and teach others about nature.

12:30 p.m.—Sushi burrito time! It's definitely filling but would've tasted even better if I'd made it this morning.

3:15 p.m.—I snack on clementines and an apple while I make a grocery list.

5:52 p.m.—I stop by the store and get celery, potatoes (regular and sweet), cauliflower, cilantro, parsley, carrots, sweet bell peppers, broccoli, bulk popcorn, bulk black beans, bulk chickpeas, goat milk for my dad, almond milk for myself, a big tub of nutritional yeast, canned coconut milk, and a bottle of Boochcraft. **$63.26**

6:34 p.m.—Back home, I make a cauliflower pizza. For the crust, I use cauliflower, oregano, salt, pepper, and flax "egg" (1 part ground flax, 2 parts water). I bake the crust, and once it's halfway done I add tomato sauce, broccoli, red onion, bell peppers, tomatoes, and shredded mozzarella cheese I found in the fridge that I think my mom bought.

8 p.m.—I spend the night playing with my cat. He lived in our offices for ten years, but he stopped eating on the weekend when no one was there. My coworker asked if I would adopt him. I'm so happy I did. I fall asleep with him on my chest around 10:30.

DAILY TOTAL: $63.26

| **DAY THREE** |

5:45 a.m.—Coffee and breakfast time! I make two breakfast sandwiches using French bread, egg, and avocado. One for breakfast and one for lunch.

10:26 a.m.—I have to submit my school schedule to my supervisors. Spring semester starts in two weeks, and it will be a bit of a challenge, scheduling-wise. During the fall, I took night classes. This semester, I could only get a microbiology lecture and lab in the mornings. I'll also be taking a Saturday class and an online class. Long days are ahead of me, but I'm determined to do everything I can to get into nursing school.

1:45 p.m.—A friend meets me at work to give me the painting I commissioned her to do of D.'s dog. It came out AWESOME! D. does so much for me, and I've been wanting to do something special for him. I also love supporting my friend's work. **$80**

2:30 p.m.—My iPhone 6 recently died. I really didn't want to dig into my savings for a new phone, but since I now handle social media for work, I decided to get an iPhone 8+ for the camera quality ($219). I also get a screen protector and a case ($76.63). I painfully transfer money from my savings account to my checking. **$251.87**

4:45 p.m.—I text D. that I'm home, and he comes over after work. I surprise him with the painting. He loves it!

6:25 p.m.—We go to dinner at a bar near the arts district. I get the vegetarian chili fries and buffalo mushrooms, and D. gets the burger special. The fries are too much for me, but D. has his eco lunch box, so I'm able to avoid unnecessary takeout waste. **$27.39**

7:03 p.m.—We can't resist ice cream from Salt & Straw. D. treats.

8:42 p.m.—Back to hang out at my place. D. heads home around 10:30. I knock out feeling super-satisfied, if you know what I mean.

DAILY TOTAL: $359.26

| DAY FOUR |

7:15 a.m.—I make coffee and almond butter toast and pack mac and cheese for lunch that my brother's girlfriend brought from Panera. I'm on my way to work by 8.

12:30 p.m.—I've been working nonstop on these presentation proposals and I almost forgot lunch.

2 p.m.—My coworker tells me her husband is out of town this weekend, and I ask if she wants to hang out. She excitedly agrees.

We both started around the same time, and we've gotten really close.

6:20 p.m.—I'm always losing socks. I stop by Target to get a couple packs. I would love to order ethically made ones, but I need socks ASAP and can't wait around for shipping. **$15.89**

7:15 p.m.—I'm feeling under the weather, so I make a veggie noodle soup with gluten-free pasta, veggie stock paste, celery, carrots, potatoes, onion, garlic, salt, and pepper. I top it off with avocado and toasted French bread with Earth Balance. It's so simple, yet incredibly delicious.

9:20 p.m.—I shower, relax, and knock out before I can text D. good night.

DAILY TOTAL: $15.89

| DAY FIVE |

6 a.m.—I wake up feeling much better. I don't know if it was the soup or the fact that I slept really good.

7 a.m.—I make a frozen banana, almond butter, flaxseed, chia seed, and almond milk smoothie. I pour it into my hydroflask and head to work.

10:35 a.m.—I get into an agency vehicle to do a quick work errand. On my way back to the office I stop to get an Americano with almond milk. The barista compliments my hydroflask. **$3.50**

1:30 p.m.—Banners for a project I'm working on arrive. I load up my car and head to the west side. With traffic, it's going to take me too long to go back to work, so I plan on being done once I finish posting the banners.

2:15 p.m.—I hang up the banners and walk around the park for a little while. I grew up riding my bike around here. I feel so nostalgic.

3 p.m.—I'm starving! I didn't pack a lunch because I've been craving Sunny Blue. This place has delicious onigiri! I order the hijiki (seaweed, shiitake mushroom, tofu, and peas), the miso mushroom (my favorite), and the spicy eggplant. **$12**

4:20 p.m.—I stop at a Goodwill on my way home but have no luck today.

5 p.m.—Back home, I warm up my veggie soup and hang out with my nephew and brother most of the night. I love being the cool aunt!

9:30 p.m.—I catch up on the latest episode of *This Is Us*, and for the first time this season, I cry.

DAILY TOTAL: $15.50

| DAY SIX |

7:45 a.m.—I wake up with my cat lying on my chest. I don't want to disturb him, so I lie in bed for almost an hour. Cat mama problems.

8:30 a.m.—I'm freaking starving, so I toast sourdough bread and make a quick raspberry chia seed jam. I also make a banana and peanut butter smoothie.

9:25 a.m.—I saw on Instagram a couple of YouTubers and Instagrammers are having a garage sale I want to check out.

10 a.m.—These people have so much cool stuff! There's a polka-dotted jumpsuit I *really* want, but the girl wants $40 for it. I try to get her to lower the price, but she snarkily says she even regrets saying $40. I'm *not* going to pay $40 for a jumpsuit that has no tags (not that I care about brands) and is well worn. Come on!

10:55 a.m.—I leave the sale with a red bucket bag ($10), sweater ($5), jacket (free), and dress (free). The girls I bought stuff from were really sweet! **$15**

1:15 p.m.—Home. I make grilled zucchini, couscous, and kale, with a ton of garlic for lunch. Can you believe this is the first time I made couscous? Love it!

1:25 p.m.—It's watering day for all my plant babies. I have about fourteen plants and one fiddle-leaf fig tree in my tiny studio. They all seem to be thriving.

6:20 p.m.—I catch an Uber to Union Station ($5) and take the train to Pasadena ($1.75) to visit my work friend. It would cost me $20+ if I took an Uber pool all the way. **$6.75**

7:35 p.m.—My friend picks me up from the station, and we go to My Vegan. We order "chicken" drumsticks to share, basil noodles for me, and a curry noodle soup for her. Everything is *delicious*, and I even have leftovers that I pack in my eco lunch box. She kindly treats me to dinner.

9:08 p.m.—We drive back to her place, drop off our leftovers, and walk over to Stone Brewery. We each get a beer and hang out in the patio talking about married life, work, and family. I pick up the tab. **$19**

10:21 p.m.—We walk to a whiskey bar, grab a drink, and people watch. She picks up the tab.

11:15 p.m.—We walk around Old Town trying to find a cool bar. We end up at Barney's Beanery. I order a Blue Moon, and we hang out on the deck. It's been a while since I went barhopping with a girlfriend. We finish our beers and go downstairs to check out the karaoke. **$8**

12:18 a.m.—I am dying of laughter seeing all these people go up onstage.

1 a.m.—We've had enough, so I get an Uber home. I text D. that I got home safe and knock out. **$7**

DAILY TOTAL: $55.75

DAY SEVEN

7:50 a.m.—Ugh! I didn't want to wake up, and I am certainly hungover. I lie around until it's time to get ready for work.

9:15 a.m.—My little brother drives me since D. will be picking me up. I eat the leftover noodles for breakfast on my way.

9:45 a.m.—Get there an hour early, which gives me plenty of time to prep for today's hike and activity with ten kids and their parents.

11 a.m.—My group arrives. They seem a bit rowdy, but I'm hoping for the best.

12 p.m.—We finished our hike, and it's time for our gardening activity. The parents have been of no help, but I stay professional.

12:45 p.m.—The gardening portion ends, and all the kids go home with potted plants.

1 p.m.—Today is our Naturalist Appreciation lunch. I missed most of it due to the hike, but I still get to enjoy the yummy cauliflower and mushroom tacos.

2 p.m.—I change out of my hiking clothes, and D. picks me up.

2:43 p.m.—We go to Urban Outfitters, and I find some earrings. When I go to buy them, my debit card isn't working. D. offers to pay, but I say no. I take this as a sign to continue staying away from fast fashion.

3 p.m.—I treat D. to ice cream at Salt & Straw. We both get sea salt and caramel. **$10.30**

3:45 p.m.—It's Free-for-All Day! We go to Descanso Gardens. It's our first visit, and we're a bit disappointed. Granted, it is winter, and many of the flowers are dormant. I put D.'s arborist skills to the test by asking what each tree is. We can be very nerdy sometimes, and I love it.

5:55 p.m.—We drive to Highland Park and walk around a bit. We wander into a men's shop. Everything looks incredibly good on D. He gets a shirt for half off, and I find the most perfect-smelling candle by tH & R Collective. **$19.20**

6:45 p.m.—We find a pizza place that has great reviews, but the wait is an hour and we're too hungry. We walk over to Highland Park Bowl and each order a personal pizza. I eat half and save the rest. D. pays.

8:35 p.m.—Back at my place, we relax, watch *Seinfeld*, and cuddle. D. leaves around 11, and I knock out right after I get his "I'm home" text.

DAILY TOTAL: $29.50

| THE BREAKDOWN |

TOTAL SPENT: $539.16

FOOD AND DRINK: $143.45

ENTERTAINMENT: $0

HOME AND HEALTH: $271.07

CLOTHES AND BEAUTY: $30.89

TRANSPORTATION: $13.75

OTHER: $80

| THE FOLLOW-UP |

You converted your parents' garage into a small studio last year. What made you decide to move back home? Was it for financial reasons?
When I decided I wanted to go back to school so I could eventually apply to a nursing program, I knew I had to start saving up to pay for school and the possibility that I might have to cut back to part-time or not work at all. My dad was also pretty sick for a while, and I just couldn't stand being away from home during that time.

How do you feel about being labeled part of the Boomerang Generation? Do you feel bad that you moved home?
Growing up in a Latino household, everyone I knew lived at home during or after college. It isn't frowned upon whatsoever. It doesn't mean you're not successful, lazy, or entitled.

How did you and your parents decide on the $400 rent?
I let my parents decide, and they thought $400 seemed fair. It helps them while also allowing me to save. I've paid some form of rent to my parents since I started working at the age of 17.

What made you decide to go back to school to become a nurse?

When I was younger, I really wanted to be a doctor, but as I got older that idea faded, and the park and outdoor education world found me. Now that I'm 27, I decided that I wanted to start something and finish it! I love people, and I want to help people in a more direct way, so nursing seemed like a good fit. I hope to combine the outdoor world and nursing at some point.

What are the challenges of working full-time and going back to school?

I have two big challenges. (1) Because I work full-time and I also do contract work, I have to be really careful with my time. (2) Although my supervisors know that I'm enrolled in school, they don't know that I'm trying to get into a nursing program. I'm worried that if they find out, they're going to let me go because they'll think I don't care about the work that I'm doing at the present. Which is not true, of course!

This is your second Money Diary. What has surprised you most about doing them?

After my first Money Diary, I realized I spent way too much on coffee. Since then I got a nice little Chemex and make most of my coffee at home. I also noticed that I like to go out to eat a lot. But I'm sure I'm not the only one!

It's curious how we define adulthood. Does it just mean you're over eighteen? Or that you've moved out of your parents' house? (And if so, does that mean the 32 percent of millennials living at home aren't technically grown-ups? That seems absurd.) Often when a diarist notes that she's still on her parents' phone plan, she'll follow up by saying that one day she'll get her own plan and then she'll be a *real* adult. Yet when I was explaining this phenomenon to a friend (who is a mother and homeowner), she admitted that she's still on her parents' plan. And she's definitely an adult. When I asked Shannon McLay of Financial Gym if she's noticed this trend with her clients, she says she actually recommends it!

In the grand scheme of things, $40 or $60 a month to cover your phone bill isn't much. It's a simple fact that a family phone plan is more cost-effective than an individual one—for everyone involved. And for some women, it's a big relief to have that small cost taken care of. "I'm fresh out of college and in grad school, so it's really nice to have one less bill to worry about," said Ally, 22, who makes $43,000. "I know I should be paying my own way, but it's the only financial support my parents give me right now, so I'll let it slide for a little while longer."

But is there a line young women can cross where they're accepting too much financial help from their parents? This is an area where it's so easy to judge others whose experiences don't match our own. We might roll our eyes at those who rely on a family plan but don't think much about women who are still on their parents' health insurance policy (which is likely a much higher monthly expense).

Then there are women whose parents help them buy a home, give them a monthly allowance, or set them up with a trust fund. As the expenses get bigger, the judgment gets more intense, and we begin to think those women should feel guilty for accepting parental support. Brooke, 27, pushes back on this notion. She lives in a one-bedroom apartment in Brooklyn that her mother bought for her, and she doesn't feel bad about it. There's no way she could afford the expense on her $45,000 salary, so she pays $1,000 of the $1,600 monthly mortgage payment.

"If you had kids, why *not* try to help?" she says. "It seems like a weird attitude to say, 'Now you're an adult, so your parents are no longer involved in your life financially.' The apartment seemed like a wise decision and benefits everyone in the long term."

A survey by Pew Research Center suggests that our parents find it rewarding to provide financial support.[4] You don't want to hurt their feelings, right? But more seriously, can we drop the judgment around parental support? Maybe I feel defensive about this topic as someone who still relies on my mom and dad (for free child care) even as I'm pushing my late thirties.

Every family is different, and each one needs to make its own financial decisions. As long as you're not Mona-Lisa Saperstein— all *"Money, please"*—it's okay if you get support from your mom and dad. Just remember to check your privilege and say thank you every once in a while. And hopefully pay it forward one day.

THIS IS A GOOD TIME TO:

Send a thank-you note to your parents—or whoever supported you financially from birth to eighteen and beyond.

While you're at it, save $26
Total saved so far: $351

The conversations I have with my sixty-something parents about money range from very specific (how much I make) to fairly vague (how much I have in my savings account), but one common thread is that though I'm pretty open with them about *my* money, I don't know very much about their financial situation.

As they get older, I realize we're probably overdue to have some serious conversations about money. From time to time, my mom will make an offhand mention of their wills, where all her account info is hidden, etc., but I only half listen because I like to believe that my parents will live forever. So when I sat down to chat with Barbara Ginty, I was keen to get her insights into the kinds of questions I should be asking my parents about their money.

Barbara acknowledges these can be emotional conversations but says it's crucial to have them when everyone is healthy. She's had a number of clients call her for help with things such as power of attorney when it's too late. "When your mom is in hospice care, you want to be by her side," Barbara says, "not sitting in a hospital cafeteria trying to figure out how you're going to pay her medical bills."

Here are the questions you should be asking your parents so you never, ever have to live through that kind of ordeal.

1. Do you have a current will?
Let's start with the will. In theory, your parents had wills drawn up when you were just a kid, and they determined who would

take care of you and your siblings should they die. But have they updated them since you graduated from high school? If not, it's definitely time to revise them.

2. Do you have a health care proxy and a power of attorney?

A **health care proxy** is a legal document that allows you to appoint another person (or persons) to make health care decisions for you if you are unable to.

A **power of attorney** is a legal document that allows you (the "principal") to appoint another person ("agent") to act on your behalf in regard to private, business, or legal affairs.

There are many types of powers of attorney, and the differences between them primarily have to do with when the POA goes into effect and how long it lasts:

1. **Conventional power of attorney:** Goes into effect as soon as the agent signs the document and ends when the principal becomes incapacitated.

2. **Durable power of attorney:** Goes into effect when the document is signed, and ends only if the principal decides to cancel it. Allows agents to maintain POA even if the principal becomes incapacitated.

3. **Springing power of attorney:** Begins only when a certain event occurs, such as if the principal becomes incapacitated.

Health care proxies and powers of attorney should be updated when your parents update their wills. These legal documents vary from state to state, so it's best to consult an attorney for the specifics.

You'll want to ask a few follow-up questions as well: If your parents have designated you and your sibling(s) as proxies, can you make decisions separately or will you need to act together? If a parent gets sick, who will manage their bills? Is there a joint family account you can access? Or will you need to use the power of attorney to gain access? This conversation is even more important if your parent is single.

Barbara notes that many people think that since they have power of attorney, they can just walk into a bank and access the accounts they need. This is not usually the case. In some states, the POA might need to be recertified by an attorney or the bank might require you to fill out certain paperwork. This can take anywhere from a few business days to a few weeks. Planning ahead and being clear on your state laws can make things much easier.

3. Do you have long-term care insurance?

The national average cost of a private room in a nursing home is a shocking $250 a day ($92,400 a year).[5] The US government estimates that 70 percent of Americans over sixty-five will need some form of long-term care.[6]

Long-term care insurance can be prohibitively expensive if you purchase it once you've reached retirement age, so if your parents don't have a policy, you'll want to discuss other ways you might cover nursing home expenses should they need it. This is especially important if they own their home—more on that below—or have limited retirement savings.

Some life insurance policies have a long-term care rider, which can either be used to cover long-term care (i.e., living in a nursing home) or be paid out as a death benefit.

4. Do you own your home outright? How much mortgage do you have remaining?

If your parents own their home, it's important to consider how much they still owe on the mortgage. If they leave the house to you, you'll have to continue making mortgage and homeowners' association/maintenance payments until you sell it.

Also, if your parents spend extended time in a nursing home and deplete their assets, there's a chance their home was used to pay for the the long-term care. In that case the state can put a lien on the home, making it difficult for you to sell. Make sure you know how the nursing home is being paid (whether that's something your parents cover or a cost you help with).

5. What accounts should I know about, and where do you keep the info?
Remember in chapter 1, when I made you write down all your account info in one place along with your passwords? Your parents should do the same thing and then tell you (and your siblings) where they keep that information.

6. Have you considered a living will?
A living will is a legal document that states what actions need to be taken should a person become incapacitated. Talking about this is perhaps one of the most stressful conversations you can have with your parents, but it's crucial. Everyone in the family should be involved so there's no confusion.

7. Can you afford retirement?
A few years ago, the writer Neal Gabler wrote a compelling piece for The Atlantic in which he talked about liquidating his 401(k) to pay for his daughter's wedding.[7]

We talked a little bit about privilege earlier in this chapter, but I wonder if Gabler's daughter knew the true cost of her wedding. A number of articles have been published about how baby boomers aren't saving enough for retirement[8]—in part because they choose to pay for their children's college tuition rather than save for themselves.[9] Check in with your parents to make sure they're on track for retirement—especially if they're still helping you out (see that $40 a month you're not paying them back for your phone bill).

8. Where do you want to live as you get older?
You plan on living in a small apartment in the middle of a city for the rest of your life, but your mom thinks you'll be moving home when she's too old to care for herself. Or maybe you have dreams of buying your childhood home *one day*, but your parents are ready to unload it *now*. It's better to have conversations about these expectations before you have to make hard decisions during an already stressful time.

9. Have you made any funeral arrangements?
A few years ago, my friend Elaine lost her father very suddenly. Her parents were divorced, her father didn't leave behind much of an estate, and she had to organize and pay for the funeral herself. That was before she was married or had kids, and she commented after the fact that dealing with her dad's funeral arrangements was the first time she had felt like an adult. Losing a parent is hard enough without trying to figure out how you can afford to pay for a funeral, which, according to the National Funeral Directors Association, can cost upward of $7,000.[10]

It can seem incredibly morbid to prepay for your funeral and grave site, but this is an example of a time when you shouldn't let your emotions prevent you from making smart financial decisions. And there are ways to bring levity to a sad conversation. Don't just talk about the financial aspects but about what kind of event you want the funeral to be. Me, personally? I'd like everyone to go to a bar, blast '90s pop hits, drink PBR, and end the evening with tequila shots in my honor. I hope everyone wakes up with a hangover.

"AS I'VE GOTTEN MORE GENEROUS . . . THEY THINK OF ME AS AN ATM"

Not all millennials are mooching off their parents—in fact, a 2015 survey suggests that more than 20 percent of millennials help support their mom and dad.[11]

Jessica Chou chatted with a money diarist from LA who makes $500,000 a year—a cool $1.25 million when combined with her husband—and has a line item in her budget to help her extended family. Unfortunately, that privilege has led to some unexpected consequences.

Would you say you're the most successful person in your family?

I have both the blessing and the curse of making the most money, and I have a lot of obligation and responsibility along with that. I definitely wish someone else outearned me to take the pressure off me. But I still hope for my siblings that their success is coming.

Have your family-related spending habits changed over time?

Early on, I'd send my grandma a little extra money on a holiday, or I'd buy my mom a pair of shoes if we were out together. It was $50 here and there. Now it's like, "Oh, you want to go to Jamaica? Okay, I'll pay for the airfare." My aunt needed to have her hip replaced and couldn't afford it, so we paid for her surgery. Today, I spent $10,000 to have my parents' kitchen redone after a flood. I couldn't have done that five years ago, but today I can with relative ease.

I have gotten a bit more generous as we've gotten more afflu-ent, but I would also say we don't live like we make that kind of money. We definitely have a nice life, don't get me wrong, but we still save 30 to 35 percent of our income.

How much do you spend on your family a year?

I think the line item right now is $15,000 for the year—it's just a bucket of money I tap into. I budgeted for it because it became a recurring part of what we were spending, especially as my parents and my husband's parents have gotten older.

I have to balance it, because at a certain point my family expects it. Yesterday, my dad called because he needed $3,000 to buy something. He said he would pay me back in a couple of days. I said no because I didn't have time to get to the bank to transfer the money. My comment to him was "You know, I don't like being your first call."

As I've gotten more generous and they perceive that I have more money, they think of me as an ATM. We go out to eat, and they expect me to pay. I wish they'd do the reach every once in a while or offer to pay the tip, you know?

Has your financial success ever caused a conflict with your family?

I'm trying to avoid the scenario where money causes a rift in the family. There have been times where it's broken down. It happens when I lend people money and they can't pay it back. They just stop communicating with me and start avoiding me.

I don't lend people money anymore. If you ask for money and I give it to you, I just give it to you. I've had to do that to ensure that I don't lose relationships over it.

Has it gotten better?

I've drawn more boundaries. I say no a lot more than I did before. I also have a new rule: if someone asks me for money, I say fine, I'll give this to you today, but you can't ask me again for another year. If it's something for your kids, for school, or health, that's fine. But you wanting a new iPhone is not grounds to call me for money.

When was the first time you had to say no?

My dad got into a habit where every time he called me he was asking me for $500 or $1,000. A lot of times, he paid me back, but he was just using me as an ATM. He's always played it paycheck to paycheck, and he never has a reserve for things. So when he was short, he would just call me. It got to a point where I was interrupting my workday to run to the bank. Finally, I said, "No, enough is enough, you can't ask me anymore." He said, "But I'm paying you back," and I said, "Yeah, but you're abusing me, too." I told him not to ask me for money for a year, and he ultimately respected it. That's when I made the once-a-year rule. And it stopped the flood of calls.

Do you have any exceptions?

If it's a medical issue or something for a kid, then there's no need to pay me back. But at one point I was getting calls from everyone—my dad, my mom, my sister, and my brother. I felt completely abused. And I said to them, you don't realize that you're not the only one calling me. I just want six months where I don't have to think every time you call, you're going to ask for money.

Do you think your family understands your point of view now that you've started to set boundaries?

I don't think they get it at all. I think this is true for everyone in my life. I was on a trip with my girlfriends once, and we were talking about our jobs. I said to them, "Oh, can I complain about money?" And they said, "No, you don't get to complain about money because you make a lot." There's this idea that because you're successful you can't complain about your success or you can't have an issue with your success or you can't say life is hard.

The thing is, my husband and I, we're still building wealth. This is all new. Yes, we make a lot of money, but we're not wealthy yet. This could stop. It's not guaranteed to be here forever, so we have to be mindful and protective of it.

FINANCIAL CHALLENGE

Talk to Your Parents About Their Finances

TIME: *~1 hour (maybe more, don't rush this)*
TOOLS: *Your parents! And maybe a notebook/laptop to take notes and contact info for an estate attorney*

Earlier, I gave you nine questions to ask your parents about their financial situation and retirement plans. Now it's time for you to ask them.

I know, I know. I do realize that I keep making you have really awkward conversations with everyone you know. And by bringing up money with your parents, there's a good chance they'll start asking you about your own finances. That's fair, but today, let's keep them on track.

I think there's also some fear that talking about money with your mom and dad—specifically what to do with their money when they become sick and/or die—can feel superweird, almost like you're trying to suss out how much you stand to inherit one day.

I'm just going to make a small suggestion: frame the conversation so it's about them, not you. You're not asking them about funeral plans or long-term care because you don't want to shoulder that financial burden one day but because you want to make sure you're by their side through the bad stuff and not, as Barbara pointed out earlier, sitting in a hospital cafeteria with a financial planner trying to pay the bills. Because that's just a sad picture for everyone.

As with every awkward conversation, timing is key. Maybe don't bring this up during a celebratory dinner. And if you do it over drinks, this is one time you should most definitely pick up the tab.

While you're at it, save $27
Total saved so far: $378

CHAPTER 9

Wealth & Money
(Or How Do I Get Rich?)

I'd like to be rich one day. Not Oprah rich but secure enough that I can stay in nice hotels, buy designer dresses, and pay for my kid's college education. I'm okay working my butt off to make a lot of money. Though I love an overnight success story, I recognize there's usually considerable behind-the-scenes hustle (and luck) to make that kind of wealth a reality.

There's a lot of complicated feelings around women earning the big bucks. Even now, in a progressive city like New York, it's hard to escape the heteronormative fairy tale that men are supposed to make money, while women raise children. It doesn't help that there's a wage gap, that the language around investing is aggressively male, and that few men have access to paid paternity leave. It's okay for women to desire wealth, but society makes us think that we're not supposed to be the sole person responsible for earning it. That kind of independence threatens to upend the balance of power that's so entrenched in our way of thinking about gender roles.

Enough. It's okay to bring home your own goddamn bacon.

In this chapter, we'll explore what it takes to get rich. Saving for your future isn't rocket science, but it does require discipline, prioritizing, hard work, and a lot of luck. Having the right tools makes it more manageable. And though you might not have a Birkin bag in time for your birthday, you could certainly have one before they go out of style. (Kidding. Like they would ever go out of style.)

A Week in Atlanta, GA, on a **$230,000** Salary

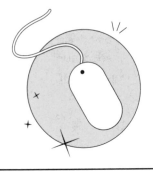

Savings Account Balance:
$30,000
Emergency Savings Contribution: $500/paycheck
General Savings Contribution:
$200/paycheck

 HOUSING:
Mortgage: $3,200
(includes taxes and insurance; my fiancé and I split this 50/50.)
Utilities: $531 (split with fiancé)
Phone: $120
Housekeeper: $88 every other week (split with fiancé)

 OCCUPATION: Sales executive
INDUSTRY: Software
AGE: 31
LOCATION: Atlanta, GA
ANNUAL SALARY: $230,000
PAYCHECK AMOUNT (TWICE A MONTH): $2,700 + quarterly commission bonuses, usually around $20,000 per quarter

FIANCÉ'S INDUSTRY:
Consulting
FIANCÉ'S ANNUAL SALARY: $125,000

 TRANSPORTATION:
Car Payment: $250
(on a $13,000 car loan)
Car Insurance: $75

 HEALTH & SELF-CARE:
Health Insurance: $20/paycheck
HSA: $100/paycheck
Gym: $169
Therapist: $275

 GENERAL FINANCIAL INFORMATION:
Checking Account Balance:
$3,500

SUBSCRIPTIONS:
Amazon Fresh: $14.99
Netflix/HBO Go: $24.99 (We don't have cable.)

 RETIREMENT:
401(k) Contribution: $350/paycheck + $5,600 every bonus

 DEBT:
Student Loan Debt
Total: $55,000
Student Loan Payment: $342

DAY ONE

7:30 a.m.—Wake up. My 100-year-old house is freezing, and it takes a ton of willpower to get out of bed. Let the dogs out, and start coffee for myself and my fiancé, M.

8 a.m.—Still dragging. M. made a gluten-free peanut butter bagel, but he hated it so I ate it instead! Grabbed an apple on my way out the door to work.

12 p.m.—Team lunch today (Indian food!), and my boss expensed it. Doesn't really matter, though, since we get breakfast and lunch for free. Saved the leftovers for M.

12:30 p.m.—Sign the contract for the photographer for our wedding brunch. She's quite expensive ($300 an hour with a three-hour minimum), but this is the only wedding event my grandparents will be able to attend, and it's important to me to get good pictures. I put it on my SPG Amex to get the extra points (trying to save up for our honeymoon!). **$450**

3:35 p.m.—I'm hunting for a pair of leather boots. I'd LOVE a Jimmy Choo pair but can't bring myself to spend that much. Find a Frye pair on Tradesy for about $165, which I could cover with credits from things I've sold. Resolve not to purchase until I go to Frye to make sure they fit.

5 p.m.—Go to a workout class. I spend $169 a month on an unlimited pass, so I try to go at least ten times to make it worthwhile. But this is the first time I've been this month. Fail.

6:30 p.m.—Really wanted to order from the Vietnamese place close to home as I'm completely wiped. However, we really went overboard eating out last week, so I'm trying to pull back for the next couple of weeks. Make pasta with pesto and a fried egg.

7:30 p.m.—Settle in to watch *Little Women* with my dogs. Decide to hit the sack early so I can get up a bit earlier in the morning.

DAILY TOTAL: $450

DAY TWO

6:21 a.m.—Forgot to set my alarm, but still manage to wake up an hour early. Sadly, waste this extra time reading emails and the news.

7:45 a.m.—Bagel from M. I'm still late getting out the door and barely make my 9:30 meeting.

12 p.m.—Grab Chinese food in the office cafeteria.

1 p.m.—Head home early to let dogs out and work from home.

2:15 p.m.—Check to see when my year-end bonus is coming in. It's a week earlier than I expected! I mentally start making plans for the $42,000 bonus (pretax). I want to put the bulk of it toward student loans, but I also want to repaint my kitchen cabinets (probably about $1,600). And Christmas gifts, of course. I also noticed that a random bonus I wasn't expecting came through last week. I usually put the bulk of my bonus into my 401(k), which is why I missed it. This extra bump means I hit the $18,000 limit a bit earlier than I anticipated, so turn off my contributions for the rest of the year.

4:38 p.m.—Read an interesting review of the book *The Gilded Years*, and buy on Kindle **$8.99**

5 p.m.—Meet with a security consultant. There's been a rash of burglaries in my still-gentrifying neighborhood, so I want to make sure the house is well protected. Decide to go whole hog, and pay him a security deposit. **$500**

6:30 p.m.—*Really* wanted Vietnamese again but resisted and made do with pasta.

DAILY TOTAL: $508.99

DAY THREE

6 a.m.—We're out of the "good" coffee, and I have to drink really overpowering Bourbon-flavored coffee. I scrounge up some toast and an apple.

7 a.m.—I use a service in Atlanta that sends stylists to your house for blowouts. I know it sounds indulgent, but it's the most efficient option. Plus, it's about the same price as going to the salon, and I *have* to get my hair done before my business trip. I work in software sales and deal with a lot of old-school men, so it's really important that I look polished in my meetings. Sadly, my naturally curly hair isn't seen as "professional" in my line of work. **$65**

10:30 a.m.—Uber to the airport. **$15** (expensed)

11 a.m.—I always buy the exact same things when I travel: two trashy magazines and a bottle of sparkling water. I avoid Chick-fil-A and grab a cup of carrots and hummus. **$25**

1:30 p.m.—Land and head straight to the hotel to scarf down lunch before afternoon meetings. Get a terrible fish sandwich at the hotel restaurant. **$17** (expensed)

2:30 p.m.—Uber to meetings. **$12** (expensed)

5:30 p.m.—Meetings over! I still have a ton of work to do, but craving pasta, so Uber Eats it is! **$26** (expensed)

6 p.m.—I order M.'s wedding ring. Luckily, he's not into jewelry, so we're going with a nontraditional wood ring that I found on Etsy. **$40**

8:30 p.m.—To bed early again, so I can finish up work in the morning.

DAILY TOTAL: $130

| DAY FOUR |

5 a.m.—Damn the alarm clock.

6:45 a.m.—Room service breakfast arrives—fried eggs, bacon, and potatoes with coffee. Hallelujah! **$28** (expensed)

8 a.m.—I am obsessive about checking our accounts on Mint. My S.O. and I have one shared checking account where we deposit money each month for our mortgage and house bills, and a joint emergency savings account for the inevitable disasters like squirrels in the attic (*so* fun), but everything else is separate. Once a week, I scrutinize our spending. We've spent almost $1,500 on food this month. *Yikes.* Definitely need to pull waaay back.

9 a.m.—I've been using the app Debitize to automatically withdraw money from my checking account when I use my credit card. In the past, I strictly used a debit card for daily purchases, since I had a pretty bad history of keeping track of my spending on credit cards. But since I'm trying to rack up points for my honeymoon, it's definitely better to do my day-to-day spending on my credit cards to get points, as long as I can stay on top of paying it all off. Debitize makes it supereasy.

9:15 a.m.—Bought a college sweatshirt from my alma mater for my nephew (he asked!), as well as some books for my brother and nephew for Christmas. **$116**

9:30 a.m.—Uber to my first meeting. **$6** (expensed)

9:45 a.m.—Get to my meeting superearly, so I pop into CVS to pick up some travel-sized toiletries. **$20**

9:50 a.m.—Stop in a coffee shop to work before my meetings. Don't like to overcaffeinate so order a matcha latte. **$6** (expensed)

11:30 a.m.—Make a pit stop in

between meetings for an excellent dollar slice. **$2** (expensed)

5 p.m.—Whew! Day of meetings finally over. Have a few minutes back at my hotel to decompress before a client dinner tonight. Got an email from the painter saying the price will double if I use two colors for the cabinets ($2,900). WTF.

6 p.m.—Fancy client dinner at a tapas restaurant. I used to be really into picking the absolute best restaurants for client dinners and never really minded staying out all hours of the night. These days, I try to keep everything to under two hours and two drinks max. Still, the food is amazing and my clients are actually pretty cool people. My boss picked up the tab.

8:30 p.m.—Boss called an Uber for us to get back to the hotel. I'm wiped, which feels really lame since it's only 8:30. To be fair, I've been working since 5 a.m. and forced social interactions completely exhaust me emotionally. Climb into bed so I can get up early to do work before *more* client meetings

DAILY TOTAL: $136

6 a.m.—Wake up and start working. Slightly annoyed because I can't get ahold of room service right away. **$29** (expensed)

7:30 a.m.—It's BONUS DAY! I'm almost scared to look at my bank account. This will be the biggest bonus check I've ever gotten: $42,000 before taxes. I'm in sales, so a big chunk of my take-home pay comes in the form of quarterly commission bonuses. This can be good and bad, but luckily last quarter was very good. I immediately put $5,600 into my 401(k) so I can max out before the end of the year. After that and taxes, I have about $20,000. I plan to put $15,000 toward my student loans, pay off my credit card balance of about $3,000, and the other $2,000 will pay for my kitchen cabinets.

9 a.m.—Headed to another day of meetings.

9:15 a.m.—Turns out the exec I was supposed to meet with had a conflict, so meeting canceled.

11 a.m.—At the airport, praying to get a seat on an earlier flight. Buy my customary magazines and water, plus a sandwich. **$20**

11:30 a.m.—Success! Made the flight!

2 p.m.—Uber home. **$16** (expensed)

5:30 p.m.—Try to knock out some more Christmas shopping. Get gifts for M., my nephew, my sister-in-law, and my future brother-in-law. I keep track of all of the gifts on a spreadsheet to make sure I don't go too over budget, but honestly Christmas is my favorite holiday. I take a lot of pride in thinking carefully about the gifts I get people and aim to buy presents they'd never buy for themselves. I have a particular soft spot for my family because I know we do a lot better than them financially, so I like to give them nice things for Christmas. **$640**

6 p.m.—Giving in to weeklong Vietnamese craving. **$26**

7:30 p.m.—Zonked out on the sofa.

DAILY TOTAL: $686

| DAY SIX |

7 a.m.—We are totally out of coffee, so I head down the block to get a couple of cups to go. Also pick up a bagel for M. **$6**

9 a.m.—Finally make it to another workout class. Not quite as brutal as Monday's, but I'm still woefully out of shape.

10 a.m.—I'm disgusting after my workout, but the paint store is on the way home, so I make a stop. Order three samples. **$22**

10:30 a.m.—Quick stop at home.

10:45 a.m.—Sitting in line at McDonald's. I actually really hate fast food and constantly nag M. about his love of processed food. I thought it would be faster than making a sandwich at home but ended up having to wait for my order. Ugh. **$4**

11:30 a.m.—Head to Anthropologie and BHLDN. I generally spend too much money at Anthro, and now that I'm planning my wedding, it's gotten even worse. I originally picked out a shawl for $180 on BHLDN, but it's back-ordered, so I need to find a replacement ASAP, as we'll be outdoors in the middle of winter for this wedding brunch. I'm finding few options that match the classic, vintage look of my dress. Finally, in distress, I find a faux fur stole that honestly looks terrible, but I buy it just in case the rest of my shopping is completely fruitless. Also throw in a sparkly headband from BHLDN because I'm a magpie. **$300**

12:45 p.m.—I find a great plaid shawl at J. Crew that makes my preppy heart sing. **$79**

1:15 p.m.—Stop by Banana to shop for M. He couldn't care less about what he wears, but I figure it wouldn't hurt for him to look nice for our pictures. Everything at Banana is 50 percent off (who buys full price at Banana?). Pick out a pair of pants, a button-up, and a sweater, plus another plaid shawl (maybe this one will work better than the J. Crew one?). **$179**

1:45 p.m.—Make a last-minute detour to Trashy Diva. I was originally hoping to find a petticoat to go under my dress, but they stopped selling them. I find a great sparkly headband for literally 1/10th the price of the one from BHLDN. **$12**

2 p.m.—Dash home to shower and change before the dinner party. It's kind of a big deal since it's with M.'s boss. Try to look relatively well put together.

3 p.m.—Dinner party is fine. It's weird: it feels so adult, but in my mind, I should still be at the kids' table. Make small talk and do the whole "What do you do? Where did you go to school? Do you know so-and-so?" Ivy League roulette, which I hate. Drink too much wine.

8:30 p.m.—Bail on plans to go out with my friend because I'm supertired. End up watching old episodes of *The West Wing* with M.

9 p.m.—Try on my purchases from today (I hate store dressing rooms). End up texting pictures to my mom, and we both agree the Banana Republic shawl is the winner, so I'll return the items from BHLDN and J. Crew.

DAILY TOTAL: $602

DAY SEVEN

6 a.m.—Wake up early. Use this sudden burst of energy to clean the house while M. sleeps.

8:30 a.m.—M. finally is up, so we go out for brunch. He picks up the tab.

10 a.m.—We need a GPS tracker for one of our dogs, so we head over to the pet store. They don't have any in stock, so we have to order online. We spend *waaay* too much money on our dogs; it's embarrassing.

10:30 a.m.—Pop into Home Depot to check out the Christmas lights.

We browse a bit, but they don't have the display we wanted, so we leave empty-handed. I'm also PMSing, so I got supercrabby. Probably 80 percent of the fights in my relationship have started in Home Depot.

11:30 a.m.—While M. stops by the grocery store, I pop into T.J.Maxx. I love a good discount, and T.J.Maxx is like my crack. I pick up a gift for my brother and a few stocking stuffers. **$123**

1 p.m.—Meet a girlfriend for lunch. The restaurant is superpacked, so we get lattes and window-shop. I love our get-togethers because we can discuss work challenges and gossip. Lots of self-care going on post–Home Depot meltdown. **$16**

1:30 p.m.—Return ill-advised accessories to BHLDN and feel supervindicated and $300 richer.

2 p.m.—Wander into an amazing flower shop (seriously dreamy) and decide to get my mom a flower-arranging class for Christmas. **$150**

2:15 p.m.—Return plaid shawl to J. Crew.

3 p.m.—Head to the paint store to pick up my samples, though I'm wondering if now is the best time to drop $2,000 on upgrades?

3:30 p.m.—Stop by the grocery store to get extra ingredients for chili (sour cream and cheese). I also get some eggs. **$16**

3:45 p.m.—My sister-in-law calls. I've been trying to arrange time to hang out with my nephew, and they are finally free.

4:15 p.m.—Nephew in tow, I head back to my house. I don't know how it happens, but my weekends just fly by with tons of errands, etc.

4:45 p.m.—We spend some quality time putting up Christmas decorations. I also bribe him with hot chocolate and marshmallows, so he'll like me more than M.—who's basically a big kid.

5:30 p.m.—Made amazing chili and beer bread from Trader Joe's.

9 p.m.—After watching *Sing* with my nephew, we take him home and hit the sack.

DAILY TOTAL: $305

| THE BREAKDOWN |

TOTAL SPENT: $2,817.99

FOOD AND DRINK: $113

ENTERTAINMENT: $8.99

HOME AND HEALTH: $522

CLOTHES AND BEAUTY: $695

TRANSPORTATION: $0

OTHER: $1,479

| THE FOLLOW-UP |

You earn a big salary for someone so young. Was there a moment when you hit a certain salary that it felt monumental?

It felt like a big accomplishment when I first made over $100,000. I was pretty young, 25 or 26. I remember, like, telling my friend, "Oh my gosh, this is how much money I made last year," and she was, like, "Me, too!" I think we both thought hitting that six-figure mark was something that would happen later in our careers. We were both pleasantly surprised, like, *Oh, okay. Okay, I can do this.*

Who do you rely on for financial advice?

I have a couple of really good girlfriends who I talk with about my finances and my financial goals. We'll talk about our salaries or how much money to expect with a certain promotion or how much to negotiate for. We want to help each other out—we're not competitive with each other at all.

Do you talk with your family about your salary?
Not really. It's not that I feel uncomfortable, we just don't talk about it. It wasn't something that my parents talked about with me growing up, and they don't ask now. They know I make good money, but they don't know how much.

How do you and your fiancé manage your money?
We talk about finances quite a bit, but it's usually me initiating the conversation. I'm definitely more of the financial geek in our relationship. My fiancé's kind of hands off, he's just, like, "Tell me how much I need to save," and that's it. So I'm the one who manages the details.

I like stuff. I like champagne flutes and tiny tumblers; kitchen gadgets and tablecloths. I like party dresses and crisp blazers. I'm a born consumer, and often the idea of buying something comes with the thought that it will make me a better person. These high heels will confirm to the world that I'm an adult. This red lipstick will make me look sexy. This clever organizer will solve my messy desk problem.

But there are two things that temper my urge to buy: (1) wanting a home that's not overrun with clutter and (2) wanting a high balance in my bank accounts.

I also realize the lipstick and heels and organizer won't make me a better person, and I definitely don't *need* them. Buying them now might prevent me from getting something I really want in the future.

That's really what we're talking about here: the money you want and need for future you versus the money you want to spend right this minute. (Note: we're not necessarily talking about "retirement age" you; it could be "next year" you.) It might be difficult to imagine a time when you will have disposable income that you can earmark for long-term goals, let alone extra cash to spend on whatever. Maybe you make a low salary, or you have a lot of student loan debt. Maybe you live in a city with a high cost of living. It's easy to make excuses why you can't save anything.

Of course, some of those excuses are really good (all that student loan debt) and others are arguably not so good (Zara had a sale). I promised that I wouldn't give you shit if you spent all your money on lattes. But *you* might give a shit about all the money you're spending on lattes once you start thinking about how a $5-a-day habit can add up to $1,825 over the course of a year. You might want to earmark that money for something else. My hope is that you will become more conscious about where your cash is going, and making some savings goals can help make money management less painful.

There's joy to be found in planning for your future, so let's take a minute to daydream about how you might spend the money you're saving. Yes, having a fully funded emergency account is crucial (see chapter 4), but let's talk about the other stuff. Maybe you want a house and a kid. Maybe your goal is to open your own business or travel the world. Maybe your dream is even more elaborate.

I talked a little bit about future Lindsey in the intro. She takes nice vacations, is paying for her kid's college education, and indulges in the occasional designer dress. She's a 401(k) millionaire, so she can work as much or as little as she wants when she reaches retirement age. She also has enough cash on hand to move to LA with future Ken and buy a little Hollywood Hills bungalow with an avocado tree in the backyard.

Right now, I'm working to achieve these goals, and sometimes that means short-term sacrifices. Of course, reaching your financial goals isn't all about savings—you also need to be investing smartly. We'll explore how later in this chapter.

What are your goals? What are you doing to achieve them? For every practical goal (retirement fund) try to come up with one that gets you excited: a puppy, a trip, a beach house (dare to dream!). It's so important to have that balance so you stay motivated on the days when skipping that latte stings the most.

Write down your savings goals. It might seem a little cheesy, but it can also be highly motivating. And by actually writing them down, you can begin to prioritize your spending and saving to make them a reality.

While you're at it, save $28
Total saved so far: $406

I've been investing some chunk of my salary for retirement for the past thirteen years, and right now I'm setting aside 10 percent every pay period. It sounds like a lot, but is it enough? I know I'm not alone in my concerns about retirement savings. It's confusing. How do these accounts work? How should I invest my money? Should I have both a 401(k) and a Roth IRA? What the hell is matching?

But confusion is not an excuse for inaction. And yeah, it's not the same instant gratification as a really nice dinner out with friends, but with some careful planning, you can save for the future and still have fun.

Maybe the most exciting part of retirement funds is when you think about how much money you'll make if you start investing in your 401(k) right this minute.

Consider this:

You're 28.

You make $50,000 per year.

Your company matches 100 percent of the first 6 percent of your salary that you deposit into a 401(k).

Your portfolio will have an 8 percent annual growth over the course of your lifetime.*

*This is just a projection based on the past one hundred years of the US mar-

Option 1: You contribute 6 percent of your salary to max your employer match (you contribute $3,000, and your employer contributes $3,000).

At 65, you will have $1,218,421.92.

Option 2: You contribute the maximum to your 401(k) (which as of this writing was $18,500), and the first 6 percent is matched dollar for dollar by your employer for a total of $21,500 a year.

At 65, you will have $4,264,476.72.

Boom! You're a freaking 401(k) millionaire!

Even if your employer isn't matching your contribution, if you invest 6 percent of your salary into your 401(k), you'll have more than $600,000 by the time you hit 65. That's assuming you never get a raise. (And if you've been reading this book, you'll definitely get a raise.)

Some of you with student loan debt might think you can't save for the future while you're still paying for the past. I'm not going to let you make that excuse anymore. Contributing to a retirement account should be a priority, even if it's just a little bit each month, especially if your employer offers a match. After all, $3,000 a year is just a little more than $8 a day.

Not convinced you need to start saving *right this minute*? Priya Malani provided these numbers to show how crucial it is. Imagine that your goal is to save $1 million by the time you turn 65.

If you start at 25, you need to save $3,860.17 a year to hit your goal.

---

kets. But every portfolio is different, and no financial adviser should promise you a certain rate of return.

If you start at 35, you need to save $8,827.45 a year to make the same amount.

That's 228 percent more!

Below we try to answer all your retirement account–related questions. If you get bored, take a page from my playbook and spend a little time looking at real estate in your dream retirement location (two words: avocado tree). Just think of it as a preview of your life after all those years of hard work. The first piña colada is on my future self.

What is a 401(k) anyway?

Defined contribution plans—401(k), Roth 401(k), and 403(b) (retirement accounts for the nonprofit sector)—are savings accounts offered by your employer so you can make contributions to save for your future. 401(k) and 403(b) plans are "qualified," meaning the money you put into the account is not taxed as part of your income but is taxed when you make withdrawals in retirement. In the case of a Roth 401(k), any money you put into the account is taxed up front but free from federal taxation when you make withdrawals in retirement.

It's important to note the money you save in your company-sponsored plan cannot be accessed without a penalty until you turn 59½ years old. The law was created this way so you won't tap those funds before retirement. There are certain exceptions, but you should consider this money off-limits. If you try to borrow from your account early, you might be jeopardizing your financial security at retirement—not to mention that you will have to pay a big fine.

What does "before taxes" mean, and why should I care?

Priya provided a simple equation to show how you can make more money by contributing to your 401(k).

Say you make $50,000 a year and are in a 25 percent tax bracket. (You can figure out your tax bracket by going to the IRS website.) If you don't contribute to your 401(k), your entire salary of $50,000 is taxable, so you'll pay $12,500 in taxes ($50,000 x .25).

If you contribute 10 percent to your 401(k), or $5,000, you can subtract that 10 percent from your total salary:

$50,000 - $5,000 = $45,000

Which means you'll pay taxes on only $45,000 of your income:

$45,000 x .25 = $11,250

You get to keep an additional $1,250 in your pocket (or, ahem, bank account) each year.

What's the difference between a 401(k) and a Roth 401(k)?
With a Roth 401(k) you pay taxes now, not in the future when you start withdrawing from the account. If you make $50,000 and have elected to make contributions only to your Roth 401(k), your entire $50,000 salary would be taxed first (at 25 percent), and then your contribution is moved to your Roth account. Sure, there's no obvious up-front benefit, but, as Priya points out, you won't have to pay *any* taxes on the money when you withdraw it in retirement (and the money should grow year over year).

Priya advises her clients to do a 50/50 split between a 401(k) and a Roth 401(k) if both are offered by your employer, to be partially protected against higher taxes in the future.

Why should I max my match?
Not all company-sponsored retirement plans are created equal. What makes some stand out is the company match. To incentivize employees to save for retirement, employers help by

matching your contribution. It's essentially like getting a raise—but you need to make sure you are maxing your contribution to take full advantage of the extra money.

It's fairly common for employers to offer to match 100 percent of your contributions up to 6 percent of your salary, Priya says. So if your annual salary is $50,000 and you contribute 6 percent of your gross income ($3,000 per year) to your company-sponsored account, your employer will contribute another $3,000 per year. That's basically a $3,000 raise. Plus it doubles your annual retirement savings to $6,000. If you choose to contribute only $2,000 for the year, your employer will make a $2,000 contribution.

This is really a no-brainer. If you're not maxing your match, you're ignoring free money. And it's not likely your employer will alert you to this fact. Don't leave money on the table.

How much should I contribute?

There's a limit to how much you can contribute, and it can change annually. In 2018, the limit is $18,500, but check the IRS website for updates. Some 401(k) enrollment forms allow you to choose the "max" option, which ensures that you contribute the full amount each year.

If your employer offers a match, you should at least max your match. (Have debt? See chapter 4 to help determine your financial priorities.) If you've paid off your debt and have a fully funded emergency account, it's really up to you to determine how much more you want to contribute beyond that goal.

How should I invest my 401(k)?

I'm very much in the set-it-and-forget-it camp, but maybe a little bit too much so (I had to double-check to see how much I was contributing each month when writing this). You should be aware of how much you're contributing and how that money is invested, even if it seems overwhelming.

According to Priya, when it comes to investing, the number one rule is diversification. When you're properly diversified, your selection of investments is uncorrelated, she explains, which means that when some are doing well, others may be doing poorly. I know that sounds counterintuitive, but you don't want everything to be doing well at the same time, because then you risk it all going bad at the same time.

Priya says the smartest way to achieve diversification in your 401(k) is by utilizing a hybrid investment called a target date fund (TDF). TDFs are a pretty common choice offered by company-sponsored retirement plans, and they are great because you don't have to overthink your investment choices (or, like me, make blind guesses and hope you chose correctly). You just choose a TDF that corresponds with the year you plan to retire and the fund manager will do the picking for you. For example, if you're 28 (in 2018) and plan to retire when you're 65 (thirty-seven years from now), you would choose TDF-2055.

As Priya explains it, the fund is automatically diversified according to the time frame you have to invest. Someone with thirty-plus years until retirement will likely have a higher allocation to equities (for growth), whereas someone with only five to ten years until retirement might have a higher allocation to bonds (for safety).

If your company plan doesn't offer target date funds, there is a general rule of thumb that you can use. Subtract your age from 120, and the remaining number is your allocation for equities (stocks). For example, if you are 27 (120 – 27 = 93), you might put 93 percent of your portfolio into stocks and the rest into bonds.

What if my company doesn't sponsor a retirement plan?
You're not off the hook if your job doesn't offer a 401(k). (I'm talking to you, full-time freelancers.) This is where personal retirement accounts come into play.

You're probably familiar with the terms *IRA* and *Roth IRA* (I know you don't live under a rock), but it's cool if you're not 100 percent sure what they are—and if you need one.

A traditional IRA (usually referred to as IRA), or individual retirement account, is a retirement investment account similar to a 401(k). Depending on several factors determined by the IRS (visit its website for the most up-to-date factors[1]), you can make a contribution to your IRA on a tax-deferred basis. Like a 401(k), this has the effect of lowering your annual tax bill.

A Roth IRA is similar to a Roth 401(k)—you pay taxes now on the amount you contribute and don't pay taxes when you access the money in retirement. Unlike with a traditional IRA, there are income limits on Roth IRA accounts. Again, we recommend that you visit the IRS website for more details or consult a tax professional.

As with a 401(k), you cannot access the money in an IRA until you're at least 59½. Additionally, there is a cap to how much you can contribute and a yearly deadline to make contributions, since there are tax benefits to investing your money in these accounts. The deadline usually falls annually on Tax Day. If you've never had an account before, it can be good to take your year-end bonus and open one before you file your income tax return so you can take advantage of the tax break.

If your company offers a retirement plan such as a 401(k), you may still make a contribution to an IRA, but it likely won't be tax deductible.

What's better, a Roth IRA or a traditional IRA?
Whether you choose a Roth IRA or a traditional IRA depends on your income. If you meet the income requirements—and you're contributing to your company's 401(k)—Priya suggests that it could be wise to contribute to a Roth IRA. Yes, you'll pay taxes up front, but you'll enjoy the earnings tax free at retirement

(when you'll be paying taxes on your 401(k) earnings). Once you no longer qualify to make deposits into your Roth IRA, the account will continue to grow until you're eligible to make withdrawals.

Do I need both a personal retirement account and a company retirement account?

It all goes back to whether your employer offers a match to your 401(k) and whether you are maxing your match. If the answer is yes to both, and you *still* want to save more money for retirement, then consider opening an IRA or Roth IRA. This will allow you to maximize what Priya calls your "tax flexibility"—you'll be paying taxes on some of your retirement funds up front and some in the future. It's good to spread those payments out so you're not saddled with a big tax bill when you start withdrawing funds at 59½.

How should I invest my IRA or Roth IRA?

It's not quite as simple to invest your money in a personal retirement account as in a 401(k). While we dig a little deeper into investing later in this chapter, you need to know some basics in order to manage your IRA. Your default might be to buy stocks in companies you're familiar with. There's nothing wrong with having a few stocks in your IRA account, Priya explains, but it's not an effective way to achieve true diversification (which we touched on in our advice on how to invest your 401(k)).

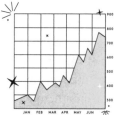

To simplify things, we'll just focus on stocks and bonds. Let's go back to the formula Priya shared earlier to determine how much you should invest in stocks versus bonds:

120 − YOUR AGE (30) = 90

So 90 percent of your investments should be in stocks and 10 percent should be in bonds. Priya suggests you start by looking at ETFs (exchange-traded funds), which have very low fees because they aren't actively managed. You'll want to research stock ETFs and bond ETFs; Vanguard, for example, offers competitively priced products, so you could start there.

When can I start using the money I've saved in a retirement account?
You cannot touch the funds in your personal retirement accounts until you turn 59½. If you withdraw the funds before-hand, you'll pay a big tax bill as well as a 10 percent penalty.

There are exceptions to the 10 percent penalty rule, known as "hardship withdrawals," that the IRS allows only in the event of "immediate and heavy financial need." These are usually things such as medical expenses, qualified education costs, and the purchase of your primary residence. In such cases, you can get around the 10 percent penalty, but it is not easy to qualify, and Priya says it's not advisable to do so. The phrase "fund it and forget it" is a helpful way to think of your contributions. They are meant to provide income in retirement, so consider them earmarked for that purpose.

THIS IS A GOOD TIME TO:

Increase your 401(k) by 1 percent. It might seem as though you can't afford to save another penny, but it's worth taking a look to see how an incremental increase to your 401(k) contributions impacts your overall lifestyle. If you can't afford to do it this month, make sure you do so next time you get a raise—before the increase even hits your bank account, so you don't get a chance to miss it.

While you're at it, save $29
Total saved so far: $435

Roll Over Your 401(k)

TIME: *15–90 minutes*
TOOLS: *Personal computer, account information, phone number of your ex-employer's benefits department*

Here's another (kind of silly) financial truth about me: until I started writing this book, I had never rolled over my 401(k) accounts. One of them had been sitting dormant for *eight years*. I might have ignored it for another eight if my editor hadn't finally said, "Enough!" I was embarrassed enough to finally take action.

Once you stop working for a company, you can no longer make contributions to your company-sponsored retirement account. Which is why it makes sense to transfer the funds into a personal retirement account that's in your own name (such as a traditional IRA), where you have many more investment options to choose from.

It's also a lot easier to manage when everything is in one place.

One of the reasons I stalled on rolling over my 401(k) is that it's a little annoying to initiate the rollover. Sometimes you can simply go through the financial institution that manages your original 401(k) account. Sometimes you'll need to contact the benefits department at your former company, advise your rep that you no longer work there, and let them know you'd like to roll over your funds. Either way, you're going to need to pick up the phone. (Sorry!) Your former employer (or the company that manages your 401(k)) will cut a check for any contributions you've made and any vested contributions that your employer made, and you're required to deposit that money in your (new) personal retirement account within sixty days.

Ask the benefits department to make the check payable to include the name of the bank or investment company where you have your personal retirement account. It should look something like this:

**Please make the check payable to
Fidelity FBO Lindsey Stanberry**

FBO stands for "for benefit of." You should also ask it to put your personal retirement account number in the memo line of the check.

For years Priya had told me that the whole process wouldn't take more than thirty minutes. I'll admit to you that it took a *little* longer, but it was really easy, and I only had to make two phone calls.

**While you're at it, save $30
Total saved so far: $465**

Whenever the media starts talking about young women and retirement, the headlines are bleak. And a 2017 survey found that 44 percent of millennial women spend more on coffee each year than they invest in their 401(k).[2] I did the math, and in 2017, I spent close to $300 at the coffee shop across the street from my office. Thankfully, I invested much more than that in my 401(k) plan. But since I started writing this book, I found myself drinking the office brew more than grabbing a latte across the street.

Taking a peek at your coffee spending versus your 401(k) investment is a good way to reconsider your spending and investing habits and an obvious way to make some changes to your priorities. Below, five women share how much they spend on coffee per month versus their 401(k) and how it makes them feel.

BLAKE, 22, KANSAS CITY, MO | ANNUAL SALARY: $38,500 | COFFEE: $40 | 401(K): $200

"Like an adult!"

JENNIFER, 35, PHOENIX, AZ | ANNUAL SALARY: $36,000 | COFFEE: $20 | 401(K): $25

"Not so good."

KELLY, 26, LOS ANGELES, CA | ANNUAL
SALARY: $110,000 | COFFEE: $118 | 401(K):
$1,500 (I MAX OUT)

"I work long hours, and if a little coffee makes my day better in the
morning, I feel like that's okay. I'm fortunate to be able to max out
my 401(k), but I definitely do treat myself a lot."

HAYDEN, 25, TALLAHASSEE, FL
| SALARY: $42,000 | COFFEE:
$16.63 | 401(K): $155

"*Really* good. I try not to buy coffee out
because I tend to order the same thing
I would make at home anyway, and I'm
so happy I can already be saving for
retirement."

AKILAH, 29, MICHIGAN | SALARY: $35,000
| COFFEE: $30–$40 | 401(K): BESIDES THE
$33 THAT'S AUTOMATICALLY TAKEN OUT OF MY
PAYCHECK, $0

"Sad."

The idea of saving $10,000 (or even $1,000) can seem really daunting, if not impossible, when you have other priorities (student loan debt, rent, your best friend's birthday dinner, etc.). But what if you stop looking at that number as a whopping five-figure behemoth and start viewing it as a daily expense, just like that latte I told you it was okay to buy?

The writer Sarah Knight penned a piece for Refinery29 in which she talked about saving $10,000 in 365 days by transferring $27.40 into her savings account each morning. She equated that number with a cab ride or a hardcover book, expenses she could easily give up.

Jean Chatzky, the *Today* show's financial expert, created a big stir on Twitter when she suggested that you should save an amount equal to your annual salary by the time you're 30. (This is a retirement savings goal created by Fidelity.) *Yeah, right*, you might be thinking. But I was curious how much you have to save every day if you want to hit $60,000 by your 30th birthday. Say you start working at 23. You've got 2,555 days to save, which means you'd need to put away $23.48 every day. And don't forget, if you're saving this amount in a 401(k), your employer may offer a match, and ideally, your investments are growing every year, which makes the amount you save each day even smaller.

Maybe that makes saving $60,000 seem not so impossible?

But if you want to start smaller, let's go back to your emergency fund goal. If you're trying to save three to six months' expenses—we'll say $11,000 to give us a nice cushion—over three years, you'll need to save around $10 a day. Maybe a good reason to give up that sad desk salad?

Of course, you might get a few year-end bonuses along the way, maybe some tax refunds. In chapter 5 we talked about putting that extra money toward paying down your high-interest debt, but once you have that squared away, you should start saving some of it, too. Use Priya's 80/20 rule, saving 80 percent and spending 20 percent.

Of course, it might not always be possible to save anything. Or maybe you don't have a job with a 401(k) right now. Jean urges people to remember that life takes twists and turns. "There are times in your life when you'll be able to save more and there are times in your life when you won't," she says. It's important to take advantage of the good times to prepare for the bad.

Don't put this savings into a plain old savings account. Anything you're putting away for short-term goals should go into a high-yield savings account. And money for those long-term goals? Read on for how to invest that money so you can live the good life one day.

Even though Ken and I are good savers, for a long time we were really nervous about investing beyond our 401(k)s. But I also realize there's a real connection between wealth and investing, and I'd like to be wealthy one day. If I'm going to send my kid to college or fulfill my fantasy of having a home in the Hollywood Hills (and, you know, retire), I can't just leave my money in a savings account.

Unfortunately, I'm not alone in this financial fear. A 2015 Fidelity report found that 92 percent of women want to learn more about financial planning, yet 80 percent aren't talking about money with anyone, and only 47 percent feel comfortable discussing money with a professional.[3] As a result, we lag behind men in how much we're investing[4] and, in the long run, how much money we're earning from those investments.

Priya knows my aversion to investing, so I asked her for help putting together this beginner's guide. Whole books are written on this topic—and we didn't have room to get into the nitty-gritty—but you also don't have to read every single one of them to get started. Sure, it's a little scary, but it's not as risky as some would like you to think. Men are already getting in on the action. It's time for us to start having some of the fun (and making all the money).

Where should I begin?
Okay, I know I said that everyone needs to invest, but there are a few exceptions. You're ready to invest if you can check the following boxes:

1. You have a fully funded emergency fund (see chapter 4)
2. Your debt repayments are under control (see chapter 5)
3. You're maxing your 401(k) match (see page 270)

If you said yes to all of the above, you should consider investing any extra money you have that isn't earmarked for short-term goals.

How much money do I need?

These days you don't need much to get started. Many robo advisers (Ellevest or Betterment, for example) have no balance minimums and low monthly fees. These platforms do a wonderful job of simplifying the investing process by doing the heavy lifting for you. You simply fill out a questionnaire to assess your risk tolerance (which takes into consideration things such as your age, income, and short- and long-term savings goals); they crunch some numbers and then allocate your money across different investments, giving you a diverse portfolio (more on diversification in a minute). Voilà, you're investing!

If you don't have a ton of money and are nervous about getting into the market—or, let's be frank, kind of uninterested in the whole thing—robo advisers are a great place to start.

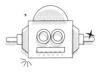

Why can't I just leave my money in a savings account?

Man, I wish. It would be so much easier. But it's kind of scary how much you lose out on if you do go that route. I asked Priya to crunch some numbers, and here's one example:

> If you start out at 25 with an annual salary of $50,000:
> Starting investment amount: $5,000
> Annual contribution: $2,500 (5 percent of annual salary, or roughly $210 a month)
> At 65 you'll have: $756,264*

---

*Based on an 8 percent rate of return.

Say you just left that money in a high-yield savings account with a 1.25 percent interest rate, you'd have only around $137,000. (Also, inflation will dilute your gains—but let's not get overly complicated here.) That's more than a $600,000 difference.

Investor.gov, a website run by the US Securities and Exchange Commission, has some really fun calculators you can play with to see just how much you need to save and invest in order to reach all your financial goals.

That said, you should keep cash for any short-term savings goals in a high-interest savings account, so it's easier to access and you won't lose it if the market takes a sudden dip.

Do I need to hire a financial adviser?

Maybe. It can be good to have someone to help you review your financial picture, create a game plan, and give feedback on ways you can invest. But it's really important to make sure that whomever you talk to abides by fiduciary standards.

I know that word *fiduciary* sounds kind of jargon-y, but I also trust you're smart enough to remember it. It's a *very* important word in the personal finance/investing world. Basically, it comes down to understanding who can sell you what financial products (from investment funds to life insurance), and what they stand to earn by selling you those products, so you can make sure you're not talked into buying something you don't need. (If you're young, healthy, and single, for example, you do not need a whole life insurance policy even though it seems as though insurance companies are constantly convincing the women I know to buy them.)

The consensus among experts is that you want to get advice from someone who follows fiduciary standards, as they are required by law to keep your best financial intentions in mind when managing your money. So when you seek out an adviser, you need to ask them, "Do you follow fiduciary standards?" and the answer needs to be "Yes."

There are so many different investing terms: ETFs, mutual funds, stocks. Why is it so confusing?

I agree, it can seem really complicated. But it's actually pretty straightforward if you keep these three things in mind:

1. Stocks are sexy, but they shouldn't make up your whole portfolio. They should be only a very small part of your overall investment strategy. Why? Because . . .
2. Diversification is everything. It turns out that diversity in your portfolio is just as important as diversity in the workplace.[5] That means you need to have a mix of investments: stocks and bonds. Which is why it's great to invest in . . .
3. ETFs! Exchange-traded funds should be your new best friends. According to Priya, they are the most straightforward cost-effective investment option that provides instant diversification.

Why are ETFs so good? Well, for one thing, Warren Buffett loves them, and who doesn't love that sweet grandfather of a financial genius? But also, research shows (and Priya agrees) that people who aren't constantly tinkering with their investments tend to do better in the market in the long run.[6] The same goes for money managers. ETFs are passively managed, which means you aren't paying a high fee to someone behind the scenes to manage your account. As Priya explains it, no one manages an ETF; it simply replicates the index it's benchmarked to.

If you just went, "Huh?" don't worry—I did the same thing the first time Priya explained it to me. She shared a more concrete example. An S&P 500 ETF tracks the performance of the S&P 500 Index (which is basically a collection of stocks from the five hundred biggest companies in the United States). Whatever the S&P 500 does, the ETF will do the same, minus a small fee. The fee is usually less than the fee charged if you have a traditional mutual fund: 0.12 percent of your investment versus closer to 0.75 percent (at the time of this writing). That might seem like a small difference in fees between ETFs and mutual funds, but Priya reassures me that it adds up.

Basically, it's cheaper to invest in ETFs over the long run, and statistically they do better than mutual funds. If you choose to work with a robo adviser, the investment plan it sets up for you will include a diverse mix of ETFs.

Can I just invest that $5,000 now and never think of it again?

This might seem obvious, but I want to reiterate just in case: you have to make monthly contributions to see that money grow. Priya uses the term "dollar-cost averaging" when she talks about coming up with a solid investment strategy. It's essentially a fancy phrase that simply means you need to invest the same amount every month.

At this point, your 401(k) investment is (or should be!) automated, and you can set up automated withdrawals from your checking account into an investment account so you can (mostly) avoid looking at the market altogether.

How much time is this all going to take?

The thing that I find most intimidating about investing is that it sounds as though it will take up a ton of time I don't have (or would rather be spending on other things). But Priya actually promotes a "set it and forget it" strategy. As she explains, individual investor portfolios don't tend to do well, because we're always reacting to the markets the wrong way. When stock prices start going up, we buy—often too late. And when they start going down, we sell—when it's actually a better opportunity to buy, because things are probably about to get better again and stocks are cheaper.

Priya says she's found that 401(k)s are often individual investors' best accounts, because the investor sets a strategy at the beginning and then doesn't think about it again. This lack of fiddling allows the account to ride untouched through good times and bad, which will leave you in better shape in the end.

That said, you should rebalance your account once a year. When the markets go up and down, Priya explains, your individual investments will go up and down, changing from their original allocation. It's a good idea to check on them annually and sell some of the winners and buy more of the losers to get back on track with your original strategy. (Remember: Buy low, sell high!)

In the end, investing requires a long-term strategy. Yes, it's intimidating, but if you're not relying on that money to tide you over the next time you feel a cash crunch, the process shouldn't stress you out. Rather, it should help you achieve those amazing goals you've been dreaming of.

THIS IS A GOOD TIME TO:

Open an investment account. You'll need to do some research to find the best plan for your needs (whether that's opening a robo adviser account or hiring a financial adviser), but the long-term benefits are huge.

While you're at it, save $31
Total saved so far: $496

FINANCIAL CHALLENGE

Do a Money Diary

TIME: *7 days!*

TOOLS: *The form on the Money Diaries website (or a pen and paper, if you prefer to keep it offline)*

Here we are. At the end. How do you feel? I'll admit, I'm a little emotional. We covered a lot in this book. It's likely you've had more than a few awkward conversations. Hopefully, you've also opened a high-yield savings account, rolled over your 401(k), and taken control of your spending and saving.

Is it time to buy a latte? Or maybe just put an extra $5 into your savings account?

The one thing we haven't done is a Money Diary. And I think that's a nice note to end on. Writing down how much you spend each day—and on what—is a really great practice in mindfulness. I have a bad habit of not looking at the total of my grocery bill before I swipe my card, and I'm sure I'm not alone.

Take the time to do your own diary—it doesn't have to be as elaborate as the diaries in this book and online. (Though I will never, ever dissuade someone from sharing their diary with us!) While you're at it, look at how your finances have changed since the beginning of the book. With this last challenge, you'll have saved $528—a nice start to an emergency account or a vacation fund.

More than the money in the bank, though, I hope you close this book feeling more confident about your money man-agement skills. It's not that hard, right? Sure, it's sometimes stressful and it's sometimes awkward and it's most definitely emotional. But being in control of your finances gives you the freedom to live the life you want. Is there a better feeling than that? I don't think so.

Before you close this book, save another $32
Total saved: $528

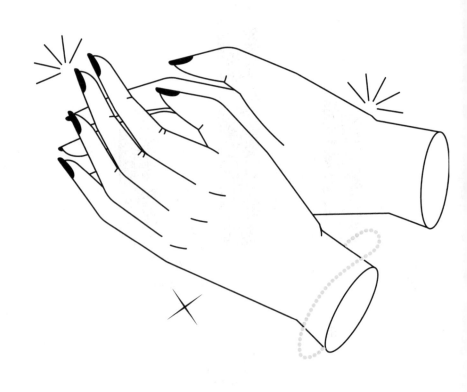

ACKNOWLEDGMENTS

This book would not have been possible without the women who generously shared their Money Diaries and experiences. Your openness and honesty inspires me endlessly. And I'm overwhelmingly grateful for the Refinery29 readers—thank you for trusting us with your hopes, dreams, and daily realities.

Christene Barberich, Refinery29's global editor in chief, came in one hot August morning and told me we needed a Money Diaries book. I will be forever grateful that she believed I could write a book and gave me the space and time and encouragement to make a crazy idea a reality. Amy Emmerich, Refinery29's chief content officer, championed this project from the very beginning and cheered us along every step of the way. Money Diaries is the brainchild of Jessica Chou, a brilliant ideas woman, who nurtured the series in its infancy. She also helped wrangle diarists and conduct interviews for the book. Brittnee Cann, former Refinery29 product manager, developed the Money Diaries form, which took this little franchise to a whole new level. Caroline Stanley read the first draft of this book, gives the best notes, and is always around to remind me to put on my big-girl pants. Bourree Lam, the Work & Money senior editor, ably manned the ship while I wrote and wrote and wrote, and was always around for an encouraging word. Paulina Canini kept me organized and this book on schedule, never fussed when I missed a deadline, and always listened to my rants. Ly Ngo Heisig and Abbie Winters are responsible for the incredible design and illustrations that makes my ideas look even better. And Linda Huang created an incredible cover that I love very, very much.

A huge thank-you to Refinery29's senior leadership team: Philippe von Borries, Justin Stefano, Piera Gelardi, Melanie Goldey, Sarah Personette, Carolyn Meacher, and Suzy Berkowitz. You helm a company that encourages women to change the world, and I'm so thankful I get to work here.

The editorial team at Refinery29 is the smartest, funniest, best group of women and men around, and I really do consider you to be my family. I have to especially call out Yael Kohen, who is hands down the best editor I've ever worked with, and Rebecca Smith, who is always ready with a thoughtful compliment when I need it most. And of course my Work & Money team (both the 2017 & 2018 iterations!): Madeline Buxton, Judith Ohikuare, Anabel Pasarow, Venus Wong, Marshall Bright, Natalie Gontcharova, and Andrea González-Ramírez. You make it a joy to come to work every day.

There are so many amazing people at Refinery29 who helped support this book: Leah Carroll, Rebekkah Easley, Andrea Velazquez, Albie Hueston, Krystle Champagne, Sara Okin Livengood, Joanna Bomberg, Steve Gordon, Stacy Eisner, Chelsea Sanders, Cody Manker, Alyssa Alward, Selina Santiago, Raffi Asdourian, Denise Meikle, Neena Koyen, and Kate Hyatt, to name just a few.

I am not a financial expert, and I'm so thankful for the amazing women who shared their advice and expertise with me: Priya Malani, Manisha Thakor, Shannon McLay, Barbara Ginty, Fran Hauser, Sallie Krawcheck, Georgia Hussey, and Farnoosh Torabi.

Thank you to Cara Bedick and her team at Touchstone, including Susan Moldow, Tara Parsons, Meredith Vilarello, Kelsey Manning, Sydney Morris, Jessica Roth, Lara Blackman, and Tom Spain. And to Eve Attermann and the team at William Morris Endeavor, including Haley Heidemann, Matilda Forbes Watson, and Siobhan O'Neill.

There are so many people behind the scenes (near and far) who have encouraged me along the way: Jennifer Prestigiacomo,

Cristina Goyanes, Elaine Ybarra, Jeffrey Kurtz, Brittany Keen, Vanessa Golembewski, Lauren Prince, Geoffrey Bickford, Allegra LaViola, Pat Feghali, Margaret Lebahn, Deb and Ken Partridge, David E. Brown, Maura Egan, Mikki Halpin, Nina Rastogi, Jacob Lewis, Chris Daly, Carol Fultz, Patrick Kelly, Claudia Mann, Colleen Blumer, Mary Griffith, and Robyn Breiman. I owe you all a drink.

At the end of the day, there are six people who make me feel like the richest woman alive: my parents, Elizabeth and Lawrence; my brother and sister-in-law, Martin and Rachel; and my husband and son, Ken and Desmond. I love you all so much.

·

Chapter 1: Life & Money

1. Andrew T. Jebb, Louis Tay, Ed Diener, and Shigehiro Oishi, "Happiness, Income Satiation and Turning Points Around the World," *Nature Human Behaviour*, January 8, 2018, https://www.nature.com/articles/s41562-017-0277-0.
2. Mike Cetera, "Survey: Surprisingly Few Millennials Carry Credit Cards," Bankrate, June 13, 2016, https://www.bankrate.com/finance/consumer-index/money-pulse-0616.aspx.

Chapter 2: Love & Money

1. "The American Family Today," Pew Research Center, December 17, 2015, http://www.pewsocialtrends.org/2015/12/17/1-the-american-family-today/).
2. Katie Lobosco, "One Thing You Should Know About Your Spouse, But 43% Don't," CNN Money, June 24, 2015, http://money.cnn.com/2015/06/24/pf/married-couples-salary/index.html.
3. "A Week in NYC on a $120k Salary," Refinery29, January 24, 2016, http://www.refinery29.com/money-diary-product-manager-new-york-city-budget?bucketed=true.
4. "The Product Manager Who Eats Greek Yogurt Every Day," Facebook, January 24, 2016, https://www.facebook.com/refinery29/posts/10153949674142922.
5. "How Much One NYC Woman Spends over Valentine's Day Weekend," Refinery29, February 15, 2016, http://www.refinery29.com/money-diary-new-york-city-budget-valentines-day.

Chapter 3: Work & Money

1. "Equal Pay Today! Campaign," 2018, http://www.equalpaytoday.org/equalpaydays/.

2. AAUW, *The Simple Truth about the Gender Pay Gap*, Spring 2018, https://www.aauw.org/aauw_check/pdf_download /show_pdf.php?file=The-Simple-Truth.

3. Kim Parker and Cary Funk, "Gender Discrimination Comes in Many Forms for Today's Working Women," Pew Research Center, December 14, 2017, http://www.pewresearch.org /fact-tank/2017/12/14/gender-discrimination-comes-in -many-forms-for-todays-working-women/.

4. Carrie Dann, "NBC/WSJ Poll: Nearly Half of Working Women Say They've Experienced Harassment," NBC News, October 30, 2017, https://www.nbcnews.com/politics/first -read/nbc-wsj-poll-nearly-half-working-women-say-they-ve -n815376.

5. Michelle Marks and Crystal Harold, "Who Asks and Who Receives in Salary Negotiation," Wiley Online Library, March 24, 2011, https://onlinelibrary.wiley.com/doi/abs/10 .1002/job.671.

6. Lydia Dishman, "Best and Worst Graduate Degrees for Jobs in 2016," *Fortune*, March 21, 2016, http://fortune .com/2016/03/21/best-worst-graduate-degrees-jobs-2016/.

7. "Is the Cost of a Graduate Degree Worth It?," Peterson's, January 9, 2018, https://www.petersons.com/blog/Is-the -Cost-of-a-Graduate-Degree-Worth-It/.

Chapter 4: Emergencies & Money

1. Zac Auter, "U.S. Uninsured Rate Steady at 12.2% in Fourth Quarter of 2017," Gallup, January 16, 2018, https://news .gallup.com/poll/225383/uninsured-rate-steady-fourth -quarter-2017.aspx.

2. "CFPB Finds Private Student Loan Borrowers Face 'Auto-Default' When Co-Signer Dies or Goes Bankrupt," Consumer Financial Protection Bureau, April 22, 2014, https:// www.consumerfinance.gov/about-us/newsroom/cfpb-finds -private-student-loan-borrowers-face-auto-default-when-co -signer-dies-or-goes-bankrupt/.

Chapter 5: Debt & Money

1. Tony Mecia, "Poll: 2 in 3 U.S. Adults with Debt Doubt They'll Ever Live Debt-Free," creditcards.com, January 10, 2018, https://www.creditcards.com/credit-card-news/debt-free -living-survey.php.
2. "Quarterly Report on Household Debt and Credit," Federal Reserve Bank of New York, August 2017, https://www.new yorkfed.org/medialibrary/interactives/householdcredit/data /pdf/HHDC_2017Q2.pdf.
3. "Millennials in Adulthood," Pew Research Center, March 7, 2014, http://www.pewsocialtrends.org/2014/03/07/millenni als-in-adulthood/#fn-18663-11.
4. Melanie Lockert, "The Complete List of Student Loan Forgiveness Programs and Options," Student Loan Hero, July 16, 2017, https://studentloanhero.com/featured/the -complete-list-of-student-loan-forgiveness-programs/.
5. Erin El Issa, "2017 American Household Credit Card Debt Study," NerdWallet, 12/2017, https://www.nerdwallet.com /blog/average-credit-card-debt-household/.
6. Holly Johnson, "Here's How Much the Average American Pays in Interest Each Year," Simple Dollar, March 22, 2017, https://www.thesimpledollar.com/heres-how-much-the-aver age-american-pays-in-interest-each-year/).
7. "PayScale's Salary Negotiation Guide," PayScale, https:// www.payscale.com/salary-negotiation-guide.
8. Vivian Giang, "You Should Plan on Switching Jobs Every Three Years for the Rest of Your Life," Fast Company, January 7, 2016, https://www.fastcompany.com/3055035 /you-should-plan-on-switching-jobs-every-three-years-for -the-rest-of-your-.
9. "Over 44 Million Americans Have a Side Hustle," Bankrate, July 12, 2017, https://www.bankrate.com/pdfs/pr/20170712 -Side-Hustles.pdf.

Chapter 6: Kids & Money

1. Mark Lino, Kevin Kuczynski, Nestor Rodriguez, and Tusa-Rebecca Schap, "Expenditures on Children by Families, 2015," Miscellaneous Report No. 1528-2015, United States Department of Agriculture, Center for Nutrition Policy and Promotion, January 2017, revised March 2017, https://www.cnpp.usda.gov/sites/default/files/crc2015.pdf.

2. Michelle J. Budig, "The Fatherhood Bonus and the Motherhood Penalty: Parenthood and the Gender Gap in Pay," Third Way, https://www.thirdway.org/report/the-fatherhood-bonus-and-the-motherhood-penalty-parenthood-and-the-gender-gap-in-pay.

3. Gretchen Livingston and D'Vera Cohn, "Childlessness Up Among All Women; Down Among Women with Advanced Degrees," Pew Research Center, June 25, 2010, http://www.pewsocialtrends.org/2010/06/25/childlessness-up-among-all-women-down-among-women-with-advanced-degrees/#.

4. "Short Term Disability Insurance and Maternity Leave: Frequently Asked Questions," FairyGodBoss, https://fairygodboss.com/career-topics/short-term-disability-insurance-pregnancy-and-maternity-leave-questions-and-answers.

5. "Left Out: How Corporate America's Parental Leave Policies Discriminate Against Dads, LGBTQ+, and Adoptive Parents," June 2017, Paid Leave for the United States, https://actionnetwork.org/user_files/user_files/000/018/898/original/plus_leftoutreport_2017-7-11.pdf.

Chapter 7: Home & Money

1. "Consumer Expenditures (Annual) News Release," Bureau of Labor Statistics, August 29, 2017, https://www.bls.gov/news.release/cesan.htm.

2. "Highlights from the Profile of Home Buyers and Sellers," National Association of Realtors, 2017, https://www.nar.realtor/research-and-statistics/research-reports/highlights-from-the-profile-of-home-buyers-and-sellers.

3. Mike Bostock, Shan Carter, and Archie Tse, "Is It Better to Rent or Buy?," *New York Times*, July 21, 2014, https://www.nytimes.com/interactive/2014/upshot/buy-rent-calculator.html.

4. "Brooklyn Home Prices & Values," Zillow, March 31, 2018, https://www.zillow.com/brooklyn-new-york-ny/home-values/.

5. "QuickFacts: Kings County (Brooklyn Borough), New York: Median Household Income (in 2016 Dollars), 2012–2016," United States Census Bureau, https://www.census.gov/quickfacts/fact/map/kingscountybrooklynboroughnewyork/INC110216.

Chapter 8: Parents & Money

1. Jillian Berman, "40 percent of Millennials Get Financial Help from Their Parents," MarketWatch, April 25, 2105, https://www.marketwatch.com/story/40-of-millennials-get-financial-help-from-their-parents-2015-04-22.

2. Richard Fry, "For First Time in Modern Era, Living with Parents Edges Out Other Living Arrangements for 18- to 34-Year-Olds," Pew Research Center, May 24, 2019, http://www.pewsocialtrends.org/2016/05/24/for-first-time-in-modern-era-living-with-parents-edges-out-other-living-arrangements-for-18-to-34-year-olds/.

3. Alessandra Malito, "Where Did Baby Boomers Go Wrong? This Generation Isn't Financially Prepared for Retirement," MarketWatch, November 18, 2017, https://www.marketwatch.com/story/where-did-baby-boomers-go-wrong-this-generation-isnt-financially-prepared-for-retirement-2017-07-05.

4. "Family Support in Graying Societies: Helping Adult Children," Pew Research Center, May 21, 2015, http://www.pewsocialtrends.org/2015/05/21/5-helping-adult-children/.

5. "Costs of Care," LongTermCare.gov, October 10, 2017, https://longtermcare.acl.gov/costs-how-to-pay/costs-of-care.html.

6. Russ Banham, "Facing the Future," *Wall Street Journal*, http://online.wsj.com/ad/article/longtermcare-future.

7. Neal Gabler, "The Secret Shame of Middle-Class Americans," *The Atlantic*, May 2016, https://www.theatlantic.com/magazine/archive/2016/05/my-secret-shame/476415/.
8. Malito, "Where Did Baby Boomers Go Wrong?"
9. Jillian Berman, "Loans Are Making It Harder for Parents to Retire," MarketWatch, March 9, 2017, https://www.marketwatch.com/story/college-loans-are-making-it-harder-for-parents-to-retire-2017-02-27.
10. "Statistics," National Funeral Directors Association, January 4, 2018, http://www.nfda.org/news/statistics.
11. "Financial Support Survey: Understanding Financial Obligations Across Generations," Ameritrade, https://s1.q4cdn.com/959385532/files/doc_downloads/research/TDA-Financial-Support-Study-2015.pdf.

Chapter 9: Wealth & Money

1. "IRA Deduction Limits," Internal Revenue Service, https://www.irs.gov/retirement-plans/ira-deduction-limits.
2. Kathryn Lindsay, "Millennials Are Officially Spending More $ on Coffee Than on Retirement Savings," Refinery29, January 17, 2017, http://www.refinery29.com/2017/01/136539/millennials-spending-more-coffee-retirement-savings.
3. "Money FIT Women Study: Executive Summary," Fidelity Investments, 2015, https://www.fidelity.com/bin-public/060_www_fidelity_com/documents/women-fit-money-study.pdf.
4. Rana Pritanjali, "Why Women Should Embrace Investing," Motley Fool, December 11, 2014, https://www.fool.com/how-to-invest/2014/12/11/put-your-boots-on-women.aspx.
5. Kim Abreu, "The Myriad Benefits of Diversity in the Workplace," *Entrepreneur*, December 9, 2014, https://www.entrepreneur.com/article/240550.
6. Carl Richards, "The Best Investment Strategy? Getting Out of Our Own Way," *New York Times*, March 3, 2014, https://www.nytimes.com/2014/03/03/your-money/stocks-and-bonds/the-best-investment-strategy-getting-out-of-our-own-way.html.

Barbara Ginty is a Certified Financial Planner professional, the owner of the New York–based financial planning services firm Independent Financial Services, and the creator of the video series *Planancial*, which summarizes key financial concepts relevant to young professionals. Barbara started her career on Wall Street working for both Bloomberg and Credit Suisse before moving to personal finance to pursue her passion. Barbara takes the fear out of money management and helps women claim their financial power by providing knowledge and access to financial planning information.

Fran Hauser is a longtime media executive, startup investor, and author of *The Myth of the Nice Girl*. She's held senior positions at some of the world's largest digital media businesses, including Time Inc.'s *People*, *InStyle*, and *Entertainment Weekly* as well as AOL and Moviefone. Now an angel investor who largely invests in female founders, Fran was named one of Refinery29's "6 Most Powerful Women in NYC's Tech Scene" and one of *Business Insider*'s "30 Women in Venture Capital to Watch in 2018." She has been featured by CNBC, *Forbes*, Vogue.com, *Ad Age*, and more.

Sallie Krawcheck is the CEO and cofounder of Ellevest, a recently launched innovative digital investment platform for women. She is the chair of Ellevate Network, a global professional woman's network, and the Pax Ellevate Global Women's Leadership Fund, which invests in the top-rated companies in the world for advancing women. She is also the best-selling author of *Own It: The Power of Women at Work*.

Priya Malani is an entrepreneur and founder of Stash Wealth, a financial planning and investment management firm for H.E.N.R.Y.s (High Earners, Not Rich Yet). Since its inception, Stash Wealth has disrupted the financial planning industry by providing highly personalized advice and guidance to twenty- and thirtysomethings who make good money and want something to show for it. Dubbed "the Rebel of Wall Street," Malani wants to change the way millennials think about money by empowering them to get their financial sh*t together. In addition to running Stash Wealth, Malani is a resident financial expert for Refinery29, as well as a featured expert on numerous platforms including *Shape* magazine, *Bustle*, PureWow, Girlboss, *QGentleman*, the *Wall Street Journal*, *Brides*, *Forbes*, the *Coveteur*, and SiriusXM.

Shannon McLay is a financial planner who left a traditional financial services firm to start her own company, Financial Gym, because she felt traditional financial services firms did not have the tools or resources to help the everyday Jack and Jill who are trying to build assets while also managing debt. Shannon realized that the key to financial success for most people is human contact and not a website or an app. People are more than algorithms, and Financial Gym is putting the personal back in to personal finance. In 2018, she opened the flagship Financial Gym in New York City, and by 2019 she plans to have gyms open across the United States. Through her blog, *Financially Blonde*, her book, *Train Your Way to Financial Fitness*, her podcast, *Martinis and Your Money*, and her company, Shannon is committed to making financial fitness fun, easy, and accessible for everyone.

Manisha Thakor, a renowned financial literacy advocate for women, is vice president of financial education at the Seattle-based wealth management firm Brighton Jones. Her mission is to help clients live a richer life—literally and figuratively. Manisha is the coauthor of two critically acclaimed personal finance books: *On My Own Two Feet: A Modern Girl's Guide to Personal Finance* and *Get Financially Naked: How to Talk Money with Your Honey*. Manisha is a member of the *Wall Street Journal*'s Wealth Experts Panel, sits on the faculty at the

Omega Institute, and serves on the board of the National Endowment for Financial Education. Her financial advice has been featured in a wide range of national media outlets including CNN, PBS, NPR, *Today*, *Rachael Ray*, the *New York Times*, the *Boston Globe*, the *Los Angeles Times*, *Real Simple*, *Woman's Day*, *Glamour*, *Marie Claire*, *Cosmopolitan*, and *Women's Health*. Her website is MoneyZen.com.

As Work & Money Director at Refinery29, **Lindsey Stanberry** provides millennial women with the smart, entertaining financial and career advice they deserve. She developed her passion for these topics after her story "How I Saved $100K to Buy an Apartment" received a massive response from R29 readers. In 2015, she launched Refinery29's first Work & Money vertical, covering everything from retirement funds and paid family leave to the inspiring female entrepreneurs she met in Haiti while interviewing Chelsea Clinton. She recently appeared on *CBS This Morning* as part of the Refinery29 series on the financial lives of millennials. She lives in Brooklyn with her frugal husband and one-year-old son. *Refinery29 Money Diaries* is her first book.

Refinery29 is the leading digital media and entertainment company focused on women with a global audience footprint of 550 million across all platforms. Through a variety of lifestyle stories, original video programming, social, shareable content, and live experiences, Refinery29 provides its audience with the inspiration and tools to discover and pursue a more independent, stylish, and informed life. "Money Diaries" has been featured on *CBS This Morning* and in the *New Yorker*, the *Wall Street Journal*, MarketWatch, and more.